THE DROLLS, TRADITIONS, AND SUPERSTITIONS OF OLD CORNWALL

(POPULAR ROMANCES OF THE WEST OF ENGLAND)

FIRST SERIES

collected & edited by
ROBERT HUNT

The Giant Bolster striding from the Beacon to Carn Brea —
— A distance of six miles —

Also published by Llanerch:

SYMBOLISM OF THE CELTIC CROSS
by Derek Bryce.

TRADITIONS & HEARTHSIDE STORIES OF
WEST CORNWALL by W. Bottrell.

TALIESIN POEMS trans. by Meirion Pennar.

A HISTORY OF THE KINGS
by Florence of Worcester.

For a complete list of our small—press
editions & facsimile reprints, write to:
LLANERCH PUBLISHERS,
FELINFACH, LAMPETER,
DYFED, SA48 8PJ.

THE DROLLS, TRADITIONS, AND SUPERSTITIONS OF OLD CORNWALL
(POPULAR ROMANCES OF THE WEST OF ENGLAND)

FIRST SERIES

collected & edited by
ROBERT HUNT

Facsimile reprint, 1993, by
LLANERCH PUBLISHERS, Felinfach
ISBN 1 897853 17 3

" ' Have you any stories like that, guidwife?'

" ' Ah, she said ; ' there were plenty of people tha could tell those stories once. I used to hear them telling them over the fire at night ; but people is so changed with pride now, that they care for nothing.' "—CAMPBELL.

PREFACE TO THE THIRD EDITION.

DURING the last few years a new interest has been awakened, and the West of England has attracted the attention of many, who had previously neglected the scenes of interest, and the spots of beauty, which are to be found in our own island.

The rugged granite range of Dartmoor, rich with the golden furze; the moorlands of Cornwall, with their mighty Tors and giant boulders fringed with ferns and framed in masses of purple heath; the stern coasts, washed by an emerald sea, quaint with rocks carved into grotesque forms by the beating of waves and winds, spread with the green samphire and coated with yellow lichens; are now found to have a peculiar —though a wild—often a savage—beauty. The wood-clad valleys, ringing with the rush of rivers, and the sheltered plains, rich with an almost tropical vegetation, present new features of interest to the stranger's eyes, in the varied characters of the organisation native to that south-western clime.

The railways give great facilities for visiting those scenes, of which the public eagerly avail themselves. But they have robbed the West of England of half its interest, by dispelling the spectres of romance which were, in hoar antiquity, the ruling spirits of the place.

The "Romances of the West of England"—collected into a volume which has served its purpose well—gives the tourist the means of restoring the giants and the fairies to their native haunts.

The growing inquiries of those who are desirous of knowing something of the ancient Cornish miners,—of the old peasantry of this peninsula, and of the aged fishermen who almost lived upon the Atlantic waters,—have convinced me that a third edition of this volume of folk-lore has become a necessity.

While correcting the pages for a new edition, a scientific friend, who was deep in the cold thrall of positivism, called upon me. He noticed the work upon which I was engaged, and remarked, "I suppose you invented most of these stories."

In these days, when our most sacred things are being sneered at, and the poetry of life is being repressed by the prose of a cold infidelity, this remark appears to render it a humiliating necessity, to assure my readers that none of the legends in this volume have been invented. They were all of them gathered in their native homes, more than half a century since, as stated fully in the Introduction to the volume.

For this edition some necessary corrections have been made; and additions will be found in the Appendix, which it is thought will increase the interest of the volume.

ROBERT HUNT.

March 1881.

CONTENTS.

First Series.

B

Contents.

INTRODUCTION.

THE beginning of this collection of Popular Romances may be truly said to date from my early childhood. I remember with what anticipations of pleasure, sixty-eight years since, I stitched together a few sheets of paper, and carefully pasted them into the back of an old book. This was preparatory to a visit I was about to make with my mother to Bodmin, about which town many strange stories were told, and my purpose was to record them. My memory retains dim shadows of a wild tale of Hender the Huntsman of Lanhydrock ; of a narrative of streams having been poisoned by the monks ; and of a legend of a devil who played many strange pranks with the tower which stands on a neighbouring hill. I have, within the last year? endeavoured to recover those stories, but in vain. The living people appear to have forgotten them ; my juvenile note-book has long been lost : those traditions are, it is to be feared, gone for ever.

Fifteen years passed away—about six of them at school in Cornwall, and nine of them in close labour in London,—when failing health compelled my return to the West of England. Having spent about a month on the borders of Dartmoor, and wandered over that wild region of Granite Tors, gathering up its traditions,—ere yet Mrs Bray* had thought of doing so,—I resolved on walking through Cornwall. Thirty-five years since, on a beautiful spring morning, I landed at Saltash, from the very ancient passage-boat which in those days conveyed men and women, carts and cattle, across the river Tamar, where now that triumph of engineering, the Albert Bridge, gracefully spans its waters. Sending my box forward to Liskeard by a van, my wanderings commenced ; my purpose being to visit each relic of Old Cornwall, and to gather up every existing tale of its ancient people. Ten months were delightfully spent in this way ; and in that period a large number of the romances and superstitions which

---

* Mrs Bray collected her "Traditions, Legends, and Superstitions of Devonshire" in 1835, and they were published in 1838. This work proves to me that even at that time the old-world stories were perishing like the shadows on the mist before the rising sun Many wild tales which I heard in 1829 appear to have been lost in 1835.

are published in these volumes were collected, with many more, which have been weeded out of the collection as worthless.

During the few weeks which were spent on the borders of Dartmoor, accidental circumstances placed me in the very centre of a circle who believed " there were giants on the earth in those days " to which the " old people " belonged, and who were convinced that to turn a coat-sleeve or a stocking prevented the piskies from misleading man or woman. I drank deeply from the stream of legendary lore which was at that time flowing, as from a well of living waters, over

" Devonia's dreary Alps ; " *

and longed to renew my acquaintance with the wild tales of Cornwall, which had either terrified or amused me when a child.

My acquaintance with the fairies commenced at an early date. When a very boy, I have often been taken by a romantic young lady, who lives in my memory—

" So bright, so fair, so wild,"†

to seek for the fairies on Lelant Towans. The maiden and the boy frequently sat for hours, entranced by the stories of an old woman, who lived in a cottage on the edge of the blown sandhills of that region. Thus were received my earliest lessons in fairy mythology.

From earthly youth accidental circumstances have led to my acquiring a taste for collecting the waifs floating upon the sea of time, which tell us something of those ancient peoples who have not a written history. The rude traditions of a race who appear to have possessed much native intelligence, minds wildly poetical, and great fertility of imagination, united with a deep feeling for the mysteries by which life is girdled, especially interested me. By the operation of causes beyond my control, I was removed from the groove of ordinary trade and placed in a position of considerable responsibility, in connection with one of the most useful institutions of Cornwall.‡ To nurse the germs of genius to maturity—to seek those gems " of purest ray serene," which the dark, though not " unfathomed caves " of the Cornish mines might produce—and to reward every effort of human industry, was the purpose of this institution. As its secretary, my duties, as well as my inclination, took me often into the mining and agricultural districts, and brought me into intimate relation with the miners and the peasantry. The bold shores of St Just—the dark and rock-clad hills of Morva,

* Carrington's " Dartmoor." † Coleridge.
‡ The Royal Cornwall Polytechnic Society.

Zennor, and St Ives—the barren regions of St Agnes—the sandy
undulations of Perranzabuloe—the sterile tracts of Gwennap—
the howling moorlands of St Austell and Bodmin—and, indeed,
every district in which there was a mine, became familiar ground.
Away from the towns, at a period when the means of communication were few, and those few tedious, primitive manners still
lingered. Education was not then, as now, the fashion. Church-
schools were few and far between ; and Wesleyan Methodism—
although it was infusing truth and goodness amongst the people
—had not yet become conscious of the importance of properly
educating the young. Always delighting in popular tales, no opportunity of hearing them was ever lost. Seated on a three-legged
stool, or in a "timberen settle," near the blazing heath-fire on the
hearth, have I elicited the old stories of which the people were
beginning to be ashamed. Resting in a level, after the toil of
climbing from the depths of a mine, in close companionship with
the homely miner, his superstitions, and the tales which he had
heard from his grandfather, have been confided to me.

To the present hour my duties take me constantly into the most
remote districts of Cornwall and Devon, so that, as boy and as man,
I have possessed the best possible opportunities for gathering up
the folk-lore of a people, who, but a few generations since, had a
language peculiarly their own,*—a people, who, like all the Celts,
cling with sincere affection to the memories of the past, and who
even now regard with jealousy the introduction of any novelty, and
accept improvements slowly.

The store of old-world stories which had been collected under
the circumstances described would, perhaps, never have taken
their present form, if Mr Thomas Wright had not shown the value
of studying the Cyclopean Walls of the promontory beyond
Penzance, popularly called "The Giant's Hedges,"—and if Mr

---

* "The Cornish dialect, one of the three branches of the old British, bears greater
affinity with the Breton or Armorican dialect of Brittany than it does with the Welsh,
although it properly forms the link of union between the Celtic dialect of France and
that of the Cambrian hills. The nature of its inflexions, both in letters and in tenses
and cases, is, generally speaking, alike, allowance being made for dialectic variations
arising from the nature of the country in which the dialect is spoken." The above quotation is from the remarkable book published by Bagster & Sons, "The Bible of every
Land : A History of the Sacred Scriptures in every Language and Dialect into which
Translations have been made." Preceding the above quotation, I find it stated that
"Dolly Pentreath, who died at Penzance in 1778, aged 102, was then said to be the only
person in Cornwall who could speak the aboriginal idiom of that province of ancient
Britain." This old woman died at Mousehole, and was buried in the churchyard of Paul.
Over her grave Prince Lucien Bonaparte has recently placed an inscribed granite obelisk.
Polwhele and some others have doubted the statement made by Daines Barrington, that
Dolly was the last person who could speak Cornish. As they contend, many other men
and women may, a hundred years since, have known the tongue, but no writer has pro-
duced good evidence to show that any person habitually spoke the language, which
Barrington informs us was the case with Dolly Pentreath.

J. O. Halliwell had not told us that his "*Rambles in Western Cornwall, by the Footsteps of the Giants,*" had led him to attempt " to remove part of a veil beyond which lies hid a curious episode in the history" of an ancient people.

In writing of the Giants, the fairies, and the spectral bands, I have often asked myself, How is it possible to account for the enduring life of those romantic tales, under the constantly-repressing influences of Christian teaching, and of the advances of civilisation ? I have, to some extent, satisfied myself by such a reply as the following:—

Those things which make a strong impression on the mind of the child are rarely obliterated by the education through which he advances to maturity, and they exert their influences upon the man in advanced age. A tale of terror, related by an ignorant nurse, rivets the attention of an infant mind, and its details are engraven on the memory. The " bogle," or " bogie," with which the child is terrified into quiet by some thoughtless servant, remains a dim and unpleasant reality to shake the nerves of the philosopher. Things like these—seeing that existence is surrounded by clouds of mystery—become a Power which will, ever and anon through life, exert considerable control over our actions. As it is with the individual, so is it with the race to which that individual belongs. When our Celtic ancestors—in the very darkness of their ignorance—were taught, through their fears, a Pantheistic religion, and saw a god in every grand phenomenon :—when not merely the atmospheric changes—the aspects of the starry sky—and the peculiarities apparent in the sun and moon, were watched with fearful anxiety ; but when the trembling of a rock—the bubbling of a spring—the agitation of the forest leaves—and the flight of a bird, were charged with sentences of life and death :—then was moulded the Celtic mind, and the early impressions have never been entirely obliterated. " There were maddening orgies amongst the sacred rites of the Britons ; orgies that, whilst they reminded one writer of the Bacchic dances, reminded another of the worship of Demeter." *

The Romans came and possessed the land. Even to the most westerly promontory, we have evidences of their rule, and indications of their superiority. The Saxons overcame the Danmonii—Athelstane drove the Cornish beyond the Tamar, and planted his banner on the Scilly Islands ;—and this Teutonic people diffused their religion and their customs over the West.† The Dane followed upon

---

* Latham.
† " Athelstane (937) handled them yet more extremely, for he drove them out of

the Saxon, and he has left his earthworks, in evidence of his possession, upon the Cornish hills.* The Norman conquerors eventually took possession of our island, and several of the existing families of Cornwall can speak of ancestors, who won their lands by favour of William, the Duke of Normandy.

Notwithstanding the influences which can be—not very obscurely —traced of Roman and Saxon, Danish and Norman civilisations, the Celtic superstitions lingered on :—varied perhaps in their clothing, but in all essentials the same. Those wild dreams which swayed with irresistible force the skin-clad Briton of the Cornish hills, have not yet entirely lost their power where even the National and the British Schools are busy with the people, and Mechanics' Institutions are diffusing the truths of science. In the infancy of the race, terror was the moving power : in the maturity of the people, the dark shadow still sometimes rises, like a spectre, partially eclipsing the mild radiance of that Christian truth which shines upon the land.

It must not be forgotten that Cornwall has, until a recent period, maintained a somewhat singular isolation. England, with many persons, appeared to terminate on the shores of the river Tamar ; and the wreckers of the coasts, and the miners of the hills, were equally regarded as indicating the semi-civilisation of this county. The difficulties of travelling in Cornwall were great. A clergyman writing in 1788, says, " Our object was now to obtain a passage to Loo, without losing sight of the noble sea. Saddle-horses would render the difficulty of this route a pleasure, but with my carriage it is deemed impracticable."† Again, he tells us he was with his guide " five hours coming the eleven miles from Loo to Lost-withiel." Within my own memory, the ordinary means of travelling from Penzance to Plymouth was by a van called a "kitterine," and three days were occupied in the journey. There was in latter years, a mail coach, but the luxury of this conveyance was, even then, reserved for the wealthier classes. This difficulty of transit in a great measure explains the seclusion of the people up to a comparatively recent period ; and to it we certainly owe the preservation of their primitive character, and most of the material to be found in these volumes. At one period indeed—but still earlier than the days of kitterines—we find the Cornish people, as a body,

---

Excester, where, till then, they bare equal sway with the Saxons, and left them only the narrow angle on the west of Tamar river for their inheritance, which hath ever since beene their fatall bound."—*Carew*, p. 96.

* " And divers round holds on the tops of hill ; some single, some double, and treble trenched, which are termed *Castellan Denis* or *Danis*, as raysed by the Danes when they were destyned to become our scourge."—*Carew*, p. 85.

† A Tour to the West of England in 1788. By the Rev. S. Shaw, M.A., London, 1789.

curiously, but completely, cut off by the river Tamar, from their countrymen. They were then informed of the active life of the world beyond them by the travelling historian only, who, as he also sought amuse the people, was called the "droll-teller."

The wandering minstrel, story-teller, and newsmonger appears to have been an old institution amongst the Cornish. Indeed Carew, in his "Survey of Cornwall," tells us that "the last of the Wideslades, whose estates were forfeited in the Rebellion, was called Sir Tristram. He led a walking life with his harp to gentlemen's houses." As the newspaper gradually found its way into this western county (the first one circulated in Cornwall being the *Sherbourne Mercury*), the occupation of this representative of the bards was taken away ; but he has only become extinct within the last twenty years. These old men wandered constantly from house to house, finding a hearty welcome at all. Board and bed were readily found them, their only payment being a song or a droll (story). A gentleman to whom I am under many obligations writes :—

" The only wandering droll-teller whom I well remember was an old blind man, from the parish of Cury,—I think, as he used to tell many stories about the clever doings of the conjurer Luty of that place, and by that means procure the conjurer much practice from the people of the west. The old man had been a soldier in his youth, and had a small pension at the time he went over the country, accompanied by a boy and dog. He neither begged nor offered anything for sale, but was sure of a welcome to bed and board in every house he called at. He would seldom stop in the same house more than one night, not because he had exhausted his stories, or ' eaten his welcome,' but because it required all his time to visit his acquaintances once in the year. The old man was called Uncle Anthony James. (Uncle is a term of respect, which was very commonly applied to aged men by their juniors in Cornwall. Aunt (A'nt or Ann), as A'nt Sally or Ann' Jenney, was used in the same manner when addressing aged women.

" Uncle Anthony James used to arrive every year in St Leven parish about the end of August. Soon after he reached my father's house, he would stretch himself on the ' chimney-stool,' and sleep until supper-time. When the old man had finished his frugal meal of bread and milk, he would tune his fiddle and ask if ' missus ' would like to hear him sing her favourite ballad. As soon as my dear mother told him how pleased she would be, Uncle Anthony would go through the ' woeful hunting' ('Chevy Chase '), from beginning to end, accompanied by the boy and the fiddle.

I expect the air was his own composition, as every verse was a different tune. The young were then gratified by hearing the 'streams' (strains) of 'Lovely Nancy,' divided in three parts.* I never saw this ballad published, yet it is a very romantic old thing, almost as long as 'Chevy Chase.' Another favourite was :—

> 'Cold blows the wind to-day, sweetheart ;
> Cold are the drops of rain ;
> The first truelove that ever I had
> In the green wood he was slain.
>
> 'Twas down in the garden-green, sweetheart,
> Where you and I did walk ;
> The fairest flower that in the garden grew
> Is withered to a stalk.
>
> 'The stalk will bear no leaves, sweetheart ;
> The flowers will ne'er return ;
> And since my truelove is dead and gone,
> What can I do but mourn ?
>
> 'A twelvemonth and a day being gone,
> The spirit rose and spoke—
> "My body is clay cold, sweetheart ;
> My breath smells heavy and strong ;
> And if you kiss my lily-white lips,
> Your time will not be long."'

" Then follows a stormy kind of duet between the maiden and her lover's ghost, who tries to persuade the maid to accompany him to the world of shadows. Uncle Anthony had also a knack of turning Scotch and Irish songs into Cornish ditties. 'Barbara Allan' he managed in the following way, and few knew but that he had composed the song :—

> 'In Cornwall I was born and bred,
> In Cornwall was my dwelling ;
> And there I courted a pretty maid,
> Her name was Ann Tremellan.

" The old man had the 'Babes in the Wood' for religious folks ; but he avoided the 'Conorums,' as he called the Methodists. Yet the grand resource was the stories in which the supernatural bore great part. The story I told you about the ancestors of the conjurer Luty finding the mermaid, who gave them the power to break the spell of witchcraft, was one of this old man's tales, which he seemed to believe ; and he regarded the conjurer with as much respect as the bard might the priest in olden time. I have a dim recollection of another old droll-teller, called Billy Frost, in St Just, who used to go round to the feasts in the neighbouring parishes, and be well entertained at the public-houses for the sake of his drolls."

* Carew, in his "Survey of Cornwall," makes especial mention of "three men's songs, as being peculiar to this county.

In 1829 there still existed two of those droll-tellers, and from them were obtained a few of the stories here preserved.

These wanderers perpetuated the traditions of the old inhabitants ; but they modified the stories, according to the activity of their fancy, to please their auditors. Not merely this : they without doubt introduced the names of people remembered by the villagers ; and when they knew that a man had incurred the hatred of his neighbours, they made him do duty as a demon, or placed him in no very enviable relation with the devil. The legends of Tregeagle are illustrations of this. The man who has gained the notoriety of being attached to a tale as old as that of Orestes,— was a magistrate in Cornwall two hundred years since. The story of the murderess of Ludgvan and her lover is another, and a very modern, example of the process by which recent events are interwoven with very ancient superstitions.*

When the task of arranging my romances was commenced, I found that the traditions of Devonshire, as far east as Exeter—the tract of country which was known as " Danmonium," or even more recently as " Old Cornwall "—had a striking family resemblance. My collection then received the name it bears, as embracing the district ordinarily known as the West of England. Although I have avoided repeating any of the traditions which are to be found in Mrs Bray's books ; I have not altered my title ; for the examples of folk-lore given in these volumes belong strictly to " Old Cornwall."

There are some points of peculiar interest connected with the Dartmoor traditions, indicating, as I conceive, a purely Saxon origin, deserving an attention which they have not yet received.

Childe's Tomb, in one of the dreariest portions of the moor, is a large cross of granite. This Childe, lord of the manor of Plymstock, was benighted on the moor in a snowstorm ; he killed his horse, and got within its body for warmth, having first written in blood on a granite slab, near which he was found dead,—

> " The first that finds and brings me to my grave,
> The lands of Plymstock he shall have."

The Benedictine monks of Tavistock are said to have found the body, and thus secured their right to the lands. This is without doubt an old Saxon legend, modified, as it has been handed down from age to age. Wistman's Wood, with its " hundred oaks one hundred yards high,"—a remnant of the old Dartmoor Forest,—

* I find in Campbell's " Popular Tales of the West Highlands " particular mention made of numerous historical events which have taken the forms of ancient legends. " There is popular history of events which really happened within the last five centuries."

is the very home of the *Wish hounds*, which hunt so fiercely over the Moor; and this Wistman appears to have been some demon creature, whose name alone remains. Mr Kemble gives *Wusc*, or *Wisc*, as one of the names of Odin. Here we have a similar name given to a strange wood in Devonshire, associated with wild superstitions; and *whish*, or *whisht*, is a common term for that weird sorrow which is associated with mysterious causes.

The stone circles, the stone avenues, and the rock tribunals,—of which Crockern Tor furnishes us with a fine example,—have yet tales to tell, which would well repay any labour that might be bestowed upon them. Ancient British rule gave way to Saxon power, and probably there was no tract in England less known to the Romans than Dartmoor. Thus we may expect to find the paganism of the Briton and the rude Christianity of the Saxon, shadowed out in the remaining legends of Dartmoor.

> "Crocker, Conwys, and Coplestone,
> When the Conqueror came, were found at home,"

is an old Devonshire rhyme. Those names are associated with many a moorland tradition, and indicate their Saxon origin.

It may appear strange to many, that having dealt with the superstitions of the Cornish people, no mention has been made of the Divining Rod (the "*Dowzing Rod*," as it is called), and its use in the discovery of mineral lodes. This has been avoided, in the first place, because any mention of the practice of "*dowzing*" would lead to a discussion, for which this work is not intended; and, in the second place, because the use of the hazel-twig is not Cornish. The divining or dowzing rod is certainly not older than the German miners, who were brought over by Queen Elizabeth to teach the Cornish to work their mines, one of whom, called Schutz, was some time Warden of the Stannaries. Indeed, there is good reason for believing that the use of this wand is of more recent date, and, consequently, removed from the periods which are sought to be illustrated by this collection. The Divining Rod belongs no more to them than do the modern mysteries of twirling hats, of teaching tables to turn, and,—in their wooden way,—to talk.

The giant stories, prefaced with the often-told tale of Gogmagog, are of a character peculiarly their own. They do not appear to resemble the giants described in Mr Campbell's "Popular Tales of the West Highlands;" but it must be admitted that there are some indications of a common origin between those of Cromarty and of Cornwall. In Mr Dasent's translation of Asbjörnsen, and Moe's collection of "Norse Tales," the giant is not like our native friends. May we venture to believe that the

Cornish giant is a true Celt, or may he not belong to an earlier race? He was fond of home, and we have no record of his ever having passed beyond the wilds of Dartmoor. The giants of Lancashire, of Cheshire, and Shropshire have a family likeness, and are, no doubt, closely related; but if they are cousins to the Cornish giants, they are cousins far removed. Dr Latham, in his " Ethnology of the British Islands," says " Tradition, too, indicates the existence of an old march or debatable land; for south of Rugby begins the scene of the deeds of Guy, Earl of Warwick, the slayer of the dun cow." The large bone which is shown in Redcliff Church, Bristol, is the last indication of the dun cow in the south. As this marvellous cow moved within prescribed limits, so was it with the giants of old Cornwall.

The fairies of Cornwall do not exhibit the same marked individuality. Allowing for the influences of physical conditions, they are clearly seen to be an offshoot from the common stock. Yet they have several local peculiarities, and possess names which are especially their own.

A few of the more popular legends of the Cornish saints are preserved, for the purpose of showing how enduringly the first impressions of power, as exhibited by the earliest missionaries, have remained fixed amongst the people; this being due mainly to the mental operation of associating mental power and physical strength with external things in the relations of cause and effect.

I cannot but consider myself fortunate in having collected these traditions thirty-five years ago. They could not be collected now. Mr J. O. Halliwell speaks of the difficulties he experienced in his endeavours to obtain a story. The common people think they will be laughed at if they tell their " ould drolls " to a stranger. Beyond this, many of the stories have died out with those who told them. In the autumn of 1862, being very desirous of getting every example of folk-lore which existed in the remote parishes of Zennor and Morva, I employed the late C. Taylor Stephens, " sometime rural postman from St Ives to Zennor," and the author of " The Chief of Barat-Anac," to hunt over the district. This he did with especial care, and the results of his labours are included in those pages. The postman and poet, although he spent many days and nights amidst the peasantry, failed to procure stories which had been told me, without hesitation, thirty years before.

When it was known that I was engaged in preparing for publication a work on the Traditions and Superstitions of Cornwall, numerous contributions, from much-valued friends, and from strangers interested in the preservation of these characteristics of the West of England, were sent to me. From these some stories have been selected, but by far the larger number were modifications of stories already told. My obligations and thanks are, nevertheless, due to all; but there are two gentlemen to whom acknowledgments beyond this are necessary. These are Mr T. Q. Couch, who had already published examples of the folk-lore of Polperro and the neighbourhood, who has communicated several original stories, and Mr W. Botterell of Caerwyn, a native of St Leven, who possesses a greater knowledge of the household stories of the Land's-End district than any man living. Mr Botterell has, with much labour, supplied me with gleanings from his store, and his stories have been incorporated, in most cases, as he told them. Beyond this, it was satisfactory to have the correctness of many in my own collection confirmed by so reliable an authority. Without the assistance which this gentleman has given, the West Cornwall stories would not have possessed the interest which will be found to belong to them.

One word on the subject of arrangement. In the First Series are arranged all such stories as appear to belong to the most ancient inhabitants of these islands. It is true that many of them, as they are now told, assume a mediæval, or even a modern character. This is the natural result of the passage of a tradition or myth from one generation to another. The customs of the age in which the story is told are interpolated for the purpose of rendering them intelligible to the listeners, and thus they are constantly changing their exterior form. I am, however, disposed to believe that the spirit of all the romances included in this series shows them to have originated before the Christian era. The romances of the Second Series belong certainly to the historic period, though the dates of many of them are exceedingly problematical.

All the stories given in these volumes are the genuine household tales of the people. The only liberties which have been taken with them has been to alter them from the vernacular—in which they were for the most part related—into modern language. This applies to every romance but one. "The Mermaid's Vengeance" is a combination of three stories, having no doubt a common origin, but varying considerably in their details. They were too much alike to bear repeating; consequently it was thought best to throw them into one tale, which should preserve the peculiarities of all. This has been done with much care; and even the songs given preserve lines which are said by the fisherman—from whom the stories were obtained—to have been sung by the mermaids.

The traditions which are told, the superstitions which are spoken of, and the customs which are described in these volumes, may be regarded as true types of the ancient Cornish mythology, and genuine examples of the manners and customs of a people who will not readily deviate from the rules taught them by their fathers.

Romances such as these have floated down to us as wreck upon the ocean. We gather a fragment here and a fragment there, and at length, it may be, we learn something of the name and character of the vessel when it was freighted with life, and obtain a shadowy image of the people who have perished.

Hoping to have been successful in saving a few interesting fragments of the unwritten records of a peculiar race, my labours are submitted to the world. The pleasure of recalling the past has fully repaid me for the labour of arranging the *Traditions of Old Cornwall.*

ROBERT HUNT.

ROMANCES AND SUPERSTITIONS

OF THE

MYTHIC AGES.

THE GIANTS.

"Of Titan's monstrous race
Only some few disturb'd that happy place.
Raw hides they wore for clothes, their drink was blood,
Rocks were their dining-rooms, their prey their food,
Caverns their lodging, and their bed their grove,
Their cup some hollow trunk."
—*Havilan's "Architrenium,"*
translated in Gough's "Camaen."

POPULAR ROMANCES OF THE
WEST OF ENGLAND.

THE AGE OF THE GIANTS.

" Eald enta geweorc
Idlu stodon."—*The Wanderer. Exeter Book.*

" The old works of giants
Stood desolate."—THOMAS WRIGHT.

IN wandering over some of the uncultivated tracts which still
maintain their wildness, austerely and sullenly, against the
march of cultivation, we are certain of finding rude masses of rock
which have some relation to the giants. The giant's hand, or the
giant's chair, or, it may be, the giant's punch-bowl, excites your
curiosity. What were the mental peculiarities of the people who
fixed so permanently those names on fantastic rock-masses?
What are the conditions—mental or otherwise—necessary for the
preservation of these ideas? are questions which I have often
asked myself when wandering amidst the Tors of Dartmoor, and
when seated upon the granite masses which spread themselves so
strangely, yet so picturesquely, over Carn Brea and other rocky
hills in Cornwall. When questions of this kind are continually
recurring, the mind naturally works out some reply, which satisfies
at least itself; and it consequently not unfrequently reposes con-
tentedly on a fallacy as baseless as the giant-spectre of the mountain mists. This may possibly be the condition at which I have
arrived, and many of my readers may smile at my dreams. It is
not in my nature to work without some hypothesis; but I endeavour to hold it as loosely as possible, that it may be yielded up
readily the moment a more promising theory is born, whoever may
be its parent—wherever its birthplace.

Giants, and every form of giant-idea, belong to the wilds of nature. I have never discovered the slightest indication of the existence of a tradition of giants, of the true legendary type, in a fertile valley or in a well-cultivated plain. Wherever there yet linger the faint shadows of the legendary giant, there the country still retains much of its native wildness, and the inhabitants have, to a great extent, preserved their primitive character In other words, they have nurtured a gloomy imagination, and permitted ignorance to continue its melancholy delusions. The untaught mind, in every age, looks upon the grander phenomena of nature with feelings of terror, and endeavours to explain them by the aid of those errors which have been perpetuated from father to son since the days when the priests of superstition sought to rule the minds of men by exciting their fears.

I shall have to tell, by and by, the story of a so-called giant, who could bestride the lovely river which flows through the luxuriant valley of Tavistock, where, also, the inquiring traveller is shown his grave. The giant's grave in Penrith churchyard is familiar to me; and in or near many a picturesque village, shadowed by noble trees, and surrounded by richly-clothed fields, I can point to mounds, and to stones, which are said to be the resting-places of giants. These, however, will invariably be found to be rude monuments to ordinary men, who were possessed of more wealth, intelligence, courage, or strength than their fellows : men who have been the objects of hero-worship, but whose names have perished amidst the wrecks of time. It may be argued that these village giants are creations of the same character as those of the true legendary type, and that both result from analogous operations in the human mind. It may be so ; but how vastly different must have been the constitution of those minds to which we owe the creations of the Titans of our mountains and the large men of our lowlands. Had I the learning necessary for the task of showing that our legendary giant is of Oriental origin, I have not the required leisure to pursue that inquiry to its end ; and I leave it to abler men, contenting myself, and, let me hope, satisfying my readers, by studying the subject in its more simple aspects.

I find, over a tract of country extending from the eastern edge of Dartmoor to the Land's End—and even beyond it, to the Scilly Islands—curious relics of the giants. This district is in many respects a peculiar one. The physical features of the country are broadly marked ; and, even after the civilising influences of centuries, wild nature contests with man, and often maintains her supremacy. On one hand we see industry taking possession of the hills, and holding them firm in its ameliorating grasp ; on the other, we find the sterile moor and the rock-spread region still resisting successfully the influences of man and his appliances. When I travel into other parts of the British Isles, and reach a district having the same general features, I usually discover some outstanding memory of the giants, often, it must be admitted, faint and ill-defined. The giant Tarquin, almost forgotten amidst the whir of spindles, " who had his dwelling in a well-fortified castle near Manchester, on the site of what is yet known by the name of Castlefield," and Carados—

> " A mighty giant, just pull'd down,
> Who lived near Shrewsbury's fair town "—

may be quoted as examples of the fading myths.*

I therefore draw the conclusion that those large masses of humanity—of whom Saturn devouring his own children would seem to be the parental type—can exist only in the memories of those races who are born and live amidst the sublime phenomena of nature.

On the rugged mountain, overspread with rocks which appear themselves to be the ruins of some Cyclopean hall, amidst which the tempests play, still harmless in their fury ;—here, where the breezes of spring and summer whistle as with some new delight— where the autumnal winds murmur the wildest music, or make the saddest wail ; and the winter storms, as if joyous in their strength, shout in voices of thunder from cairn to cairn ;—here does the giant dwell ! On the beetling cliff, where coming tempests delight to send those predicating moanings, which tell of the coming war of winds and waves ;—on rocks which have frowned for ages on the angry sea, and in caverns which mock, by repeating, the sounds of air and water—be they joyous as the voice of birds, or wild and solemn as the howl of savages above the dead ; —here does the giant dwell !

In the valley, too, has he sometimes fixed his home ; but the giant has usually retired from business when he leaves the hills. Even here we miss not the old associations. Huge boulders are spread on every side ; rock-masses are overgrown with furze, ferns, mosses, and heaths ; and torrents rush from the hills, bringing, as it were, their native music with them. Wherever, indeed, the giants have made a home, we find a place remarkable for the grand scale on which the works of nature are displayed.

* See " Popular Traditions of Lancashire," by J. Roby, Esq., M.R.S.L. Bohn, 1843

The giants of Danmonium—as that region was once named to which I have confined my inquiries—will be found to be a marked race. They appear to bear about them the characteristics of the giants of the East. They have the peculiarities which may be studied in those true Oriental Titans, Gog and Magog, who still preside so grimly and giantly at our City feasts. They have none of that stony, cold-hearted character which marks the giants of Scandinavia; and although Mr Keightley* would connect the mighty Thor with the no less mighty giants of the Arabian stories, I think it can be shown that all those of the West of England resemble their Northern brethren only in the manner in which the sensual monsters succumb to the slightest exercise of thought.

Mr J. O. Halliwell appears to have been a little surprised at discovering, during a very short residence in the West of Cornwall, that the Land's End district was "anciently the chosen land of the giants;" that it was "beyond all other the favourite abode and the land of the English giants." Peculiarly fitted for the inquiry as Mr Halliwell is, by his life-long studies, it is to be regretted that he spent so brief a period amidst "what still remains of these memorials of a Titan race." †

Who were the giants? Whence came they? ‡ I asked myself these questions when, seated in the Giant's Chair, I have looked down upon a wide expanse of "furzy downs," over which were scattered in picturesque confusion vast masses of granite rocks, every one of them standing in monumental grandeur, inscribed by the finger of tradition with memorials of this mighty race. Did Cormelian and Cormoran really build St Michael's Mount? Did Thunderbore walk the land, inspiring terror by his extreme ugliness? Did Bolster persecute the blessed St Agnes, until she was compelled by stratagem to destroy him? Did, indeed, our British Titans play at quoits and marbles with huge rocks? Is it a fact that all the giants died of grief after Corineus overthrew Gog Magog on Plymouth Hoe? Let us, if only for amusement—and to give to a light work some appearance of

---

* Tales and Popular Fictions: their Resemblance and Transmission from Country to Country. By Thomas Keightley. 1834.

† Rambles in Western Cornwall by the Footsteps of the Giants, with Notes on the Celtic Remains of the Land's End District, and the Islands of Scilly. By J. O. Halliwell, F.R.S. 1861.

‡ That these Titans lived down to historic times is suggested by the following :—

"Guy, Earl of Warwick, fought at the request of Athelstan a combat with Colbrand, a Danish giant, and slew him."—*Gilbert*, quoting Carew, who again quotes Walter of Exeter. Vol. iv., p. 111.

research—examine a few antiquated authorities, who may be said —in their own way—indirectly to answer those questions.

M. Pezron, D.D., and abbot of *La Charmoye,* wrote a strange book, "The Antiquities of Nations," which in 1706 was "Englished by Mr Jones."*

In his Epistle Dedicatory to Charles Lord Halifax, speaking of the "Famous Pezron," Mr Jones asks, "Was there ever any before him that attempted to Trace the Origin of the *Celtæ,* who with Great Probability of Truth, were the same People, and spoke the same Language, as our Ancient *Britains* did. and their Descendants continue to do to this Day, so high as *Gomer* and the *Gomarians ?* "

This authority, with a great display of learning, proves that Gomer, the eldest son of Japhet, was the chief of the Gomarians, and that these Gomarians afterwards were called Galatians, or Gauls. We further learn from him that a section of the Gomarians were called Sacæ, and that the Sacæ went into Phrygia, and afterwards assumed the name of TITANS. This race, "and especially the Princes that commanded them, exceeded all others in Bulk and Strength of Body ; and hence it is that they have been looked upon to be terrible people, and, as it were, Giants. The Scripture itself, the Rule of Truth, even gives such an Idea as this, of those famous and potent men, who, according to it, ruled over all the Earth. *Judith,* speaking of them in her fine Song, called them *Giants* the sons of the *Titans.*† And the Prophet Isaiah informs us, also, that these Giants were anciently Masters of the World."

This mighty race dwelt in mountains, woods, and rough and inaccessible places, and " they lay in the Hollows of Valleys, and the like Places of Shelter and retirement, because they had no Houses in those Times." The learned abbot proceeds, exerting all his powers to prove that the Titans were the true Celtæ—that a people of Greece were the descendants of the Titans—that Gomer was "the true stock of the Gauls"—and that Magog, his brother, " is also looked upon to be the Origin of the *Scythians,* or People of *Great Tartary.*"‡

To seize on another authority, who appears to connect the Oriental with the British cromlech, and through those the people

---

* The Antiquities of Nations : more particularly of the Celtæ or Gauls, taken to be originally the same People as our Ancient Britains.

† Judith xvi. 7 : "Neither the sons of the Titans smite him, nor high giants set upon him."

‡ Those who are curious in this matter may examine also, "Gomer ; or, A Brief Analysis of the Language and Knowledge of the Ancient Cymry. By John Williams, A.M., Oxen., Archdeacon of Cardigan."

whose remains they cover, we will quote Dr E. D. Clarke, who describes* a Cyclopean structure visited by him near Kiel, consisting of three upright stones, supporting horizontally an enormous slab of granite. After mentioning several cromlechs of a similar character, and other "stupendous vestiges of Cyclopean architecture," he says—"There is nothing *Gothic* about them— nothing denoting the *Cimbri* or the *Franks*, or the old *Saxons*— but rather the ancient *Gaulish*, the ancient *British*, and the ancient *Irish;* and if this be admitted, they were *Titan-Celts:* the GIANTS of the *sacred*, and the CYCLOPS of the *heathen* historians." I am informed that Mr Christy has lately examined several cromlechs in Algeria ; beneath each he found a human skeleton.

Such may be presumed to be the sources from which sprang the giants of Cornwall, whose labours—of which relics still remain —prove them to have been a race by the side of whom

> " In stature the tall Amazon
> Had stood a pigmy's height."

Everything they have left us informs us that they were men who

> " Would have ta'en
> Achilles by the hair, and bent his neck,
> Or with a finger stay'd Ixion's wheel." †

With these evidences, who then dares say that the *Samotheans,* who, under the reign of *Bardus*, people this island, were not subdued by *Albion*, a giant son of Neptune, "who called the land after his own name, and reigned forty-four years."‡ Let us not forget the evidence also given by Milton in his "Lycidas," when he asks, in his poetic sorrow, if his friend

> " Sleep'st by the fable of Bellerus old,
> Where the great Vision of the guarded Mount
> Looks towards Namancos and Bayona's hold."

Bellerian was the name formerly given to the promontory of the Land's End. It was the home of a mighty giant, after whom, in all probability, the headland was called.§

---

* Travels in Various Countries of Europe, Asia, and Africa, vol. ix., p. 59.
† Hyperion. By John Keats.
‡ The History of Britain. By John Milton. Second edition, 1678.
§ Keightley, who of all men should have traced this Bellerus to his home, in his "Life of Milton" confuses St Michael's Mount and the Land's End, and "conceives the giant Bellerus to have been an invention of Milton's." The evidence of the "History

Tradition throws a faint light back into those remote ages, and informs us that Cyclopean walls, vast earthworks, and strangely-piled masses of rock, which still remain, imperishable monuments of animal power, in various parts of the ancient Danmonium, were the works of the giants. With the true history of Jack the Giant-Killer—of him of the Bean-Stalk—and some others, we are all acquainted. We listened to those histories ere yet the dark seed of that troublesome weed—doubt—had germinated. They were poured forth from loving lips into believing ears ; and often in the sleep of innocency have we buried our heads in the maternal bosom to hide the horrid visage of some Cormoran Blunderbore, or Thunderbore, and escape the giant's toils. By this process the stories were imprinted on memory's tablets with an indelible ink, and for long years, the sponge and water—which is employed by the pioneers in the great March of Intellect—has been used almost in vain. Notwithstanding the influences which have been brought to bear, with no kindly spirit, upon the old-world tales, we have still lingering, though in ruins, the evidences by which they were supported. Mr Thomas Wright, in his " Memoir on the Local Legends of Shropshire," quotes from (and translates his quotation) an Anglo-Saxon poem, which bears the title of " The Ruin," in the " Exeter Book . "—

> " Wondrous is this wall-stone,
> The fates have broken it,
> Have burst the burgh-place ;
> The work of giants is perishing."

From the Land's End* to the eastern edge of Dartmoor, the perishing works of the giants—wondrous wall-stones—are yet to be found. In many instances the only records by which we can mark the homes of the giants are the names which yet cling to the rocks on the hills where they dwelt. The Giant's Cradle, on Trecrobben Hill, reminds us of the great man's infancy, as does also the Giant's Spoon, which is near it. The giant of Trecrobben

of Britain" shows with how much diligence the legendary lore which existed in 1678 had been sought out by the poet ; and his grand epic proves with how much reverence Milton studied our own mythology. I could lead the reader to twenty places around the Land's End which were not discovered even by Mr J. O. Halliwell when rambling " In Western Cornwall by the Footsteps of the Giants," upon which Bellerus, although he has not left his name, has left a long-enduring record. See Appendix A.

* " Not far from the land's ende there is a little village called *Trebegean*—in English, *the towne of the Giant's Grave*,—near whereunto, and within memory (as I have been informed), certain workmen, searching for Tynne, discovered a long square vault, which contained the bones of an excessive bigge carkas, and verified this Etimology of the name."—*Carew's Survey of Cornwall.*

was, beyond question, a temperate one, as the Giant's Well, without the walls of his castle, incontestibly proves. But what shall we say of his neighbour, who dwelt at Beersheba, where the Giant's Bowl is still suggestive of imbibitions deep. The monumental mass of granite on Dartmoor, known as *Bowerman's Nose*, may hand down to us the resting-place and name of a giant whose nose was the index of his vice; though Carrington, in his poem of " Dartmoor," supposes these rocks to be

> " A granite god,—
> To whom, in days long flown, the suppliant knee
> In trembling homage bow'd."

Let those, however, who are curious in this problem visit the granite idol ; when, as Carrington assures us, he will find that the inhabitants of

> " The hamlets near
> Have legends rude connected with the spot
> (Wild swept by every wind), on which he stands,
> The Giant of the Moor."

Of the last resting-places of the giants there are many. Mardon, on Dartmoor, has a *Giant's Grave*,* and from that rude region, travelling westward, we find these graves—proving the mortality of even this Titan race—rising on many a moor and mountain, until, crossing the sea, we see numerous giants' graves in the Scilly Islands ; as though they had been the favourite resting-places of the descendants of those who dreamed of yet more western lands, beneath the setting sun, which were, even to them, " the Islands of the Blest." †

---

* See Shortt's Collection, p. 28.

† Mr Augustus Smith, in the Reports of the Royal Institution of Cornwall, has described one of the graves opened by him during a visit paid by the Cambrian Archæological Society to the Scilly Isles.

Hugh Miller, in his " Scenes and Legends of the North of Scotland," tells us a story of the giants of Cromarty, which shows us that they were intimately related to the giants of Cornwall. Moreover, from him we learn something of the parentage of our giants, for we presume the Scottish myth may be applied with equal truth to the Titans of the south. " Diocletian, king of Syria, say the historians, had thirty-three daughters, who, like the daughters of Danaus, killed their husbands on their wedding-night. The king, their father, in abhorrence of their crime, crowded them all into a ship, which he abandoned to the mercy of the waves, and which was drifted by tides and winds, until it arrived on the coast of Britain, then an uninhabited island. There they lived solitary, subsisting on roots and berries, the natural produce of the soil, until an order of demons, becoming enamoured of them, took them for their wives, and a tribe of giants, who must be regarded as the true aborigines of the country, if indeed the demons have not a prior claim, were the fruits of those marriages. Less fortunate, however, than even their prototypes, the Cyclops, the whole tribe was extirpated a few years after by Brutus, the

There is scarcely a pile of rocks around our western shore upon which the giants have not left their impress. At Tol-Pedden-Penwith we have the Giant's Chair ; at Carn Boscawen we see the Giant's Pulpit. If we advance nearer to the towns, even the small mass of rocks behind Street-an-Noan, near Penzance, called Tolcarne, has the mark of the Giant's Foot. The priests, however, in the season of their rule, strove to obliterate the memories of those great pagans. They converted the footprint at Tolcarne—and similar indentations elsewhere—into the mark of the devil's hoof, when he stamped in rage at the escape of a sinner, who threw himself from the rock, strong in faith, into the arms of the Church. In more recent times, this footmark has been attributed to the devil jumping with joy, as he flew off, from this spot, with some unfortunate miller, who had lost his soul by mixing china clay with his flour. The metamorphosis of ancient giants into modern devils is a curious feature in our inquiry. At Lemorna we have the Giant's Cave. On Gulval Cairn we find also the giant's mark, which the magic of Sir H. Davy's science could not dispel.* On Carn Brea are no end of evidences of these Titans—the Giant's Hand rivalling in size any of the monstrous monuments of the Egyptian gods. Thus, in nearly every part of the country where granite rocks prevail, the monuments of the giants may be found. Why do the giants show such a preference for granite ? At Looe, indeed, the Giant's Hedge is a vast earthwork; but this is an exception,† unless the Bolster in St Agnes is a giant's work. In pursuing the dim lights which yet remain to guide us to the history of the giants, we must not forget the record of the *Fatal Wrestling* on Plymouth Hoe.

parricide, who, with a valour to which mere bulk could render no effectual resistance, overthrew Gog, Magog, and Termagol, and a whole host of others with names equally terrible." The Cromarty legends give accounts of a ponderous stone flung from the point of a spindle across Dornoch Firth ; and of another yet larger, still to be seen, a few miles from Dingwall, which was thrown equally far, and which bears the impress of the giant's finger and thumb. Also, they tell us of the *cailliach-more*, or great woman, who "from a pannier filled with earth and stones, which she carried on her back, formed almost all the hills of Ross-shire." The Sutars, as the promontories of Cromarty are named, served as the work-stools of two giants, who were shoemakers, or soutars, and hence, says Hugh Miller, "in process of time the name soutar was transferred by a common metonymy from the craftsmen to their stools, the two promontories, and by this name they have ever since been distinguished."

* Sir H. Davy, when a youth, would frequently steal to Gulval Cairn, and in its solitude pursue his studies.

† See Davies Gilbert's History, vol. iv., p. 29.

CORINEUS AND GOGMAGOG.

WHO can dare question such an authority as John Milton? In his " History of Britain, that part especially now called England. From the first Traditional beginning continued to the Norman Conquest. Collected out of the antientest and best authors thereof," he gives us the story of Brutus and of Corineus, " who with the battele Ax which he was wont to manage against the *Tyrrhen Giants,* is said to have done marvells." With the adventures of these heroes in *Africa* and in *Aquitania* we have little concern. They suffer severe defeats; and then " Brutus, finding now his powers much lessn'd, and this not yet the place foretold him, leaves Aquitain, and with an easy course arriving at Totness in *Dev'nshire,* quickly perceivs heer to be the promis'd end of his labours." The following matters interest us more closely :*—

" The Iland, not yet *Britain,* but *Albion,* was in a manner desert and inhospitable, kept only by a remnant of *Giants,* whose excessive Force and Tyrannie had consumed the rest. Them Brutus destroies, and to his people divides the land, which, with some reference to his own name, he thenceforth calls *Britain.* To *Corineus, Cornwall,* as now we call it, fell by lot; the rather by him lik't, for that the hugest Giants in Rocks and Caves were said to lurk still there; which kind of Monsters to deal with was his old exercise.

" And heer, with leave bespok'n to recite a grand fable, though dignify'd by our best Poets : While *Brutus,* on a certain Festival day, solemnly kept on that shoar where he first landed (*Totness*), was with the People in great jollity and mirth, a crew of these savages, breaking in upon them, began on the sudden another sort of Game than at such a meeting was expected. But at length by many hands overcome, *Goëmagog,* the hugest, in hight twelve cubits, is reserved alive; that with him Corineus, who desired nothing more, might try his strength, whom in a Wrestle the Giant catching aloft, with a terrible hugg broke three of his Ribs : Nevertheless Corineus, enraged, heaving him up by main force, and on his shoulders bearing him to the next high rock, threw him hedlong all shatter'd into the sea, and left his name on the cliff, called ever since *Langoëmagog,* which is to say, the Giant's Leap." The same story has been somewhat differently told, although there is but little variation in the main incidents. When Brutus and

---

* For a discussion of the question relative to Brutus, see Gough's "Camden's Britannia." vol. i., pp. xlix. to lv.

Corineus, with their Trojan hosts, landed at Plymouth, these chiefs wisely sent parties into the interior to explore the country, and to learn something of the people. At the end of the first day, all the soldiers who had been sent out as exploring parties, returned in great terror, pursued by several terrific giants. Brutus and Corineus were not, however, to be terrified by the immense size of their enemies, nor by the horrid noises which they made, hoping to strike terror into the armed hosts. These chieftains rallied their hosts and marched to meet the giants, hurling their spears and flinging their darts against their huge bodies. The assault was so unexpected that the giants gave way, and eventually fled to the hills of Dartmoor. Gogmagog, the captain of the giants, who was sadly wounded in the leg, and, unable to proceed, hid himself in a bog; but there, by the light of the moon, he was found by the Trojan soldiers, bound with strong cords, and carried back to the Hoe at Plymouth, where the camp was. Gogmagog was treated nobly by his victors, and his wounds were speedily healed. Brutus desired to make terms with the giants; and it was at length proposed by Gogmagog to try a fall with the strongest in the host, and that whoever came off the conqueror should be proclaimed king of Cornwall, and hold possession of all the western land. Corineus at once accepted the challenge of the monster. Notwithstanding, the giant,

> "Though bent with woes,
> Full eighteen feet in height he rose;
> His hair, exposed to sun and wind,
> Like wither'd heath, his head entwined,"

and that Corineus was but little above the ordinary size of man, the Trojan chief felt sure of a victory. The day for the wrestling was fixed. The huge Gogmagog was allowed to send for the giants, and they assembled on one side of a cleared space on Plymouth Hoe, while the Trojan soldiers occupied the other. All arms were thrown aside; and fronting each other, naked to the waist, stood the most lordly of the giants, and the most noble of men. The conflict was long, and it appeared for sometime doubtful. Brute strength was exerted on one side, and trained skill on the other. At length Corineus succeeded in seizing Gogmagog by the girdle, and by regularly-repeated impulses he made the monster undulate like a tree shaken by a winter storm, until at length, gathering all his strength into one effort, the giant was forced to his back on the ground, the earth shaking with his weight, and the air echoing with the thunder of his mighty groan, as the breath was forced from his body by the terrible momentum of his fall. There lay the giant, and there were all the other giants, appalled at the power which they could not understand, but which convinced them that there was something superior to mere animal strength. Corineus breathed for a minute, then he rushed upon his prostrate foe, and seizing him by the legs, he dragged him to the edge of the cliff, and precipitated him into the sea. The giant fell on the rocks below, and his body was broken into fragments by the fall; while the

> " Fretted flood
> Roll'd frothy waves of purple blood."

" Gogmagog's Leap " has been preserved near the spot which now presents a fortress to the foes of Britain ; and there are those "who say that, at the last digging on the Haw for the foundation of the citadel of Plymouth, the great jaws and teeth therein found were those of Gogmagog." *

THE GIANTS OF THE MOUNT.

THE history of the redoubtable Jack proves that St Michael's Mount was the abode of the giant Cormelian, or, as the name is sometimes given, Cormoran. We are told how Jack destroyed the giant, and the story ends. Now, the interesting part, which has been forgotten in the narrative, is not only that Cormoran lived *on*, but that he built the Mount, his dwelling-place. St Michael's Mount, as is tolerably well known, is an island at each rise of the tide—the distance between it and the mainland being a little more than a quarter of a mile. In the days of the giants, however, it was some six miles from the sea, and was known as *the White Rock in the wood*, or in Cornish, " Carreg luz en kuz." Of the evidences in favour of this, more will be said when the traditions connected with physical phenomena are dealt with. In this wood the giant desired to build his home, and to rear it above the trees, that he might from the top keep watch over the neighbouring country. Any person carefully observing the structure of the granite rocks will notice their tendency to a cubical form. These stones were carefully selected by the giant from the granite of the neighbouring hills, and he was for a long period employed in carrying and piling those huge masses, one on the other, in which labour he compelled his wife to aid him. It has been suggested, with much show of probability, that the confusion of the two names

* See Appendix B for the " Poem of the Wrestling," &c.

alluded to has arisen from the fact that the giant was called Cormoran, and that the name of his wife was Cormelian ; at all events, there is no harm in adopting this hypothesis. The toil of lifting those granitic masses from their primitive beds, and of carrying them through the forest, was excessive. It would seem that the heaviest burthens were imposed upon Cormelian, and that she was in the habit of carrying those rocky masses in her apron. At a short distance from the " White Rock," which was now approaching completion, there exists large masses of greenstone rock. Cormelian saw no reason why one description of stone would not do as well as another ; and one day, when the giant Cormoran was sleeping, she broke off a vast mass of the greenstone rock, and taking it in her apron, hastened towards the artificial hill with it, hoping to place it without being observed by Cormoran. When, however, Cormelian was within a short distance of the " White Rock," the giant awoke, and presently perceived that his wife was, contrary to his wishes, carrying a green stone instead of a white one. In great wrath he arose, followed her, and, with a dreadful imprecation, gave her a kick. Her apron-string broke, and the stone fell on the sand. There it has ever since remained, no human power being sufficient to remove it. The giantess died, and the mass of greenstone, resting, as it does, on clay slate rocks, became her monument. In more recent days, when the light of Christianity was dawning on the land, this famous rock was still rendered sacred : " a lytle chapel "* having been built on it ; and to this day it is usually known as the " The Chapel Rock."†

THE KEY OF THE GIANT'S CASTLE.

THE giant's castle at Treryn, remarkable as a grand example of truly British Cyclopean architecture, was built by the power of enchantment. The giant to whom all the rest of his race were indebted for this stronghold was in every way a remarkable mortal. He was stronger than any other giant, and he was a mighty necromancer. He sat on the promontory of Treryn, and by the power of his will he compelled the castle to rise out of the sea. It is only kept in its present position by virtue of a magic key. This the giant placed in a holed rock, known as the Giant's Lock, and whenever this key, a large round stone, can be taken out of the lock, the promontory of Treryn and its castle will disappear beneath the waters. There are not many people who obtain even a sight of this wonderful key. You must pass at low

---

* Leland.   † See Appendix C for the Irish legend of Shara and Sheela.

brought to bear upon the extraction of tin and copper from the earth. Beyond this thickly-peopled region the eye wanders yet eastward, and eventually reposes on the series of granite hills which rise beyond St Austell and stretch northward,—the two highest hills in Cornwall, which are known as Roughtor and Brownwhilly,* being in this range.

Let the observer now turn his face northward, and a new and varied scene lies before him. Within two miles the waters of St Ives' Bay break against the cliffs. On the left is the creek of Hayle, which has been fashioned by the energy of man into a useful harbour, and given rise to the foundation of two extensive iron-foundries. Between those and the sea are the hills of blown sand, which have ever been the homes of the Fairy people. The lighthouse of Godrevy stands, a humble companion, to balance in this bay the "Mount," which adorns the bay, washing the southern slope of this "narrow neck of land." Godrevy marks the region of sand extending to the eastward. To the north the shores become more and more rugged, culminating in St Agnes' Beacon,—a hill of graceful form rising somewhat rapidly to a considerable elevation. From this the "beetling cliffs" stretch away northward, until the bold promontory Trevose Head closes the scene, appropriately displaying another of those fine examples of humanity—a lighthouse.

To the left, towards the sea, rises the cenotaph of Knill, an eccentric man, who evidently sought to secure some immortality by this building, and the silly ceremonials carried on around it; the due performance of which he has secured by bequests to the Corporation of St Ives. Around this the mining district of St Ives is seen, and her fishing-boats dotting the sea give evidence of another industry of vast importance to the town and neighbourhood. Westward of St Ives, hills more brown and rugged than any which have yet been viewed stretch away to Zennor, Morva, and St Just, and these, girding the scene beneath our feet, shut out from us the region of the Land's End.

On the summit of this hill, which is only surpassed in savage grandeur by Carn Brea, the giants built a castle—the four entrances to which still remain in Cyclopean massiveness to attest the Herculean powers by which such mighty blocks were piled upon each other. There the giant chieftains dwelt in awful state. Along the serpentine road, passing up the hill to the principal gateway, they dragged their captives, and on the great flat rocks within the castle they sacrificed them. Almost every rock still bears some name connected with the giants—"a race may perish,

* *Bryn-whella,* the highest hill, according to Mr Bellows.

but the name endures." The treasures of the giants who dwelt here are said to have been buried in the days of their troubles, when they were perishing before the conquerors of their land. Their gold and jewels were hidden deep in the granite caves of this hill, and secured by spells as potent as those which Merlin placed upon his "hoarded treasures." They are securely preserved, even to the present day, and carefully guarded from man by the Spriggans, or Trolls, of whom we have to speak in another page.

THE GIANTS AT PLAY.

IN several parts of Cornwall there are evidences that these Titans were a sportive race. Huge rocks are preserved to show where they played at trap-ball, at hurling, and other athletic games. The giants of Trecrobben and St Michael's Mount often met for a game at bob-buttons. The Mount was the "bob," on which flat masses of granite were placed to serve as buttons, and Trecrobben Hill was the "mit," or the spot from which the throw was made. This order was sometimes reversed. On the outside of St Michael's Mount, many a granite slab which had been knocked off the "bob" is yet to be found; and numerous piles of rough cubical masses of the same rock, said to be the granite of Trecrobben Hill,* show how eagerly the game was played.

Trecrobben Hill was well chosen by the giants as the site of their castle. From it they surveyed the country on every side; and friend or enemy was seen at a considerable distance as he approached the guarded spot. It is as clear as tradition can make it, that Trecrobben was the centre of a region full of giants. On Lescudjack Hill, close to Penzance, there is "The Giant's Round," evidently the scene of many a sanguinary conflict, since the Cornish antiquarian authority Borlase informs us, that Lesgudzhek signifies the "Castle of the Bloody Field." On the cairn at Gulval are several impressions on the rocks, all referable to the giants. In Madron there is the celebrated "Giant's Cave;" and the well-known Lanyon cromlech is reported by some to be the "Giant's Coit," while others declare it to be the "Giant's Table." Cairn Galva, again, is celebrated for its giant; and, indeed, every

---

* Mr O. Halliwell, who carefully followed in the "Footsteps of the Giants," referring to this game as played by them, says:—

"Doubtlessly the Giant's Chair on Trink Hill was frequently used during the progress of the game, nor is it improbable that the Giant's Well was also in requisition. Here, then, were at hand opportunities for rest and refreshment—the circumstances of the various traditions agreeing well with, and, in fact, demonstrating the truth of each other."

hill within sight has some monument preserving the memory of those, " the Titans fierce."

HOLIBURN OF THE CAIRN.*

HOLIBURN, according to tradition, was a very amiable and somewhat sociable gentleman ; but, like his brethren, he loved to dwell amongst the rocks of Cairn Galva.   He made his home in this remote region, and relied for his support on the gifts of sheep and oxen from the farmers around—he, in return, protecting them from the predatory incursions of the less conscientious giants of Trecrobben.   It is said that he fought many a battle in the defence of his friends, and that he injured but one of his neighbours during his long lifetime.   This was, however, purely an accident.   The giant was at play with the human pigmies, and in the excitement of the moment, being delighted at the capital game made by a fine young peasant, he tapped him on the head, and scattered his brains on the grass.   I once heard that Holiburn had married a farmer's daughter, and that a very fine race, still bearing a name not very dissimilar, was the result of this union. Holiburn, like his brethren, was remarkably fond of quoits ; indeed, go where we will within the Land's End district, the " Giant's Quoit " is still shown.   Other—shall we call them *household*—relics of the giants occur.   From Cairn Galva to Zennor we find a series of " Giant's Chairs ;" and, careful to preserve each remarkable relic of this interesting race, here is also the " Giant's Dinner-plate."   That St Ives, too, was not without its giant, although the record of his name is lost, is evident from the fact that a tooth, an inch broad, was taken from a " Giant's Grave." †

* " Somewhere amongst the rocks in this cairn is the Giant's Cave—in ages long gone by the abode of a giant named Holiburn."—HALLIWELL. Mr Halliwell was fortunate in securing a name.   I have often heard of the giant in question, but I never heard his name.

† The following extract from a note written by the late Zennor postman and poet, shows how enduringly the giants have left their names on the rocks of Cornwall :—

" Some districts in Cornwall were said to have been peopled in olden times by giants, and even Zennor district possesses the largest quoit—three Logan rocks—whilst Trecrobben Hill still exhibits the Bowl in which the giants of the west used to wash.   The large granite boulder near to the residence of the Rev. Mr S——, curate of Morva, is said to be the Giant's Dinner-plate.   Farther down the hill, and hard by the Zennor vicarage, the seats of the giants are still shown by the inhabitants.   Indeed, so strong is the belief that giants inhabited the hills of the west, that a young lady in this neighbourhood assayed, a month or two ago, to deliver a lecture, or address, on the subject, taking for her text, ' There were giants in those days.'   But the giants were not immortal; colossal as were their frames, they too had to ' sleep with their fathers.'   Whether Jack the Giant-killer took any part in ridding the earth of this wonderful race of men

THE GIANT OF NANCLEDRY.*

IN Nancledry Bottoms, about a mile from the famous hill Castle-an-Dinas, there stood at one time a thatched house near the brook which runs murmuring down the valley. Rather more than thirty years since, some mouldering "clob" (mud) walls, indicating the existence at one time of a large dwelling, were pointed to as the former residence of a terrible giant. He appears to have led a solitary life, and to have lived principally on little children, whom he is said to have swallowed whole. His strength was indicated by several huge masses of granite which were scattered around the Bottoms, and in the neighbouring fields. These were carried by him in his pockets, to defend himself from the giants of Trecrobben, with whom he appears to have been on unfriendly terms. This giant is noteworthy as the only one recorded who lived in a house.

TREBIGGAN THE GIANT *

TREBEGEAN is the name of a village near the Land's End. This name, as we have already stated, signifies the town of the giant's grave. The giant's existence was confirmed by the discovery of a vault and some large bones in it, on this spot.†

Trebiggan divides with Tregeagle the honourable immortality of being employed to frighten children into virtue. Often have I heard the unruly urchins of this neighbourhood threatened with Trebiggan. They are told that Trebiggan was a vast man, with arms so long that he could take men out of the ships passing by the Land's End, and place them on the Longships ; but that sometimes he would, having had his fun with them, good-humouredly place them on board their ships or boats again. He is said to have dined every day on little children, who were generally fried on a large flat rock which stood at a little distance from his cave.

THE LORD OF PENGERSWICK AND THE GIANT OF ST MICHAEL'S MOUNT.

THE giant who dwelt on St Michael's Mount had grown very old, and had lost all his teeth; still he was the terror of the neighbouring villages. The horrid old monster—who had but one

we cannot positively state ; but thus much is certain, the giants were succeeded by a numerous race of small people, and so small as not to be observable by the eye."

* See Appendix D.   † See Heath's Description of Cornwall, 1750.

eye, and that one in the middle of his forehead—would, whenever he required food—which was pretty often—walk or wade across to Market-Jew, as the tide might be, select the best cow in the neighbourhood, and, swinging it over his shoulders, return to his island. This giant had often taken cattle from the Pengerswick estate ; and one day he thought he should like another of this choice breed. Accordingly, away he went, across the sea, to Pengerswick Cove. The giant did not know that the lord of Pengerswick had returued from the East, a master of " white-witchcraft," or magic. The lord had seen the giant coming, and he began to work his spells. The giant was bewildered, yet he knew not how. At last, after much trouble, he caught a fine calf, tied its four feet together, passed his great head between the fore and hind legs, and, with the calf hanging on his shoulders, he trod in joy towards the shore. He wandered on in perfect unconsciousness of the path, and eventually he found himself on the precipitous edge of the great black rock which still marks the western side of Pengerswick Cove. As if the rock had been a magnet, the giant was chained fast. He twisted, turned, and struggled in vain. He found himself gradually becoming stiff, so that at last he could neither move hand nor foot ; yet were his senses more keenly alive than ever. The giant had to remain thus, during a long winter's night, with the calf bleating, as never calf bleated before, into his ear. In the morning when the enchanter thought he had punished the giant sufficiently, he mounted his mare, and rode down to the shore. He disenchanted the giant, by giving him a severe horse-whipping, and he then made him drop the calf. He continued to flog the giant until he leaped off the rock into the sea, through which in great agony he waded to the Mount ; and from that day to this he has never ventured on the mainland.

We learn, however, from undoubted authority, that some time after this, Tom, the giant of Lelant, visited the giant on the Mount, and, finding him half starved, he took his aunt Nancy from Gulval to see his friend, with a large supply of butter and eggs. The old giant was exceedingly glad to see the farmer's wife, bought all her store at a very extravagant price, and bargained and paid in advance for more. He had a store of wealth in the caverns of the Mount. The knowing old woman kept him well supplied as long as the giant had money to pay her ; and aunt Nancy's family became the wealthiest in the parish of Gulval.

THE GIANT OF ST MICHAEL'S MOUNT LOSES HIS WIFE.

THE giant on the Mount and the giant on Trecrobben Hill were very friendly. They had only one cobbling-hammer between them, which they would throw from one to the other, as either required it. One day the giant on the Mount wanted the hammer in a great hurry, so he shouted, " Holloa, up there ! Trecrobben, throw us down the hammer, woost a'?"

" To be sure," sings out Trecrobben ; " here ! look out, and catch 'm."

Now, nothing would do but the giant's wife, who was very near-sighted, must run out of her cave to see Trecrobben throw the hammer. She had no hat on ; and coming at once out into the light, she could not distinguish objects. Consequently, she did not see the hammer coming through the air, and received it between her eyes. The force with which it was flung was so great that the massive bone of the forehead of the giantess was crushed, and she fell dead at the giant's feet. You may be sure there was a great to-do between the two giants. They sat wailing over the dead body, and with their sighs they produced a tempest. These were unavailing to restore the old lady, and all they had to do was to bury her. Some say they lifted the Chapel Rock and put her under it, others, that she is buried beneath the castle court, while some—no doubt the giants' detractors—declare that they rolled the body down into the sea, and took no more heed of it.

*TOM AND THE GIANT BLUNDERBUSS; OR, THE WHEEL AND EXE FIGHT.**

A YOUNG giant, who does not appear to have been known by any other name than Tom, lived somewhere westward of Hayle, probably in Lelant. Tom would eat as much meat as

---

* The similarity of this story to the well-known tale of " Tom Hickathrift " will strike every one. It might be supposed that the old story of the strong man of the Isle of Ely had been read by some Cornish man, and adapted to the local peculiarities. This may possibly have been the case, but I do not think it probable. I first heard the story from a miner, on the floors of Ding-Dong Mine, during my earliest tour in search of old stories. I have since learned that it was a common story with the St Ives nurses, who told it to amuse or terrify their children. Recently, I have had the same tale communicated to me by a friend, who got it from a farmer living in Lelant. This story is confined to the parishes of Lelant, St Ives, Sancreed, Towednach, Morva, and Zennor.

three men, and when he was in the humour he could do as much work as half a dozen. Howbeit, Tom was a lazy fellow, and spent most of his time wandering about the parish with his hands in his pockets. Occasionally Tom would have an industrious fit; then, if he found any of his neighbours hedging, he would turn to and roll in all the largest rocks from over the fields, for "grounders." * This was the only work Tom took delight in; he was won't to say, he could feel his strength about such work as that. Tom didn't appear so very big a man in those days, when all men were twice the size they are now. He was about four feet from shoulder to shoulder, square built, and straight all the way down from shoulder to cheens (loins).

Tom's old mother was constantly telling her idle son to do something to earn his food, but the boy couldn't find any job to his mind for a long time. At last he undertook to drive a brewer's wain, in the hope of getting into plenty of strong drink, and he went to live in Market-Jew, where the brewery was. The first day he was so employed, he was going to St Ives with his load of beer, and on the road he saw half a score of men trying to lift a fallen tree on to a "draw." It was, however, more than the whole of them could do.

"Stand clear!" shouts Tom.

He put his hands, one on each side of the tree, and lifted it on the "draw," without so much as saying "Ho!" to his oxen, or looking behind him. The feat was performed in Ludgvan Lees, and a little farther on was a giant's place diverting the road, which should have gone straight to St Ives but for it. This place was hedged in with great rocks, which no ten men of these times could move. They call them the Giant's Hedges to the present day. There was a gate on that side of the giant's farm which was nearest Market-Jew, and another on that side which joined the highway leading on to St Ives. Tom looked at the gate for some time, half disposed to drive through, but eventually he decided on proceeding by the ordinary road. When, however, Tom was coming

---

Mr Halliwell thinks the adventures of Tom Hickathrift are connected with "some of the insurrections in the Isle of Ely, such as that of Herewood, described in Wright's 'Essays,' ii. 91." Now, Herewood the Saxon is said to have taken refuge in the extreme part of Cornwall, and we are told of many romantic adventures, chiefly in connection with the beautiful daughter of Alef, a Cornish chief. May it not be, that here we have the origin of the story as it is told in Lincolnshire and in Cornwall?

* In making the really Cyclopean hedges which prevail in some parts of Cornwall, the large boulders of granite, or other stones, which lie scattered on the moors are used for the foundation. Indeed, one purpose, and a very important one, served by those hedges, has been the removal of the stones from the ground which has been enclosed, and the disposal of the stones so removed.

back from St Ives with his empty wain, his courage screwed up by the influence of some three or four gallons of strong beer which he had drunk, he began to reason with himself thus :—

"The king's highway ought not to be twisting and turning like an angle-twitch.* It should go straight through here. What right has the giant to keep his place closed, stopping honester men than he ever was longer on the road home? If everybody were of my mind, the road would soon be opened. Faith, I'll drive through. He wouldn't eat me, I suppose. My old mammy never told me I was to come to my end that way. They say the giant has had scores of wives. What becomes of them nobody can tell; yet there are always more ready to supply their place. Well, that's no business of mine. I never met the man to make me turn back yet; so come along, Neat and Comely," shouts Tom to the oxen, opening the great gate for them to pass through. On went Tom, without seeing anything of the giant or of anybody else, except the fat cattle of all sorts in the fields. After driving about a mile, Tom came to a pair of gates in a high wall, which was close to and surrounding the giant's castle. There was no passing round those, as deep ditches, full of water, were on either side of these gates. So at them went Tom. The huge gates creaked on their hangings, and the wheels of Tom's wain rattled on over the causey.† A little ugly midgan of a cur began to bark, and out tore the giant, a great ugly unshapely fellow, all head and stomach.

"You impudent little villain," roared the giant, "to drive into my grounds, disturbing my afternoon's nap. What business have you here?"

"I am on the road," says Tom, "and you—nor a better man than you—shan't put me back. You ha' no right to build your hedges across what used to be the king's highway, and shall be again."

"I shan't bemean myself to talk with such a little saucy black-guard as thee art," said the giant; "I'll get a twig, and drive thee out faster than thee came in."

"Well," says Tom, "you may keep your breath to cool your porridge; but, if that's the game you are up to, I can play at that as well as you."

The giant had pulled up a young elm-tree, about twenty feet high or so, and he began stripping the small branches from the head of the tree, as he came up the hill, gaping (yawning) all the time, as if he were half asleep. Tom, seeing what he was up to,

* A worm. † Causeway, pavement.

upset his wain. This he did without the oxen moving, as the tuntsy (pole) turned round in the ring of the yoke. He then slipped off the further wheel in a wink, hauled out the exe (axle-tree) fast in the other wheel, against the giant came up. (In old time the axle was made to work in gudgeons under the carts or wains.)

"Now then," says Tom, "fair play for the buttons. If you can beat me, I 'll go back. The exe and wheel is my sword and buckler, which I 'll match against your elm-tree." Then Tom began whistling.

The giant got round the uphill side, lifted his tree, and tore towards Tom without saying a word, as if he would cleave him from head to heel.

Tom lifted the axle-tree, with the wheel, up, to guard off the blow of the giant's twig—the giant being in such a towering passion to hear Tom coolly whistling all the time, that he couldn't steady himself. He missed Tom's head, struck the edge of the wheel, and, the ground being slippery, the giant fell upon his face on the ground. Tom might have driven the "exe" through him as he lay sprawling in the mud, and so have nailed him to the earth; but no, not he! Tom would rather be killed than not fight fair, so he just tickled the giant under the ribs with the end of the "exe." "Come, get up," says Tom, "let 's have another turn." The giant rose very slowly, as if he were scarcely able to stand, bent double, supporting himself on his twig. He was only dodging—the great cowardly skulk—to get the uphill side again, and take Tom unawares; but he was waiting with his right hand grasping the "exe," the wheel resting on the ground. Quick as lightning the giant raised his tree. Tom fetched him a heavy kick on the shins, he slipped, fell forward, and Tom so held the "exe," that it passed through his body like a spit. Good Lord, how the giant roared!

"Thee stop thy bleating," says Tom. "Stand quiet a moment. Let 's draw the exe out of thy body, and I 'll give thee a chance for another round. Thee doesn't deserve it, because thee aren't playing fair."

Tom turned the giant over, laid hold of the wheel, and dragged out the "exe." In doing this he was nearly blinded with the blood that spouted out of the hole. Blunderbuss rolled on the ground like an empty sack, roaring amain all the time in great agony.

"Stop thy bleating," says Tom, "and put thy hands in the hole the 'exe' has made in thee, to keep in the blood, until I can cut a turf to stop up the place, and thee will'st do again yet."

As Tom was plugging the wound with the turfs, the giant groaned and said, " It 's all no good ; I shall kick the bucket. I feel myself going round land ; but with my last breath I 'll do thee good, because I like thee better than anybody else I ever met with, for thy fair play and courage. The more thee wouldst beat me, the better I should like thee. I have no near relations. There is heaps of gold, silver, copper, and tin down in the vaults of the castle, guarded by two dogs. Mind there names are Catchem and Tearem. Only call them by these names and they 'll let thee pass. The land from this to the sea is all mine. There is more head of oxen, cows, sheep, goats, and deer, than thee canst count. Take them all, only bury me decent."

" Did you kill all your wives ? " asked Tom.

" No," sighed the giant, " they died natural. Don't let them abuse me after death. I like thee as a brother."

" Cheer up," says Tom, " you 'll do again."

He then tried to raise the giant up, but the plug of turf slipped from the wound, and all was over.

Tom put the wheel and axle in order, turned over the wain, and drove home to Market-Jew. The brewer was surprised and well pleased to see Tom back so early, and offered him good wages to stop for the year.

" I must leave this very night," says Tom, " for my old granfer, who lived up in the high countries, is dead. I am his nearest relation. He lived all alone. He 's left me all his money and lands, so I must go and bury my old granfer this very night." The brewer was about to pay him for his day's work—" Oh, never mind that," says Tom ; " I 'll give up that for as much beer as I can drink with supper."

After supper Tom went and took possession of the giant's castle and lands—nobody the wiser except a little woman, the giant's last wife, who came from some place not far from the castle. Some name Crowlas, some Tregender, others Bougiehere, as the place where she dwelt. Howbeit, she knew all about the giant's overthrow, and thought it the wisest course to " take up " at once with Tom ; and she being a tidy body, Tom was by no means unwilling. Tom and this woman took possession of the castle. They buried the giant down in the bottom, and placed a block of granite to keep him down. They gave the carcass of a sheep to Catchem and Tearem, visited the caves of the castle, found lots of treasure, and fairly got into the giant's shoes.

TOM THE GIANT, HIS WIFE JANE, AND JACK THE TINKEARD, AS TOLD BY THE "DROLLS." *

WHEN Tom and his wife had settled themselves in the giant's castle, they took good care not to allow any one to make a king's highway across their grounds. Tom made the hedges higher, and the gates stronger than ever, and he claimed all the run of land on the sea-side, and enclosed it. Tom's wife, Jane, was a wonderful cleanly body—the castle seemed to be always fresh swept and sanded, while all the pewter plates and platters shone like silver. She never quarrelled with Tom; except when he came in from hedging covered with mud; then in a pet she would threaten to go home to her mother. Jane was very famous for her butter and cheese, and Tom became no less so for his fine breed of cattle, so that he fared luxuriously, and all went on happily enough with Tom and his wife. They had plenty of children, and these were such fine healthy babies, that it took two or three of the best cows to feed them, when but a few weeks old. Tom and Jane thought that they had all that part of the world to themselves, and that no one could scale their hedges or break through their gates. They soon found their mistake. Tom was working one morning, not far from the gate, on the Market-Jew side of his property, when he heard a terrible rattle upon the bars. Running up, he saw a man with a hammer smashing away, and presently down went the bars, and in walked a travelling tinkeard, with his bag of tools on his back.

" Holla ! where are you bound for ? " says Tom.

" Bound to see if the giant, whom they say lives up here, wouldn't let a body pass through where the road ought to be," says the tinkeard.

" Oh, ay ! are you ? " says Tom.

" He must be a better man than I am who stops me," says the tinkeard. " As you are a fine stout chap, I expect you are the giant's eldest son. I see you are hedging. That's what all the people complain of. You are hedging in all the country."

* In some of the old *geese dances* (guise dances, from *danse déguisé*) the giant Blunderbuss and Tom performed a very active part. Blunderbuss was always a big-bellied fellow—his smoke-frock being well stuffed with straw. He fought with a tree, and the other giant with the wheel and axle. The giant is destroyed, as in the story, by falling on the axle. The tinker, of whom we have yet to tell, with his unfailing coat of darkness, comes in and beats Tom, until Jane comes out with the broom and beats the tinker; and then,—as in nearly all these rude plays,—St George and the Turkish knight come in ; but they have no part in the real story of the drama.—See note, page 66. Appendix E.

" Well," says Tom, " if I am his son, I can take my dad's part any way ; and we 'll have fair play too. I don't desire better fun than to try my strength with somebody that is a man. Come on. Any way you like—naked fists, single-stick, wrestling, bowling, slinging, or throwing the quoits."

" Very well," says the tinkeard, " I 'll match my blackthorn stick against anything in the way of timber that you can raise on this place."

Tom took the bar which the tinker had broken from the gate, and said, " I 'll try this piece of elm if you don't think it too heavy."

" Don't care if it 's heavier. Come on !"

The tinkeard took the thorn-stick in the middle, and made it fly round Tom's head so fast that he couldn't see it. It looked like a wheel whizzing round his ears, and Tom soon got a bloody nose and two black eyes. Tom's blows had no effect on the tinkeard, because he wore such a coat as was never seen in the West Coun-try before. It was made out of a shaggy black bull's hide, dressed whole with the hair on. The skin of the forelegs made the sleeves, the hind quarters only were cut, pieces being let in to make the spread of the skirts, while the neck and skin of the head formed a sort of hood. The whole appeared as hard as iron ; and when Tom hit the tinkeard, it sounded, as if the coat roared, like thunder. They fought until Tom got very hungry, and he found he had the worst of it. " I believe thee art the devil, and no man," says Tom. " Let 's see thy feet before thee dost taste any more of my blood."

The tinkeard showed Tom that he had no cloven foot, and told him that it depended more on handiness than strength to conquer with the single-stick ; and that a small man with science could beat a big man with none. The tinkeard then took the clumsy bar of the gate from Tom, gave him his own light and tough blackthorn, and proceeded to teach him to make the easiest passes, cuts, &c. Whilst the two men were thus engaged, Jane had prepared the dinner, and called her husband three times. She wondered what could be keeping Tom, as he was always ready to run to his dinner at the first call. At length she went out of the castle to seek for him, and surprised she was, and—if truth must be told—rather glad to see another man inside the gates, which no one had passed for years. Jane found Tom and the tinkeard tolerable friends by this time, and she begged them both to come into dinner, saying to the tinkeard that she wished she had some-thing better to set before him. She was vexed that Tom hadn't sent her word, that she might have prepared something better

than the everlasting beef and pease ; and vowed she would give
him a more savoury mess for supper, if she had to go to the hills
for a sheep or a kid herself.

At length the men were seated at the board, which groaned
beneath the huge piece of boiled beef, with mountains of pease-
pudding, and they soon got fairly to work. Jane then went to
the cellar, and tapped a barrel of the strongest beer, which was
intended to have been kept for a tide (feast). Of the meat, Tom
ate twice as much as the tinkeard, and from the can of ale he took
double draughts. The tinkeard ate heartily, but not voraciously ;
and, for those days, he was no hard drinker. Consequently, as
soon as dinner was over, Tom fell back against the wall, and was
quickly snoring like a tempest. His custom was to sleep two or
three hours after every meal. The tinkeard was no sleepy-head,
so he told Jane to bring him all her pots and pans which required
mending, and he would put them in order. He seated himself
amidst a vast pile, and was soon at work. The louder Tom
snored, the more Jack rattled and hammered away at the kettles ;
and ere Tom was awake, he had restored Jane's cooking vessels
to something like condition.

At length Tom awoke, and, feeling very sore, he begged the
tinkeard to put off until to-morrow a wrestling-match which they
had talked of before dinner. The tinkeard, nothing loath, agreed ;
so Tom took him up to the topmost tower of the castle, to show
him his lands and his cattle. For miles and miles, farther over
the hill than the eye could reach, except on the southern side,
everything belonged to Tom. In this tower they found a long
and strong bow. Tom said none but the old giant could bend it.
He had often tried, and fretted because he could not bring the
string to the notch. The tinkeard took the bow ; he placed one
end to his toe, and, by what appeared like sleight-of-hand to Tom,
he bent the bow, brought the string to the notch, sent the arrow off
—thwang,—and shot a hare so far away that it could hardly be
seen from the heath and ferns. Tom was surprised, until the
tinkeard showed him how to bend the bow, more by handiness
than strength, and again he killed a kid which was springing from
rock to rock on the cairns far away. The hare and kid were
brought home, cooked for supper, and the tinkeard was invited to
stop all night.

The story ordinarily rambles on, telling of the increasing friendship between the three, and giving the tinkeard's story of himself,
which was so interesting to Tom and Jane that they stayed up
nearly all night to hear it. He told how he was born and bred in

a country far away—more than a score days' journey from this land, far to the north and east of this, from which it was divided by a large river. This river the tinkeard had swam across ; then there was a week's journey in a land of hills and cairns, which were covered with snow a great part of the year. In this land there were many giants, who digged for tin and other treasures. With these giants he had lived and worked,—they always treated him well ; indeed, he always found the bigger the man the more gentle. Half the evil that's told about them by the cowardly fools who fear to go near them is false. Many, many more strange things did the tinkeard tell. Amongst other matters, he spoke of wise men who came from a city at no great distance from this land of tin for the purpose of buying the tin from the giants, and they left them tools, and other things, that the diggers required in exchange. One of these merchants took a fancy to the tinkeard, named him Jack—he had no name previously—and removed him to the city, where Jack was taught his trade, and many other crafts. The tinkeard had left that city four months since, and worked his way down to Market-Jew. Being there, he heard of the giant, and he resolved to make his acquaintance. The rest has been told.

While this, which was a long story, was being told, Jack the Tinkeard was enjoying Jane's new barley-bread, with honey and cream, which he moistened with metheglin. " Good night, Tom," says he at last ; " you see you have lived all your days like a lord on his lands, and know nothing. I never knew father or mother, never had a home to call my own. All the better for me, too. If I had possessed one, I would never have known one-thousandth part of what I have learned by wandering up and down in the world."

Morning came ; and, after breakfast, Tom proposed to try "a hitch " on the grass in the castle court. Jack knew nothing of wrestling ; so he told Tom he had never practised, but still he would try his strength. Tom put the tinkeard on his back at every " hitch," but he took all the care he could not to hurt him. At last the tinkeard cried for quarter, and declared Tom to be best man.

Jane had made a veal-and-parsley pie, and put it down to bake, when, being at leisure, she came out to see the sport. Now, it must be remembered the tinkeard had broken down the gate, and no one had thought of repairing it, or closing the opening. Two men of Tregender were coming home from Bal,* and passing the

* Popular name for a mine : " *Bal,* a place of digging—*Balas,* to dig."—Pryck.

giant's gate, they thought it very strange that it should be broken down. After consulting for some time, they summoned all their courage, and—it must be confessed, with fear and trembling—they crawled into the grounds, and proceeded towards the castle. Now, no one in that country except Tom and Jane knew that the old giant was dead.

The two men turned round a corner, and saw three very large children playing. The baby, a year old, was riding an old buck-goat about the field. The two elder children, Tom Veān * and young Jane, were mounted on a bull, back to back, one holding on by the horns, and the other by the tail, galloping round the field like mad, followed by the cows and dogs,—a regular " cow's courant."

" Lord, you," says one of the men to the other, " what dost a' think of that for a change ? "

" But to think," says the other, " that the old giant should ever have a wife and young chil'ren here, and the people knaw nothing about it."

" Why, don't everybody say that he ate all his wives and chil'-ren too. What lies people tell, don't they, you ? "

" Le 's go a little farther ; he won't eat we, I suppose."

" I 'll throw my pick and sho'el down the throat of an, as soon as a' do open as [his] jaws."

" Look you," now shouts the other, " you come round a little farther : just peep round the corner and thee meest see two fellows wrestling, and a woman looking on."

" Can I believe my eyes, you ? Don't that woman look some-thing like Jane I used to be courson of ? "

The miners satisfied themselves that it was Jane, sure enough, and quietly beat a retreat. Soon was St Ives in a state of excite-ment, and all Jane's cousins, believing from the accounts given by the miners that Jane was well off, resolved to pay her a visit. These visits worked much confusion in Tom's castle and family. He and his wife quarrel, but the tinkeard is the never-failing friend. All this part of the story is an uninteresting account of fair-weather friends.

Jack the Tinkeard taught Tom how to till his ground in a proper manner. He had hitherto contented himself with gathering wild herbs,—such as nettles, wild beet, mallows, elecampane, various kinds of lentils, and chick or cat-peas. Jack now planted a garden for his friends,—the first in Cornwall,—and they grew all kinds of good vegetables. The tinkeard also taught Jane to make malt and

---

* *Veān*, a term of endearment.

to brew beer; hitherto they had been content with barley-wort, which was often sour. Jack would take the children and collect bitter herbs to make the beer keep, such as the alehoof (ground ivy), mugwort, bannell (the broom), agrimony, centuary, wood-sage, bettony, and pellitory. Jane's beer was now amongst the choicest of drinks, and her St Ives cousins could never have enough of it. Tom delighted in it, and often drank enough to bewilder his senses.

Tom had followed the example of the old giant, and killed his cattle by flinging rocks at them. The giant's "bowls" are seen to this day scattered all over the country. Jack gave Tom a knife of the keenest edge and finest temper, and taught him how to slaughter the beasts. When a calf was to be skinned, he instructed Tom how to take the skin off whole from the fore legs, by un-jointing the shoulders, and to remove it entirely clear of grain, and without the smallest scratch. In addition to all this, Tomy Veän (who was now a boy four years old, but bigger than many at ten) must have a coat possessing all the virtues which belonged to the tinkeard's. So a bull-calf's skin was put on to the boy, and Jane had special instructions how she was to allow the coat to dry on his back, and tan and dress it in a peculiar way. The skin thus treated would shrink and thicken up until it came to his shape. Nobody can tell how proud the young Tom was of his coat when all was done, though the poor boy suffered much in the doing.

Now Jack the Tinkeard desired the intrusion of strangers as little as did Tom and Jane, so he set to work to repair the gate which he had broken down. He not only did this, but he con-structed a curious latch with the bobbin; it was so contrived that no stranger could find the right end of it, and if they pulled at any other part, the latch was only closed the tighter. While he was at work a swarm of Jane's St Ives cousins came around him; they mistook Jack for Tom, and pointed out how the children, who were playing near him, were like their father. Jack "parlayed" with them until he had completed his task, and then he closed the gate in their faces.

Much more of this character is related by the "drolls;" but with the exception of constant alternations of feasting and fighting, there is little of novelty in the story, until at last a grand storm arises be-tween Tom and his wife, who is believed by the husband to be on too intimate terms with Jack the Tinkeard. The result of this is, that Jane goes home to Crowlas, fights with her mother, old Jenny, because old Jenny abuses Tom, which Jane will not allow in her presence. While yet at Crowlas another boy is born, called Honey;

E

and, as the cow was not at hand as when she was in the castle, he was nursed by a goat, and it is said a class of his descendants are yet known as the Zennor goats.

HOW TOM AND THE TINKEARD* FOUND THE TIN, AND HOW IT LED TO MORVA FAIR.

WHEN Tom had fairly thrown the tinkeard in the wrestling match, which, it must be remembered, was seen by the miners of Tregender, at which Tom was much pleased, although he did not express his pleasure, it was settled that Tom was the best man.   This was sealed over a barrel of strong ale, and a game of quoits was proposed, while Jane was taking up the dinner. Tom had often wished, but never more so than now, that the green sloping banks against the inside of the castle walls had not been there, that he might have a fair fling of the quoits from end to end of the court.   Tom's third throw in this game was a very strong one, and the quoit cut a great piece of turf from the banks, laying bare many gray-looking stones, small rounded balls, and black sandy stuff.

"Look here you, Jack," says Tom; "whatever could possess the old fools of giants to heap up such a lot of black and gray mining-stones against the wall? wherever could they have found them all?"

Jack carefully looked at the stuff thus laid bare, clapped his hands together, and shouted—

---

* I have preserved the pronunciation of this word, which was common in Cornwall between twenty and thirty years since, and which still prevails in some of the outlying districts.

In Webster's English Dictionary we find tinker oddly enough derived from the Welsh *tincera*, the ringer, from *tinciaw*, to ring, "a mender of brass kettles, pans, and the like."   The word being so obviously *tin-ceard*, or *tin-cerdd*,—the original having been in all probability *staen*, or *ystaen-cerdd*, a worker in tin.   The Gaelic still retains "ceard" and "caird" to represent the English smith.*

In the present case, we have to deal, there can be little doubt, not with the modern tinker, but the ancient worker in tin, as is shown in this division of the legend, although the story has suffered some modern corruption, and Jack is made to mend Jane's pots and pans.

The old Cornish saying—

> *Stean San Agnes an quella stean in Kernow,*
> St Agnes' tin is the best tin in Cornwall—

gives the original Cornish term for tin.

Jack the Tinkeard partakes of the character of Wayland Smith in many of his peculiarities.   See Appendix F.

---

* Gomer; or, A Brief Analysis of the Language and Knowledge of the Ancient Cymry. By John Williams, A.M., Oxon.

" By the gods, it 's all the richest tin ! "

Now Tom, poor easy-going soul, " didn't knaw tin ; " so he could scarcely believe Jack, though Jack had told him that he came from a tin country.

" Why, Tom," says Jack, " thee art a made man. If these banks are all tin, there is enough here to buy all the land, and all the houses, from sea to sea."

" What do I care for the tin ; haven't I all a man can desire ? My lands are all stocked with sheep and horned cattle. We shall never lack the best beef and mutton, and we want no better than our honest homespun."

Jane now made her appearance, announcing that dinner was ready. She was surprised at seeing so much tin, but she didn't say anything. She thought maybe she would get a new gown out of it, and go down to St Ives Fair. Notwithstanding that Tom and Jane professed to treat lightly the discovery of the tin, it was clear they thought deeply about it, and their thoughts spoiled their appetites. It was evidently an accession of wealth which they could not understand.

Tom said he didn't know how to dress tin, it was of little use to him. Jack offered to dress it for the market on shares. Tom told him he might take as much as he had a mind to for what he cared. After dinner, the giant tried to sleep, but could not get a snore for the soul of him. Therefore, he walked out into the court, to get some fresh air, as he said, but in reality to look at the tin. Jane saw how restless Tom was, so she unhung his bows and arrows, and told him he must away to the hills to get some kids and hares.

" I shan't trouble myself with the bows and arrows," says Tom; " all I want are the slings Jack and I have in our pockets. Stones are plenty enough, hit or miss, no matter ; and we needn't be at the trouble to gather up the stones again."

Off went Tom and Jack, followed by young Tom and Jane, to the Towednack and Zennor hills. They soon knocked down as many kids, hares, and rabbits as they desired ;—they caught some colts, placed the children on two of them and the game on the others, and home they went. On their return, whilst waiting for supper, Jack wandered around the castle, and was struck by seeing a window which he had not before observed. Jack was resolved to discover the room to which this window belonged, so he very carefully noticed its position, and then threw his hammer in through it, that he might be certain of the spot when he found the tool inside of the castle. The next day, after dinner, when

Tom was having his snooze, Jack took Jane with him, and they commenced a search for the hammer near the spot where Jack supposed the window should be, but they saw no signs of one in in any part of the walls. They discovered, however, a strangely-fashioned, worm-eaten oak hanging-press. They carefully examined this, but found nothing. At last Jack, striking the back of it with his fist, was convinced, from the sound, that the wall behind it was hollow. He and Jane went steadily to work, and with some exertion they moved the press aside, and disclosed a stone door. They opened this, and there was Jack's hammer lying amidst a pile of bones, evidently the relics of some of old Blunderbuss's wives, whom he had imprisoned in the wall, and who had perished there. Jane was in a great fright, and blessed her good fortune that she had escaped a similar end. Jack, however, soon consoled her by showing her the splendid dresses which were here, and the gold chains, rings, and bracelets, with diamonds and other jewels, which were scattered around. It was agreed that Tom for the present should be kept in ignorance of all this. Tom awoke, his head full of the tin. He consulted with Jack and Jane. They duly agreed to keep their secret, and resolved that they would set to work the very next day to prepare some of the tin stuff for sale. Tom as yet scarcely believed in his wealth, which was magnified as much as possible by Jack, to bewilder him. However, several sacks of tin were duly dressed, and Tom and Jack started with them for Market-Jew, Tom whispering to Jack before he left the castle, that they would bring home a cask of the brewer's best ale with 'em. " It is a lot better than what Jane brews with her old-fashioned yerbes ; but don't 'e tell her so."

The brewer of Market-Jew was also mayor, and, as it appears, tin-smelter, or tin merchant. To him, therefore, Tom went with his black tin,* and received not only his cask of beer, but such an amount of golden coin—all of it being a foreign coinage—as convinced him that Jack had not deceived him. This brewer is reputed to have been an exceedingly honest and kind-hearted man, beloved by all. It was his practice, when any of the townspeople came before him, begging him to settle their disputes,—even when they "limbed" one another,— to shut them up in the brewery-yard, give them as much beer as they could drink, and keep them there until they became good friends. Owing to this practice he seldom had enough beer to sell, and was frequently troubled to pay for his barley. This brewer, who was reputed to be " the best mayor

* " *Black tin,*" tin ore ; oxide of tin.

that ever was since the creation of gray cats," gave rise, from the above practice of his, to the proverb still in daily use, " Standing, like the mayor of Market-Jew, in his own light."

The mayor was always fat and jolly. He was an especial favourite, too, with the Lord of Pengerswick, who is believed to have helped him out of many troubles. He had bought his tin of Tom and Jack, such a bargain, that he resolved to have some sport, so a barrel of beer was broached in the yard, and the crier was sent round the town to call all hands to a " courant " (merrymaking). They came, you may be certain, in crowds. There was wrestling, hurling,—the length of the Green from Market-Jew to Chyandour, and back again,—throwing quoits, and slinging. Some amused themselves in pure wantonness by slinging stones over the Mount ; so that the old giant, who lived there, was afraid to show above ground, lest his only eye should get knocked out. The games were kept up right merrily until dusk ; when in rode the Lord of Pengerswick on his enchanted mare, with a colt by her side. The brewer introduced Tom and Jack, and soon they became the best of friends. Tom invited Pengerswick to his castle, and they resolved to go home at once and make a night of it. Pengerswick gave Tom the colt, and, by some magic power, as soon as he mounted this beautiful animal, he found himself at home, and the lord, the brewer, and Jack with him. How this was brought about Tom could never tell, but Jack appeared to be in the secret. Tom was amazed and delighted to find Jane dressed like a queen, in silks and diamonds, and the children arrayed in a manner well becoming the dignity of their mother.

Jane, as soon as Tom and Jack had left her, had proceeded to the room in the wall, and with much care removed the jewels, gold, and dresses, caring little, as she afterwards said, for the dead bones, although they rattled as she shook them out of the robes. In a little time she had all the dresses in the main court of the castle, and having well beaten and brushed them, she selected the finest—those she now wore—and put the rest aside for other grand occasions.

The condescension of the great Lord of Pengerswick was something wonderful. He kissed Jane until Tom was almost jealous, and the great lord romped about the court of the castle with the children. Tom was, on the whole, however, delighted with the attention paid to his wife by a real lord, but our clear-headed Jack saw through it all, and took measures accordingly.

Pengerswick tried hard to learn the secret of the stores of tin, but he was foiled by the tinkeard on every tack. You may well suppose how desirous he was of getting Jack out of the way, and eventually he began to try his spells upon him.   The power of his necromancy was such, that all in the castle were fixed in sleep as rigid as stones, save Jack.   All that the enchanter could do produced no effect on him.   He sat quietly looking on, occasionally humming some old troll, and now and then whistling to show his unconcern.   At last Pengerswick became enraged, and he drew from his breast a dagger and slyly struck at Jack.   The dagger, which was of the finest Eastern steel, was bent like a piece of soft iron against Jack's black hide.

"Art thou the devil?" exclaimed Pengerswick.

"As he's a friend of yours," says Jack, "you should know his countenance."

"Devil or no devil," roared Pengerswick, "you cannot resist this," and he held before Jack a curiously-shaped piece of polished steel.

Jack only smiled, and quietly unfastening his cow's hide, he opened it.   The cross, like a star of fire, was reflected in a mirror under Jack's coat, and it fell from Pengerswick's grasp.   Jack seized it, and turning it full upon the enchanter, the proud lord sank trembling to the ground, piteously imploring Jack to spare his life and let him go free.   Jack bade the prostrate lord rise from the ground.   He kicked him out of the castle, and sent the vicious mare after him.   Thus he saved Tom and his family from the power of this great enchanter.   In a little time the sleep which had fallen upon them passed away, and they awoke, as though from the effects of a drunken frolic.   The brewer hurried home, and Tom and Jack set to work to dress their tin.   Tom and Jane's relations and friends flocked around them, but Jack said, "Summer flies are only seen in the sunshine," and he shortly after this put their friendship to the test, by conveying to them the idea that Tom had spent all his wealth.   These new friends dropped off when they thought they could get no more, and Tom and Jane were thoroughly disgusted with their summer friends and selfish relations.   The tinkeard established himself firmly as an inmate of the castle.   No more was said about the right of the public to make a king's highway through the castle grounds.   He aided Tom in hedging in the waste lands, and very carefully secured the gates against all intruders.   In fact, he also quite altered his politics.

Jack had a desire to go home to Dartmoor to see his mother, who had sent to tell him that the old giant Dart was near death.   He started at once, on foot.   Tom wished him to have Pengerswick's colt, but Jack preferred his legs. It would be too long a tale to tell the story of his travels. He killed serpents and wild beasts in the woods, and when he came to rivers, he had but to take off his coat, gather up the skirts of it with a string, and stretch out the body with a few sticks,—thus forming a cobble,—launch it on the water, and paddle himself across. He reached home. The old giant was at his last gasp. Jack made him give everything to his mother before he breathed his last. When he died, Jack carefully buried him. He then settled all matters for his mother, and returned to the West Country again.

Tom's daughter became of marriageable years, and Jack wished to have her for a wife. Tom, however, would not consent to this, unless he got rid of a troublesome old giant who lived on one of the hills in Morva, which was the only bit of ground between Hayle and St Just which Tom did not possess. The people of Morva were kept in great fear by this giant, who made them bring him the best of everything. He was a very savage old creature, and took exceeding delight in destroying every one's happiness. Some of Tom's cousins lived in Morva, and young Tom fell in love with one of his Morva cousins seven times removed, and by Jack's persuasion, they were allowed by Tom and Jane to marry. It was proclaimed by Jack all round the country that great games would come off on the day of the wedding. He had even the impudence to stick a bill on the giant's door, stating the prizes which would be given to the best games. The happy day arrived, and, as the custom then was, the marriage was to take place at sundown. A host of people from all parts were assembled, and under the influence of Jack and Tom, the games were kept up in great spirit. Jack and Tom, by and by, amused themselves by pitching quoits at the giant's house on the top of the hill. The old giant came out and roared like thunder. All the young men were about to fly, but Jack called them a lot of scurvy cowards, and stayed their flight. Jack made faces at the giant, and challenged him to come down and fight him. The old monster thought he could eat Jack, and presently began to run down the hill,—when, lo ! he disappeared. When the people saw that the giant was gone, they took courage, and ran up the hill after Jack, who called on them to follow him.

There was a vast hole in the earth, and there, at the bottom of it, lay the giant, crushed by his own weight, groaning like a vol-cano and shaking like an earthquake.

Jack knew there was an adit level driven into the hill, and he had quietly, and at night, worked away the roof at one particular part, until he left only a mere shell of rock above, so it was, that, as the giant passed over this spot, the ground gave way. Heavy rocks were thrown down the hole on the giant, and there his bones are said to lie to this day.

Jack was married at once to young Jane, her brother Tom to the Morva girl, and great were the rejoicings. From all parts of the country came in the wrestlers, and never since the days of Gogmagog had there been such terrific struggles between strong men. Quoits were played; and some of the throws of Tom and the tinkeard are still shown to attest the wonderful prowess of this pair. Hurling was played over the wild hills of those northern shores, and they rung and echoed then, as they have often rung and echoed since, with the brave cry, " *Guare wheag yw guare teag,*" which has been translated into " Fair play is good play," *
—an honourable trait in the character of our Celtic friends. All this took place on a Sunday, and was the origin of Morva Feast and Morva Fair. We are, of course, astonished at not finding some evidence of direct punishment for these offences, such as that which was inflicted on the hurlers at Padstow. This has, however, been explained on the principle that the people were merely rejoicing at the accomplishment of a most holy act, and that a good deed demanded a good day.†

THE GIANT OF MORVA.‡

IN the Giant's Field in Morva still stand some granite fragments which once constituted the Giant's House. From this we see the Giant's Castle at Bosprenis, and the Giant's Cradle, thus perpetuating the infancy of the great man, and his subsequent power. The quoits used by this giant are numerous indeed. This great man, on the 1st day of August, would walk up to Bosprenis Croft, and there perform some magical rites, which were either never known, or they have been forgotten. On this day,—for when thus engaged the giant was harmless,—thousands of people would congregate to get a glimpse of the monster; and as he passed them,—all being seated on the stone hedges,—every one drank " to the health of Mr Giant." At length the giant died, but the gathering on the 1st of August has never been given up,

---

* Or, " Sweet play is fair play," *i.e.,* it is not fair to play roughly.
† See Appendix G for Mr Wright's story of "The Wonderful Cobbler of Wellington."
‡ The above notices were collected for me in Morva by the late C. Taylor Stephens, author of "The Chief of Barat-Anac," and "some time rural postman from St Ives to Zennor." Their connection with the traditions of Jack and Tom will be evident to every reader.

or rather, the day shifts, and is made to agree with Morva Feast, which is held on the first Sunday in August.

A Morva farmer writes :—" A quarter of an acre would not hold the horses ridden to the fair,—the hedges being covered by the visitors, who drink and carouse as in former times. Morva Fair is, however, dying out."

The parish-clerk informed me that the giant had twenty sons ; that he was the first settler in these parts ; and that he planted his children all round the coast. It was his custon to bring all his family together on the 1st of August, and hence the origin of the fair. Whichever may be the true account of the cause which established the fair and the feast, these romances clearly establish the fact that the giants were at the bottom of it.

THE GIANT BOLSTER.

THIS mighty man held especial possession of the hill formerly known as *Carne Bury-anacht* or *Bury-anack*,* " the spar-stone grave," sometimes called *St Agnes' Ball* and *St Agnes' Pestis*, but which is now named, from the use made of the hill during the long war, St Agnes' Beacon. He has left his name to a very interesting, and undoubtedly most ancient earthwork, which still exists at the base of the hill, and evidently extended from Trevaunance Porth to Chapel Porth, enclosing the most important tin district in St Agnes. This is constantly called " The Bolster."

Bolster must have been of enormous size : since it is stated that he could stand with one foot on St Agnes' Beacon and the other on Carn Brea; these hills being distant, as the bird flies, six miles,† his immensity will be clear to all. In proof of this, there still exists, in the valley running upwards from Chapel Porth, a stone in which may yet be seen the impression of the giant's fingers. On one occasion, Bolster, when enjoying his usual stride from the Beacon to Carn Brea, felt thirsty, and stooped to drink out of the well at Chapel Porth, resting, while he did so, on the above-mentioned stone. We hear but little of the wives of our giants; but Bolster had a wife, who was made to labour hard by her tyrannical husband. On the top of St Agnes' Beacon there yet exist the evidences of the useless labours to which this unfortunate giantess was doomed, in grouped masses of small stones. These, it is said, have all been gathered from an estate at the foot of the hill, immediately adjoining the village of St Agnes. This farm is to

* *Bury*, Saxon for *grave*. This does not appear to be Cornish, which is *bedh*; Welsh, *braid*.

† See Appendix H.

the present day remarkable for its freedom from stones, though situated amidst several others, which, like most lands reclaimed from the moors of this district, have stones in abundance mixed with the soil.   Whenever Bolster was angry with his wife, he compelled her to pick stones, and to carry them in her apron to the top of the hill.   There is some confusion in the history of this giant, and of the blessed St Agnes to whom the church is dedi-cated.   They are supposed to have lived at the same time, which, according to our views, is scarcely probable, believing, as we do, that no giants existed long after their defeat at Plymouth by Brutus and Corineus.   There may have been an earlier saint of the same name ; or may not Saint Enns or Anns, the popular name of this parish, indicate some other lady ?

Be this as it may, the giant Bolster became deeply in love with St Agnes, who is reputed to have been singularly beautiful, and a pattern woman of virtue.   The giant allowed the lady no repose. He followed her incessantly, proclaiming his love, and filling the air with the tempests of his sighs and groans.   St Agnes lectured Bolster in vain on the impropriety of his conduct, he being already a married man.   This availed not ; her prayers to him to relieve her from his importunities were also in vain.   The persecuted lady, finding there was no release for her, while this monster ex-isted, resolved to be rid of him at any cost, and eventually succeeded by the following stratagem :—Agnes appeared at length to be persuaded of the intensity of the giant's love, but she told him she required yet one small proof more.   There exists at Chapel Porth a hole in the cliff at the termination of the valley.   If Bolster would fill this hole with his blood the lady would no longer look coldly on him.   This huge bestrider-of-the-hills thought that it was an easy thing which was required of him, and felt that he could fill many such holes and be none the weaker for the loss of blood.   Consequently, stretching his great arm across the hole, he plunged a knife into a vein, and a torrent of gore issued forth. Roaring and seething the blood fell to the bottom, and the giant expected in a few minutes to see the test of his devotion made evident, in the filling of the hole.   It required much more blood than Bolster had supposed ; still it must in a short time be filled, so he bled on.   Hour after hour the blood flowed from the vein, yet the hole was not filled.   Eventually the giant fainted from exhaustion.   The strength of life within his mighty frame enabled him to rally, yet he had no power to lift himself from the ground, and he was unable to stanch the wound which he had made. Thus it was, that after many throes, the giant Bolster died !

The cunning saint, in proposing this task to Bolster, was well aware that the hole opened at the bottom into the sea, and that as rapidly as the blood flowed into the hole it ran from it, and did

> " The multitudinous seas incarnadine,
> Making the green one red."

Thus the lady got rid of her hated lover; Mrs Bolster was released, and the district freed from the presence of a tyrant. The hole at Chapel Porth still retains the evidences of the truth of this tradition, in the red stain which marks the track down which flowed the giant's blood.

There is another tradition, in some respects resembling this one, respecting a giant who dwelt at Goran, on the south coast.

THE HACK AND CAST.

IN the parish of Goran is an intrenchment running from cliff to cliff, and cutting off about a hundred acres of coarse ground. This is about twenty feet broad, and twenty-four feet high in most places.

Marvellous as it may appear, tradition assures us that this was the work of a giant, and that he performed the task in a single night. This fortification has long been known as *Thica Vosa*, and the Hack and Cast.

The giant, who lived on the promontory, was the terror of the neighbourhood, and great were the rejoicings in Goran when his death was accomplished through a stratagem by a neighbouring doctor.

The giant fell ill through eating some food—children or otherwise—to satisfy his voracity, which had disturbed his stomach. His roars and groans were heard for miles, and great was the terror throughout the neighbourhood. A messenger, however, soon arrived at the residence of the doctor of the parish, and he bravely resolved to obey the summons of the giant, and visit him. He found the giant rolling on the ground with pain, and he at once determined to rid the world, if possible, of the monster.

He told him that he must be bled. The giant submitted, and the doctor moreover said that, to insure relief, a large hole in the cliff must be filled with the blood. The giant lay on the ground, his arm extended over the hole, and the blood flowing a torrent into it. Relieved by the loss of blood, he permitted the stream to flow on, until he at last became so weak, that the doctor

kicked him over the cliff, and killed him. The well-known promontory of The Dead Man, or Dodman, is so called from the
dead giant. The spot on which he fell is the " Giant's House,"
and the hole has ever since been most favourable to the growth of
ivy.

THE GIANT WRATH, OR RALPH.

NOT far from Portreath there exists a remarkable fissure, or
gorge, on the coast, formed by the wearing out, through
the action of the sea, of a channel of ground softer than that
which exists on either side of it. This is generally known as
Ralph's Cupboard ; and one tale is, that Ralph was a famous
smuggler, who would run his little vessel, even in dark nights,
into the shelter afforded by this gorge, and safely land his goods.
Another is, that it was formerly a cavern in which dwelt Wrath—
a huge giant—who was the terror of the fishermen. Sailing from
St Ives, they ever avoided the Cupboard; as they said, " Nothing
ever came out of it which was unfortunate enough to get into it."
Wrath is reputed to have watched for those who were drifted
towards his Cupboard by currents, or driven in by storms. It is
said that wading out to sea, he tied the boats to his girdle, and
quietly walked back to his den, making, of course, all the fishermen his prey. The roof of the cavern is supposed to have fallen
in after the death of the giant, leaving the open chasm as we now
see it.

ORDULPH THE GIANT.

THIS *Tavistock* Sampson is far removed from our fine old
legendary giant ; yet we perceive in the stories of Ordulph
precisely the same process as that which has given immortality to
Blunderbuss and others. In the church of the monastery of
Tavistock, built by Orgar in 960, and consecrated by St Rumon,
was buried Orgar, and also his son Edulf, or Ordulph, to whom,
by some writers, the foundation of the abbey is attributed
Ordulph was a man of giant size, and possessing most remarkable
strength. He once appeared before the gates of the city of
Exeter in company with King Edward, and demanded admission.
His demand was not immediately complied with. He tore away
the bars of the portcullis with his hands—burst open the gates
with his foot—rent the locks and bolts asunder—and broke down
a considerable portion of the wall—walking into the city over the
ruins, and occasioning great alarm amidst the inhabitants.

The king is said to have attributed this extraordinary feat of strength to the chieftain's having entered into a compact with the devil ; and the people generally believed the king to be correct.

At Tavistock, it was the custom of Ordulph to stand with one foot on either side of the Tavy, which is about twenty feet wide, and having the wild beasts driven in from the Dartmoor forests, he would—with the seemingly insignificant blows of a small knife —strike their heads off into the stream.*

* William of Malmesbury tells us that both father and son were buried at Tavistock, which is thus described :—" Est in Domnonia cænobium monachorum, juxta Tau fluvium, quod Tauistock vocator ; quod per Ordgarum, comitem Domnoniensem, patrem Elfrida, qui fuit uxor regis Edgari, surgendi exordium, per Livingum episcopum, cresendi accepit auspicium; locus, amænus opportunitate nemorum, captura copiosa piscum, Ecclesiæ congruente fabrica, fluvialibus rivis per officinas monachorum decurrentibus, qui suo impetu effusi, quidquid invenerint superflum, portant in exitum." Quoted by Pedler in his " Episcopate of Cornwall."

Mrs Bray, in her " Traditions, Legends, Superstitions, and Sketches of Devonshire," says,—" But notwithstanding the superiority of his strength and stature, Ordulph died in the flower of his age. He gave orders to be buried at his abbey at Herton, in Dorsetshire ; but was interred in or near the Abbey Church of Tavistock, where a mausoleum or tomb of vast dimensions was erected to his memory, which is represented to have been visited as a wonder. _ ' The thigh-bone of Ordulph is still preserved in Tavistock Church.' "

THE FAIRIES.

"Elves, urchins, goblins all, and little fairyes."—*Mad Prankes.*

"I do wander everywhere,
   Swifter than the moone's sphere ;
And I serve the fairy queen,
   To dew her orbs upon the green."—SHAKESPEARE.

"By the moon we sport and play ;
   With the night begins our day ;
As we dance the dew doth fall—
Trip it little urchins all ;
Lightly as the little bee,
Two by two, and three by three,
And about go we, and about go we."
                    —LYLIE, *Maydes' Metamorphoses.*

ROMANCES OF THE FAIRIES.

THE ELFIN CREED OF CORNWALL.

> "To thee the fairy state
> I with discretion dedicate;
> Because thou prizest things that are
> Curious and unfamiliar."
>
> *Oberon's Feast.*—ROBERT HERRICK.

TO the "Fairy Mythology" of Thomas Keightley, I must refer all those who are desirous of examining the metamorphoses which this family of spiritual beings undergo, in passing from one country to another. My business is with the Cornish branch of this extensive family, and I shall be in a position to show that, notwithstanding Mr Keightley has entirely excluded Cornwall from consideration, there exists, even to the present day, a remarkable fairy mythology in that county. Between thirty and forty years since, ere yet the influences of our practical education had disturbed the poetical education of the people, every hill and valley, every tree, shrub, and flower was peopled with spiritual creations, deriving their characteristics from the physical peculiarities amidst which they were born. Extending over the whole district which was formerly known as Danmonium,*—embracing not only Cornwall, but Devonshire, to the eastern edge of Dartmoor,—we find a mythology, which varies but little in its main features. Beyond an imaginary line, drawn in a north-westerly direction from the mouth of the Teign to the rise of the Torridge, the curiously wild and distinguishing superstitions of the "Cornwallers"† fade away, and we have those which are common to Somersetshire and the more fertile counties of mid-England.

---

* "If Alfred, as is probable, fixed the limits of Devon where the ancient eastern boundary was, between the Belgæ and Durotriges on the east, and Danmonii on the west, ancient Cornwall will have included all Devon, as well as what is west of the Tamar."—*Camden's Britannia.* Gough, vol. i., p. 1.

† "The 'Cornwallers' overpowered by the Saxons."—*Camden's Britannia*, vol. i., p. cxxxix.

The Piscy or Pixy of East Devon and Somersetshire is a different creature from his cousin of a similar name in Cornwall.
The former is a mischievous, but in all respects a very harmless
creation, who appears to live a rollicking life amidst the luxuriant scenes of those beautiful counties.   The latter, the piskies of
Cornwall, appear to have their wits sharpened by their necessities,
and may be likened to the keen and cunning " Arab " boy of the
London streets, as seen in contrast with the clever child who has
been reared in every comfort of a well-regulated home.   A gentleman, well known in the literary world of London, very recently
told me, that he once saw in Devonshire a troop of fairies.   It
was a breezy summer afternoon, and these beautiful little creatures
were floating on the circling zephyrs up the side of a sunlit hill,
and fantastically playing

> "Where oxlips and the nodding violet grow."

They are truly the fairies of " Midsummer Night's Dream."   They
haunt the most rural and romantic spots, and they gather

> " On hill, in dale, forest, or mead,
> By paved fountain, or by rushy brook,
> Or on the beached margent of the sea,
> To dance their ringlets to the whistling wind."

No such fairies are ever met with on Dartmoor.   A few, judging
from Mrs Bray's tales,* may have been tempted into the lovely
valley of the Tavy, but certainly they never crossed the Tamar.
The darker shades in the character of the Cornish fairy almost
dispose me to conclude that they belong to an older family than
those of Devonshire.

It should be understood that there are in Cornwall five varieties
of the fairy family, clearly distinguishable—

1. The Small People.
2. The Spriggans.
3. Piskies, or Pigseys.
4. The Buccas, Bockles, or Knockers.
5. The Browneys.

Of the *Small People* I have heard two accounts.   Indeed, it is
by no means clear that the tradition of their origin does not apply
to the whole five branches of this ancient family.   The Small
People are believed by some to be the spirits of the people who

---

* Traditions, Legends, Superstitions, and Sketches of Devonshire, on the Borders of
the Tamar and the Tavy, by Mrs Bray.

inhabited Cornwall many thousands of years ago—long, long before the birth of Christ. That they were not good enough to inherit the joys of heaven, but that they were too good to be condemned to eternal fires. They were said to be "poor innocents" (this phrase is now applied to silly children). When they first came into this land, they were much larger than they are now, but ever since the birth of Christ they have been getting smaller and smaller. Eventually they will turn into muryans (ants), and at last be lost from the face of the earth. These Small People are exceedingly playful amongst themselves, but they are usually demure when they know that any human eye sees them. They commonly aid those people to whom they take a fancy, and, frequently, they have been known to perform the most friendly acts towards men and women. The above notion corresponds with the popular belief in Ireland, which is, "that the fairies are a portion of the fallen angels, who, being less guilty than the rest, were not driven to hell, but were suffered to dwell on earth."* In Cornwall, as in Wales, another popular creed is, that the fairies are Druids becoming—because they will not give up their idolatries—smaller and smaller. These Small People in many things closely resemble the Elves of Scandinavia.

The *Spriggans* are quite a different class of beings. In some respects they appear to be offshoots from the family of the Trolls of Sweden and Denmark. The Spriggans are found only about the cairns, coits, or cromlechs, burrows, or detached stones, with which it is unlucky for mortals to meddle. A correspondent writes: "This is known, that they were a remarkably mischievous and thievish tribe. If ever a house was robbed, a child stolen, cattle carried away, or a building demolished, it was the work of the Spriggans. Whatever commotion took place in earth, air, or water, it was all put down as the work of these spirits. Wherever the giants have been, there the Spriggans have been also. It is usually considered that they are the ghosts of the giants; certainly, from many of their feats, we must suppose them to possess a giant's strength. The Spriggans have the charge of buried treasure."

The *Piskie.*—This fairy is a most mischievous and very unsociable sprite. His favourite fun is to entice people into the bogs by appearing like the light from a cottage window, or as a man carrying a lantern. The Piskie partakes, in many respects, of the character of the Spriggan. So wide-spread were their depredations, and so annoying their tricks, that it at one time was neces-

* See Keightley's "Fairy Mythology."

F

sary to select persons whose acuteness and ready tact were a match for these quick-witted wanderers, and many a clever man has become famous for his power to give charms against Pigseys. It does not appear, however, that anything remarkable was required of the clever man. " No Pigsey could harm a man if his coat were inside-out, and it became a very common practice for persons who had to go from village to village by night, to wear their jacket or cloak so turned, ostensibly to prevent the dew from taking the shine off the cloth, but in reality to render them safe from the Pigseys." *

They must have been a merry lot, since to " laugh like a Piskie " is a popular saying. These little fellows were great plagues to the farmers, riding their colts and chasing their cows.

The Buccas or Knockers.—These are the sprites of the mines, and correspond to the Kobals of the German mines, the Duergars, and the Trolls. They are said to be the souls of the Jews who formerly worked the tin-mines of Cornwall. They are not allowed to rest because of their wicked practices as tinners, and they share in the general curse which ignorant people believe still hangs on this race.

The Browney.—This spirit was purely of the household. Kindly and good, he devoted his every care to benefit the family with whom he had taken up his abode. The Browney has fled, owing to his being brought into very close contact with the schoolmaster, and he is only summoned now upon the occasion of the swarming of the bees. When this occurs, mistress or maid seizes a bell-metal, or a tin pan, and, beating it, she calls " Browney, Browney ! " as loud as she can until the good Browney compels the bees to settle.

Mr Thoms has noticed that in Cornwall " the moths which some regard as departed souls, others as fairies, are called *Pisgies.*" This is somewhat too generally expressed ; the belief respecting the moth, so far as I know, is confined to one or two varieties only. Mr Couch informs us that the local name, around Polperro, of the weasel is *Fairy.* So that we have evidence of some sort of metempsychosis amongst the elf family. Moths, ants, and weasels it would seem are the forms taken by those wandering spirits.

* The Cornish had formerly a great belief in piskays or fairies. If a traveller happened to lose his way, he immediately concluded he was "piskay led." To dispel the charm with which the "piskay-led" traveller was entangled, nothing was deemed sufficient but that of his turning one of his garments inside-out. This generally fell upon one of his stockings ; and if this precaution had been taken before the commencement of the journey, it was fully believed that no such delusion would have happened.—*Drew and Hitchins' History of Cornwall*, p. 97.

We read in Bishop Corbet, whose work was published in 1648, and was reprinted many years after by Bishop Percy—

> " The fairies
> Were of the old profession;
> Their songs were *Ave Maries,*
> Their dances were procession.
> But now, alas ! they all are dead,
> Or gone beyond the seas,
> Or, further, for religion fled,
> Or else they take their ease."

Other writers have supposed that at the time of the Reformation the fairies departed from the land. This hypothesis is not warranted by evidence. It is possible that they may have taken possession of some of the inferior creatures, but they are certainly still to be found in those regions which lie beyond the reach of the railway-giant, with his fiery mouth, or of that electric spirit who, travelling on his mysterious wires, can beat the wildest elf that ever mounted " night-steeds."

NURSING A FAIRY.

A THRIFTY housewife lived on one of the hills between Zennor Church-town and St Ives. One night a gentleman came to her cottage, and told her he had marked her cleanliness and her care : that he had a child whom he desired to have brought up with much tenderness, and he had fixed on her. She should be very handsomely rewarded for her trouble, and he showed her a considerable quantity of golden coin. Well, she agreed, and away she went with the gentleman to fetch this child. When they came to the side of Zennor hill, the gentleman told the woman he must blindfold her and she, good, easy soul, having heard of such things, fancied this was some rich man's child, and that the residence of its mother was not to be known, so she gave herself great credit for cunning in quietly submitting. They walked on some considerable distance. When they stopped the handkerchief was taken from her eyes, and she found herself in a magnificent room, with a table spread with the most expensive luxuries, in the way of game, fruits, and wines. She was told to eat, and she did so with some awkwardness, and not a little trembling. She was surprised that so large a feast should have been spread for so small a party,—only herself and the master. At last, having enjoyed luxuries such as she never tasted before or since, a silver bell was rung, and a troop of servants came in, bearing a cot covered with satin, in which was sleeping the most beautiful babe that human eyes ever gazed on. She was told this child was to be committed to her charge ; she should not want for anything ; but she was to obey certain laws. She was not to teach the child the Lord's Prayer ; she was not to wash it after sundown : she was to bathe it every morning in water, which she would find in a white ewer placed in the child's room : this was not to be touched by any one but herself, and she was to be careful not to wash her own face in this water. In all other respects she was to treat the child as one of her own children. The woman was blinded again, and the child having been placed in her arms, away she trudged, guided by the mysterious father. When out on the road, the bandage was removed from her eyes, and she found she had a small baby in her arms, not remarkably good-looking, with very sharp, piercing eyes, and but ordinarily dressed. However, a bargain is a bargain ; so she resolved to make the best of it, and she presented the babe to her husband, telling him so much of the story as she thought it prudent to trust him with. For years the child was with this couple. They never wanted for anything ; meat, and even wines, were provided,—as most people thought,—by wishing for them ; clothes, ready-made, were on the child's bed when required ; and the charmed water was always in the magic ewer. The little boy grew active and strong. He was remarkably wild, yet very tractable, and he appeared to have a real regard for his " big mammy," as he called the woman. Sometimes she thought the child was mad. He would run, and leap, and scream, as though he were playing with scores of boys, when no soul was near him. The woman had never seen the father since the child had been with them ; but ever and anon, money was conveyed to them in some mysterious manner. One morning, when washing the boy, this good woman, who had often observed how bright the water made the face of the child, was tempted to try if it would improve her own beauty. So directing the boy's attention to some birds singing on a tree outside the window, she splashed some of the water up into her face. Most of it went into her eye. She closed it instinctively, and upon opening it, she saw a number of little people gathered round her and playing with the boy. She said not a word, though her fear was great ; and she continued to see the world of small people surrounding the world of ordinary men and women, being with them, but not of them. She now knew who the boy's playmates were, and she often wished to speak to the beautiful creatures of the invisible world who were his real companions ; but she was discreet, and kept silence.

Curious robberies had been from time to time committed in St Ives Market, and although the most careful watch had been kept, the things disappeared, and no thief detected. One day our good housewife was at the market, and to her surprise she saw the father of her nursling. Without ceremony she ran up to him,— at a moment when he was putting some choice fruit by stealth into his pocket,—and spoke to him. " So, thou seest me, dost thou ? " " To be sure I do, and know 'ee too," replied the woman. " Shut this eye," putting his finger on her left eye. " Canst see me now ? " " Yes, I tell 'ee, and know 'ee too," again said the woman.

> " Water for elf, not water for self ;
> You 've lost your eye, your child, and yourself,"

said the gentleman. From that hour she was blind in the right eye. When she got home the boy was gone. She grieved sadly, but she never saw him more, and this once happy couple became poor and wretched.

CHANGELINGS.

A CORRESPONDENT, to whom I am much indebted for many curious examples of the folk-lore of the people in the remote districts to the west of Penzance, says, in reference to some stories of fairy changelings—" I never knew but one child that had been kept by the Spriggans more than three days. It was always complaining, sickly, and weakly, *and had the very face of a changeling.*"

It has been my fortune, some thirty or forty years since, to have seen several children of whom it had been whispered amongst the peasantry that they were changelings. In every case they have been sad examples of the influence of mesenteric disease—the countenance much altered—their eyes glassy and sunk in their sockets—the nose sharpened—the cheeks of a marble whiteness, unless when they were flushed with hectic fever—the lips sometimes swollen and of a deep, red colour, and small ulcers not unfrequently at the angles of the mouth. The wasted frame, with sometimes strumous swellings, and the unnatural abdominal enlargement which accompanies disease of mesenteric glands, gives a very sad, and often a most unnatural appearance to the sufferer. The intense ignorance which existed in many of the districts visited by me, at the period named, has been almost dispelled by the

civilising influences of Wesleyanism. Consequently, when a scrofulous child is found in a family, we no longer hear of its being a
changeling; but, within a very recent period, I have heard it said
that such afflicted children had been " ill-wished."

THE LOST CHILD.

IN the little hamlet of Treonike, in the parish of St Allen, has
long lingered the story of a lost child, who was subsequently
found. All the stories agree in referring the abduction of the
child to supernatural agency, and in some cases it is referred to
the "Small People or Piskies,"—in others, to less amiable spiritual
creatures. Mr Hals* has given one version of this story, which
differs in some respects from the tale as I heard it, from an old
woman some thirty years since, who then lived in this parish.
Her tale was to the following effect. It was a lovely evening, and
the little boy was gathering flowers in the fields, near a wood.
The child was charmed by hearing some beautiful music, which
he at first mistook for the song of birds; but, being a sharp boy,
he was not long deceived, and he went towards the wood to
ascertain from whence the melodious sounds came. When he
reached the verge of the wood, the music was of so exquisite a
character, that he was compelled to follow the sound, which
appeared to travel before him. Lured in this way, the boy penetrated to the dark centre of the grove, and here, meeting with
some difficulties, owing to the thick growth of underwood, he
paused and began to think of returning. The music, however,
became more ravishing than before, and some invisible being
appeared to crush down all the low and tangled plants, thus forming for him a passage, over which he passed without any difficulty.
At length he found himself on the edge of a small lake, and,
greatly to his astonishment, the darkness of night was around him,
but the heavens were thick with stars. The music ceased, and,
wearied with his wanderings, the boy fell asleep on a bed of ferns.
He related, on his restoration to his parents, that he was taken by
a beautiful lady through palaces of the most gorgeous description.
Pillars of glass supported arches which glistened with every colour,
and these were hung with crystals far exceeding anything which
were ever seen in the caverns of a Cornish mine. It is, however,
stated that many days passed away before the child was found by his
friends, and that at length he was discovered, one lovely morning,
sleeping on the bed of ferns, on which he was supposed to have

* See Davies Gilbert's Parochial History of Cornwall.

fallen asleep on the first adventurous evening. There was no reason given by the narrator why the boy was " spirited away " in the first instance, or why he was returned. Her impression was, that some sprites, pleased with the child's innocence and beauty, had entranced him. That when asleep he had been carried through the waters to the fairy abodes beneath them ; and she felt assured that a child so treated would be kept under the especial guardianship of the sprites for ever afterwards. Of this, however, tradition leaves us in ignorance.

A NATIVE PIGSEY STORY.

" D'YE see that 'ere hoss there ? " said a Liskeard farmer to a West-Country miner.

" What ov it ? " asked the miner.

" Well, that 'ere hoss he 'n been ridden to death a'most by the pigsies again."

" Pigsies ! " said the miner ; " thee don't b'leve in they, do 'ee ? "

" Ees I do ; but I specks you 're a West-Country bucca, ain't 'ee ? If you 'd a had yourn hosses wrode to death every nite, you 'd tell another tayl, I reckon. But as sure as I 'se living the pigsies do ride on 'em whenever they 've a mind to."

THE NIGHT-RIDERS.

I WAS on a visit when a boy at a farmhouse situated near Fowey river. Well do I remember the farmer with much sorrow telling us one morning at breakfast, that " the piskie people had been riding Tom again ; " and this he regarded as certainly leading to the destruction of a fine young horse. I was taken to the stable to see the horse. There could be no doubt that the animal was much distressed, and refused to eat his food. The mane was said to be knotted into fairy stirrups ; and Mr —— told me that he had no doubt at least twenty small people had sat upon the horse's neck. He even assured me that one of his men had seen them urging the horse to his utmost speed round and round one of his fields.

THE FAIRY TOOLS; OR, BARKER'S KNEE.

THE buccas or knockers are believed to inhabit the rocks, caves, adits, and wells of Cornwall. In the parish of Towednack there was a well where those industrious small people might every day be heard busy at their labours—digging with pickaxe and shovel. I said, every day. No; on Christmas-day —on the Jews' Sabbath—on Easter-day—and on All-Saints' day— no work was done. Why our little friends held those days in reverence has never been told me. Any one, by placing his ear on the ground at the mouth of this well, could distinctly hear the little people at work.

There lived in the neighbourhood a great, hulking fellow, who would rather do anything than work, and who refused to believe anything he heard. He had been told of the Fairy Well—he said it was "all a dream." But since the good people around him reiterated their belief in the fairies of the well, he said he'd find it all out. So day after day, Barker—that was this hulk's name— would lie down amidst the ferns growing around the mouth of the well, and, basking in the sunshine, listen and watch. He soon heard pick and shovel, and chit-chat, and merry laughter. Well, "he'd see the out of all this," he told his neighbours. Day after day, and week after week, this fellow was at his post. Nothing resulted from his watching. At last he learned to distinguish the words used by the busy workers. He discovered that each set of labourers worked eight hours, and that, on leaving, they hid their tools. They made no secret of this; and one evening he heard one say, he should place his tools in a cleft in the rock; another, that he should put his under the ferns; and another said, he should leave his tools on *Barker's knee*. He started on hearing his own name. At that moment a heavy weight fell on the man's knee; he felt excessive pain, and roared to have the cursed things taken away. His cries were answered by laughter. To the day of his death Barker had a stiff knee; he was laughed at by all the parish; and "Barker's knee" became a proverb.

THE PISKIES IN THE CELLAR.

THE following story, for which I am indebted to Mr T. Q. Couch, will remind the reader of "The Cluricaun" and "The Haunted Cellar," in "Fairy Legends and Traditions of the South of Ireland." By T. Crofton Croker, Esq.

On the Thursday immediately preceding Christmas-tide (year

not recorded), were assembled at "The Rising Sun" the captain and men of a stream work * in the Couse below. This Couse was a flat, alluvial moor, broken by gigantic mole-hills, the work of many a generation of tinners. One was half inclined, on looking at the turmoiled ground, to believe with them that the tin grew in successive crops, for, after years of turning and searching, there was still enough left to give the landlord his dole, and to furnish wages to some dozen streamers. This night was a festival observed in honour of one *Picrous*,† and intended to celebrate the discovery of tin on this day by a man of that name. The feast is still kept, though the observance has dwindled to a supper and its attendant merrymaking.

Our story has especially to do with the adventures of one of the party, John Sturtridge, who, well primed with ale, started on his homeward way for Luxulyan Church-town. John had got as far as Tregarden Down without any mishap worth recording, when, alas! he happed upon a party of the little people, who were at their sports in the shelter of a huge granite boulder. Assailed by shouts of derisive laughter, he hastened on frightened and bewildered, but the Down, well known from early experience, became like ground untrodden, and after long trial no gate or stile was to be found. He was getting vexed, as well as puzzled, when a chorus of tiny voices shouted, "Ho! and away for Par Beach!" John repeated the shout, and was in an instant caught up, and in a twinkling found himself on the sands of Par. A brief dance, and the cry was given, "Ho! and away for Squire Tremain's cellar!" A repetition of the Piskie cry found John with his elfish companions in the cellars at Heligan, where was beer and wine galore. It need not be said that he availed himself of his opportunities. The mixture of all the good liquors so affected him that, alas! he forgot in time to catch up the next cry of "Ho! and away for Par Beach!" In the morning John was found by the butler, groping and tumbling among butts and barrels, very much muddled with the squire's good drink. His strange story, very incoherently told, was not credited by the squire, who committed him to jail for the burglary, and in due time he was convicted and sentenced to death.

The morning of his execution arrived; a large crowd had assembled, and John was standing under the gallows-tree, when a commotion was observed in the crowd, and a little lady of com-

---

* A "stream work" is a place where tin is obtained from the drift deposits. "Streamers" are the tinners who wash out the tin.

† Picrous day is still kept up in Luxulyan. See Appendix L.

manding mien made her way through the opening throng to the scaffold. In a shrill, sweet voice, which John recognised, she cried, "Ho! and away for France!" Which being replied to, he was rapt from the officers of justice, leaving them and the multitude mute with wonder and disappointment.

THE SPRIGGANS OF TRENCROM HILL.

IT is not many years since a man, who thought he was fully informed as to the spot in which a crock of the giant's gold was buried, proceeded on one fine moonlight night to this enchanted hill, and with spade and pick commenced his search. He proceeded for some time without interruption, and it became evident to him that the treasure was not far off. The sky was rapidly covered with the darkest clouds, shutting out the brilliant light o the moon—which had previously gemmed each cairn—and leaving the gold-seeker in total and unearthly darkness. The wind rose, and roared terrifically amidst the rocks; but this was soon drowned amidst the fearful crashes of thunder, which followed in quick succession the flashes of lightning. By its light the man perceived that the spriggans were coming out in swarms from all the rocks. They were in countless numbers; and although they were small at first, they rapidly increased in size, until eventually they assumed an almost giant form, looking all the while, as he afterwards said, "as ugly as if they would eat him." How this poor man escaped is unknown, but he is said to have been so frightened that he took to his bed, and was not able to work for a long time.

THE FAIRY MINERS—THE KNOCKERS.

AT Ransom Mine the "Knockers" were always very active in their subterranean operations. In every part of the mine their "knockings" were heard, but most especially were they busy in one particular "end." There was a general impression that great wealth must exist at this part of the "lode." Yet, notwithstanding the inducements of very high "tribute" were held out to the miners, no pair of men could be found brave enough to venture on the ground of the "Bockles." An old man and his son, called Trenwith, who lived near Bosprenis, went out one midsummer eve, about midnight, and watched until they saw the "Smae People" bringing up the shining ore. It is said they were possessed of some secret by which they could communicate with the fairy people. Be this as it may, they told the little miners that they would save them all the trouble of breaking down the ore, that they would bring "to grass" for them, one-tenth of the "richest stuff," and leave it properly dressed, if they would quietly give them up this end. An agreement of some kind was come to. The old man and his son took the "pitch," and in a short time realised much wealth. The old man never failed to keep to his bargain, and leave the tenth of the ore for his friends. He died. The son was avaricious and selfish. He sought to cheat the Knockers, but he ruined himself by so doing. The "lode" failed; nothing answered with him; disappointed, he took to drink, squandered all the money his father had made, and died a beggar.

THE SPRIGGAN'S CHILD,

AS TOLD BY A CORNISH DROLL.

I 'LL tell you a tale, an you've patience to hear an,
    'Bout the Spriggans, that swarm round Partinney still—
You knew Janey Tregeer, who lives in Brea Vean,
    In the village just under the Chapel-Hill.

One arternoon she went out for to reap,
And left the child in the cradle asleep :
Janey took good care to cover the fire ;—
Turn'd down the brandis on the baking-ire   (iron),
Swept up the ashes on the hearthstone,
And so left the child in the house all alone—
The boys had all on 'em gone away,
Some to work and some to play.
Janey work'd in the field as gay as a lark,
And when she came home it was nearly dark ;
The furst thing she saw when she open'd the door
Was the cradle upset—all the straw on the floor.

But no child in sight—
    She search'd all round—
    Still no child was found :
    And it got dark night.
    So great was Jane's fright,
    That for more than an hour
    She hadn't the power
To strike a light.

However, she kindled the fire at last,
And threw in a faggot to make a blast.

As she stoop'd over the wood-corner stone,
She heard a sound 'tween a cry and a moan—
  It clearly came from a bundle of ferns—
    The two bigger boy's bed—
  And there, sure enough, as frighten'd she turns,
    Janey saw the child's head.

'Twas very queer.   How the child got there,
        Nobody could say ;
Yet ever since that day, the babe pined away—
It was at all times crying, or sucking, or eating,
And blinking and peeping, when it ought to be sleeping,
    But seldom it closed its eyes.
  Jane said for a child it look'd too wise—
  That she thought it a changeling
  She didn't disguise—
  And often and often she gave it a beating,
  To stop—but she couldn't—its cussed bleating.

    Janey resolved to work the spell,
      And whene'er she could stay,
    She bath'd the brat in the Chapel Well—
      Which he thought rare play.

On the three first Wednesdays in flow'ry May
She plunged it deep at the dawn of day—
Pass'd it slowly three times against the sun,
Went three times round,—and when all was done,
The imp of a child roar'd aloud for fun.
      No tongue can tell
        The trouble it gave her
        To dip the shaver,
      And work the spell.

From Brea to Chapel-Uny is a mile or more,
And surely it tried Janey's patience sore
To trudge forth and back from the Chapel Well,
With this brat on her back, to work the spell.

She wish'd it dead ; but it wouldn't die :
It ate its bread, it would pine and cry ;
And Janey was nearly beside herself
With this plague of her life—this wicked elf.

  Well, one rainy day,—as it rains in May,—
    Janey set out with the child in her arms
    Once more to work the holy charms.

When very close to the top of the hill,
　Where she was sure there was nobody near,
　She heard the strangest voice in her ear,
　Saying these words, quite clear and shrill—
" *Tredrill, Tredrill ! thy wife and children greet thee well.*"

Oh, Janey's heart-strings were like to crack,
When up spake the thing in her arms, good lack !—
　　" For wife or child little care I,
　　They may laugh,
　　Or they may cry,—
　　While milk I quaff,
　　When I am dry—
　　Get of my pap my fill
　　Whenever I will,
　　On the dowdy's back ride,
　　With my legs astride,
　　When we work the spell
　　At the Chapel Well."

Janey dropp'd the cussed thing on the ground,
And turn'd round, and round, and round ;
You may be sure she was in a fright
To hear the sound, and nobody in sight,
And to hear a child talk
Months before it could walk.
　She has said o'er and o'er,
　　And I am sure you can't wonder,
　'Twouldn't frighten her more,
　　Had the rocks burst asunder,
　　And the earth belch'd forth thunder.

When Janey at length got over the fright
From hearing the sound and nobody in sight,
And the brat which lay crying, as if it was dying,
Talking out like a man of his wife and his child,
She felt all bedazzled as if she was wild—
Took the brat by the arm, flung it over her shoulder—
Wouldn't believe it her child if the parson had told her—
　　Thought the devil was in it,
　　　As she ran the hill down,
　　Without stopping a minute
　　　Till she came to Brea town.

The old women came out, and all on 'em agreed
'Twas the strangest thing that ever they seed ;
They stood in a row, and each one had a word—
'Twas the wonderfull'st story that ever they heard ;
'Twas a Spriggan's brat—they were all sure of that—
No more like Jane's child than an old ram-cat.
She must beat it black, she must beat it blue,
Bruise its body all o'er with the heel of her shoe—
Then lay it alone beneath the church stile,
And keep out of hearing and sight for a while—
When every one said, as every one thought,
That Janey's child would again be brought :
Some said 'twould be living—some said 'twould be dead —
But the Spriggan's base brat she no longer need dread.

 Jane beat the babe black,
 And she beat the babe blue,
  On the ashes' pile before the door ;
  And she would have beaten it ten times more,
 But out of her hand she lost her shoe,
 Struck away all at once—by she couldn't tell who.

The brat had roar'd—it could roar no more—
 So they carried it off to the old church stile,
And laid it under the stones—some swore
 That when placed on the earth it was seen to smile—
Then all turn'd back, and kept far out of sight :—
 And Janey declared she was almost wild :
But they kept her back till the turn o' the night,
 When she rush'd to the stile and found her own child.

'Twas there, sure enough, her own dear child :—
 But when first she saw it,
 She did not know it—
It look'd so frighten'd—it seem'd so wild.

 Then the old women said,
  If it keeps its wits,
 We're sadly afraid
  The poor babe will have fits.

A friend writes me :—" I saw an account in a newspaper the other day of an Irishwoman who was brought before the magistrates, in New York, for causing the death of a child by making it stand on *hot coals,* to try if it were her own truly-begotten child, or a changeling. I think the notion was, that her own child

would stand fire, but an imp would either die, to all *appearance*,
or be spirited away. This is much worse than the plan of the
woman of Brea Vean, who put the brat on the ashes' pile, and
beat it black with the broom." *

THE PISKIES' CHANGELING.

THIS story is told by Mr T. Q. Couch, as an example of the
folk-lore of a Cornish village, in " Notes and Queries,"
under the name of " Coleman Gray : "—

" There is a farmhouse of some antiquity with which my family
have a close connection ; and it is this circumstance, more than
any other, that has rendered this tradition concerning it more
interesting to us, and better remembered than many other equally
romantic and authentic. Close to this house, one day, a little
miserable-looking bantling was discovered alone, unknown, and
incapable of making its wants understood. It was instantly
remembered by the finder, that this was the way in which the
piskies were accustomed to deal with those infants of their race
for whom they sought human protection ; and it would have been
an awful circumstance if such a one were not received by the
individual so visited. The anger of the piskies would be certain,
and some direful calamity must be the result ; whereas, a kind
welcome would probably be attended with great good fortune.
The miserable plight of this stranger, therefore, attracted attention
and sympathy. The little unconscious one was admitted as one
of the family. Its health was speedily restored, and its renewed
strength, activity, intelligence, and good-humour, caused it to
become a general favourite. It is true the stranger was often
found to indulge in odd freaks ; but this was accounted for by a
recollection of its pedigree, which was not doubted to be of the
piskie order. So the family prospered, and had banished the
thought that the foundling would ever leave them. There was to
the front door of this house, a hatch, which is a half-door, that is
kept closed when the whole door behind it is open, and it then
serves as a guard against the intrusion of dogs, hogs, and ducks,
while air and light are freely admitted. This little being was one
day leaning over the top of this hatch, and looking wistfully
outward, when a clear voice was heard to proceed from a neigh-

---

* " The Father of Eighteen Elves," in " Legends of Iceland," is, in all its chief
features, similar to this story, even to the beating him without mercy. " Icelandic
Legends. Collected by John Arnason : Translated by George E. J. Powell and
Eirikur Magmisson." Bentley, 1864.

bouring part of the *townplace*, calling, ' Coleman Gray, Coleman Gray!' The piskie immediately started up, and with a sudden laugh, clapped its hands, exclaiming, ' Aha ! my daddy is come !' It was gone in a moment, never to be seen again."

THE PIXIES OF DARTMOOR.

THERE is a celebrated piskie haunt at Costellas in Cornwall (says Mrs Bray), where they have been seen sitting in a ring —the men smoking after the most approved fashion of the Dutch burgomaster, and the women spinning, perhaps in emulation of the frugal vrow.

I never heard of this place. Like the rest of the "good people," piskies are fond of music, and the sound of their " harp and pipe and symphony," is occasionally heard at nightfall. It is said that a man once passing one of the piskie rings, and hearing them dancing and singing within it, threw a large stone into the midst of the circle, when the music at once ceased and a dreadful shriek arose.

The appearance of the *pixies* of Dartmoor is said to resemble that of a bale or bundle of rags. In this shape they decoy children to their unreal pleasure. A woman, on the northern borders of the moor, was returning home late on a dark evening, accompanied by two children, and carrying a third in her arms, when, on arriving at her own door, she found one missing. Her neighbours, with lanthorns, immediately set out in quest of the lost child ; whom they found sitting under a large oak-tree, well known to be a favourite haunt of the pixies. He declared that he had been led away by two large bundles of rags, which had remained with him until the lights appeared, when they immediately vanished.*

The pixies of Dartmoor, notwithstanding their darker character, aided occasionally in household work. A washerwoman was one morning greatly surprised, on coming down-stairs, to find all her clothes neatly washed and folded. She watched the next evening, and observed a pixie in the act of performing this kind office for her : but she was ragged and mean in appearance, and Betty's gratitude was sufficiently great to induce her to prepare a yellow petticoat and a red cap for the obliging pixie.

* For additional information respecting the pixies of the banks of the Tamar and the Tavy, the reader is referred to Mrs Bray's " Traditions, Legends, Superstitions, and Sketches of Devonshire."

THE FAIRY FAIR IN GERMOE.

BAL LANE in Germoe was a notorious place for piskies. One night Daniel Champion and his comrade came to Godolphin Bridge,—they were a little bit " overtook " with liquor. They said that when they came to " Bal Lane," they found it covered all over from end to end, and the Small People holding a fair there with all sorts of merchandise—the prettiest sight they ever met with. Champion was sure he saw his child there ; for a few nights before, his child in the evening was as beautiful a one as could be seen anywhere, but in the morning was changed for one as ugly and wizened as could be ; and he was sure the Small People had done it. Next day, telling the story at Croft Gothal, his comrade was knocked backward, thrown into the bob-pit, and just killed. Obliged to be carried to his home, Champion followed, and was telling of their adventure with the Small People, when one said, " Don't speak about them ; they 're wicked, spiteful devils." No sooner were the words uttered than the speaker was thrown clean over stairs and bruised dreadfully, —a convincing proof to all present of the reality of the existence of the Small Folks.

ST MARGERY AND THE PISKIES.

WE have no reliable information of the birth, parentage, or education of Margery Daw, but we have a·nursery rhyme which clearly indicates that she must have been a sloven—perhaps an ancient picture of a literary lady, who was by her sad habit reduced to extreme necessity.

See saw, Margery Daw,

clearly indicates a lazy woman rocking herself, either in deep thought, or for want of thought.

Sold her bed and lay on the straw ;

this was stage the first of her degradation.

She sold her straw and lay in the smut,

the second and final stage, which may well induce the poet to inquire—

Was not she a dirty slut ?

Another version of Margery's story is more distinct as to her end :—

> See saw,
> Margery Daw,
> Sold her bed
> And lay on the straw ;
> She sold her straw,
> And lay upon hay,
> So *piskies* came
> And carried her away.

A friend, in writing to me on this dirty Cornish saint, is disposed to regard St Margery Daw as a very devout Roman Catholic, and to refer the version of her story which I have given first to the strong feeling shown by many Protestants against those pious women who rejected the finery of the world, and submitted for the sake of their souls to those privations which formed at one time the severe rule of conventual life. Margery and the fairies are supposed to have left England together at the time of the Reformation, but she has left her name to several Cornish mines.

THE FAIRY REVELS ON THE " GUMP," ST JUST.

LONG has the Gump been the reputed playground of the Small People. Many of the good old people were permitted to witness their revels, and for years they have delighted their grandchildren with tales of the songs they have heard, and of the sights they have seen. To many of their friends those fairies have given small but valuable presents ; but woe to the man or woman who would dare to intrude upon the ground occupied by them at the time of their high festivals. There was a covetous old hunks in St Just—never mind his name, he was severely punished, let that suffice—well, this old fellow had heard so much of the riches displayed by the little people, when holding holiday on the Gump, that he resolved to get some of the treasures. He learned all he could learn from his neighbours, but kept his intention to himself. It was during the harvest-moon—the night was a softened day—and everything abroad on such a night should have been in harmony with its quiet brilliancy. But here was a dark soul passing along, making a small eclipse with his black shadow. The old man stole towards the rendezvous of the " good people," as some were fond of calling them, anxiously looking out for the treasures which he coveted. At length, when he had not advanced far on the Gump, he heard music of the most ravishing kind. Its influence was of a singularly mysterious character. As the notes were solemn and slow, or quick and gay, the old man was moved from tears to laughter ; and on more than one occasion he was compelled to dance in obedience to the time.   Notwithstanding that he was almost bewildered by the whirling motion to which he was compelled, the old man " kept his wits awake," and waited his opportunity to seize some fairy treasure ; but as yet nothing remarkable had presented itself.   The music appeared to surround him, and, as he thought, to come closer to him than it was at first; and although its sound led him to believe that the musicians were on the surface, he was impressed with an idea that they were really beneath the earth   Eventually there was a crash of sound, startling beyond description, and the hill before him opened.   All was now ablaze with variously-coloured lights.   Every blade of grass was hung with lamps, and every furze bush was illuminated with stars   Out from the opening in the hill marched a host of spriggans, as if to clear the road.   Then came an immense number of musicians playing on every kind of instrument.   These were followed by troop after troop of soldiers, each troop bearing aloft their banner, which appeared to spread itself, to display its blazonry, without the assistance of any breeze.   All these arranged themselves in order over the ground, some here and some there. One thing was not at all to our friend's liking ; several hundreds of the most grotesque of the spriggans placed themselves so as to enclose the spot on which he was standing.   Yet, as they were none of them higher than his shoe-tie, he thought he could " squash " them easily with his foot if they were up to any mischief, and so he consoled himself.   This vast array having disposed of themselves, first came a crowd of servants bearing vessels of silver and vessels of gold, goblets cut out of diamonds, rubies, and other precious stones.   There were others laden, almost to overflowing, with the richest meats, pastry, preserves, and fruits.   Presently the ground was covered with tables and everything was arranged in the most systematic order,—each party falling back as they disposed of their burdens.

The brilliancy of the scene nearly overpowered the old man ; but, when he was least prepared for it, the illumination became a thousand times more intense.   Out of the hill were crowding thousands upon thousands of lovely ladies and gentlemen, arrayed in the most costly attire.   He thought there would be no end to the coming crowd.   By and by, however, the music suddenly changed, and the harmonious sounds which fell upon his ears appeared to give new life to every sense.   His eyes were clearer, his ears quicker, and his sense of smell more exquisite.

The odours of flowers, more delicious than any he had ever smelt, filled the air.   He saw, without any disturbing medium, the brilliant beauty of the thousands of ladies who were now upon the Gump ; and their voices were united in one gush of song, which was clear as silver bells—a hymeneal symphony of the utmost delicacy.   The words were in a language unknown to him, but he saw they were directed towards a new group now emerging from the hill.

First came a great number of female children clothed in the whitest gauze, strewing flowers on the Gump.   These were not dead or cut flowers, for the moment they touched the ground they took root and grew.   These were followed by an equally large number of boys, holding in their hands shells which appeared to be strung like harps, and from which they brought forth murmurs of melody, such as angels only could hope to hear and live.   Then came—and there was no end to their coming—line upon line of little men clothed in green and gold, and by and by a forest of banners, which, at a signal, were all furled.   Then, seated on thrones, carried upon a platform above the heads of the men, came a young prince and princess who blazed with beauty and jewels, as if they were suns amidst a skyey host of stars.   There was much ceremonial marching to and fro, but eventually the platform was placed upon a mound on the Gump, which was now transformed into a hillock of roses and lilies ; and around this all the ladies and gentlemen walked, bowing, and each one saying some-thing to the princess and the prince,—passing onward and taking their seats at the tables.   Although no man could count the number of this fairy host, there was no confusion ; all the ladies and gentle-men found, as if by instinct, their places.   When all were seated, a signal was given by the prince ; servants in splendid liveries placed tables crowded with gold-plate and good things on the platform, and every one, the prince and princess included, began to feast with a will.   Well, thought the old man, now is my time ; if I could only crawl up to the prince's table, I should have a catch sure enough, and become a rich man for life.   With his greedy mind fixed on this one object, and unobservant of everything else, he crouched down, as though by so doing he could escape ob-servation, and very slowly and stealthily advanced amongst the revellers.   He never saw that thousands of spriggans had thrown little strings about him, and that they still held the ends of the threads.   The presence of this selfish old mortal did not in any way discompose the assembly ; they ate and drank and were as merry as though no human eye was looking on them.   The old man was wondrous cautious lest he should disturb the feasters, consequently a long time was spent in getting, as he desired, to the back of the mound. At length he reached the desired spot, and, to his surprise, all was dark and gloomy behind him, but in front of the mound all was a blaze of light. Crawling like a serpent on his belly, trembling with anxiety, the old man advanced close to the prince and princess. He was somewhat startled to find, as he looked out over the mound, that every one of the thousands of eyes in that multitude was fixed on his. He gazed a while, all the time screwing his courage up ; then, as a boy who would catch a butterfly, he took off his hat and carefully raised it, so as to cover the prince, the princess, and their costly table, and, when about to close it upon them, a shrill whistle was heard, the old man's hand was fixed powerless in the air, and everything became dark around him.

Whir ! whir ! whir ! as if a flight of bees were passing him, buzzed in his ears. Every limb, from head to foot, was as if stuck full of pins and pinched with tweezers. He could not move, he was changed to the ground. By some means he had rolled down the mound, and lay on his back with his arms outstretched, arms and legs being secured by magic chains to the earth ; therefore, although he suffered great agony, he could not stir, and, strange enough, his tongue appeared tied by cords, so that he could not call. He had lain, no one can tell how long, in this sad plight, when he felt as if a number of insects were running over him, and by the light of the moon he saw standing on his nose one of the spriggans, who looked exceedingly like a small dragon-fly. This little monster stamped and jumped with great delight ; and having had his own fun upon the elevated piece of humanity, he laughed most outrageously, and shouted, " Away, away, I smell the day !" Upon this the army of small people, who had taken possession of the old man's body, moved quickly away, and left our discomfited hero alone on the Gump. Bewildered, or, as he said, bedevilled, he lay still to gather up his thoughts. At length the sun arose, and then he found that he had been tied to the ground by myriads of gossamer webs, which were now covered with dew, and glistened like diamonds in the sunshine.

He shook himself, and was free. He rose wet, cold, and ashamed. Sulkily he made his way to his home. It was a long time before his friends could learn from the old man where he had passed the night, but, by slow degrees, they gathered the story I have related to you.

THE FAIRY FUNERAL.

THIS and two or three other bits of folk-lore were communicated to the *Athenæum* by me, when Ambrose Merton (Mr
Thoms) solicited such contributions.

The parish church of Lelant is curiously situated amidst hills
of blown sand, near the entrance of the creek of Hayle. The
sandy waste around the church is called the Towen ; and this
place was long the scene of the midnight gambols of the Small
People. In the adjoining village—or, as it is called in Cornwall,
the " church-town "—lived an old woman who had been, according to her own statement, a frequent witness to the use made by
the fairies of the Towen. Her husband, also, had seen some
extraordinary scenes on the same spot. From her—to me, oft-
repeated description—I get the following tale :—It was the fishing season ; and Richard had been to St Ives for some fish. He
was returning, laden with pilchards, on a beautiful moonlight
night ; and as he ascended the hill from St Ives, he thought he
heard the bell of Lelant Church tolling. Upon a nearer approach,
he saw lights in the church ; and most distinctly did the bell
toll—not with its usual clear sound, but dull and heavy, as
if it had been muffled, scarcely awakening any echo. Richard
walked towards the church, and cautiously, but not without fear,
approaching one of the windows, looked in. At first he could not
perceive any one within, nor discover whence the light came by
which everything was so distinctly illuminated. At length he
saw, moving along the centre aisle, a funeral procession. The
little people who crowded the aisle, although they all looked very
sorrowful, were not dressed in any mourning garments—so far
from it, they wore wreaths of little roses, and carried branches of
the blossoming myrtle. Richard beheld the bier borne between
six—whether men or women he could not tell—but he saw that
the face of the corpse was that of a beautiful female, smaller than
the smallest child's doll. It was, Richard said, " as if it were a
dead seraph,"—so very lovely did it appear to him. The body
was covered with white flowers, and its hair, like gold threads,
was tangled amongst the blossoms. The body was placed within
the altar ; and then a large party of men, with picks and spades,
began to dig a little hole close by the sacramental table. Their
task being completed, others, with great care, removed the body
and placed it in the hole. The entire company crowded around,
eager to catch a parting glimpse of that beautiful corpse, ere yet
it was placed in the earth. As it was lowered into the ground,

they began to tear off their flowers and break their branches of myrtle, crying, " Our queen is dead ! our queen is dead ! " At length one of the men who had dug the grave threw a shovelful of earth upon the body ; and the shriek of the fairy host so alarmed Richard, that he involuntarily joined in it. In a moment, all the lights were extinguished, and the fairies were heard flying in great consternation in every direction. Many of them brushed past the terrified man, and, shrieking, pierced him with sharp instruments. He was compelled to save his life *by the most rapid flight.*

THE FAIRY REVEL.

R ICHARD also once witnessed a fairy revel in the Towen— upon which tables were spread, with the utmost profusion of gold and silver ornaments, and fruits and flowers. Richard, however, according to the statement of " Aunt Alcey " (the name by which his wife was familiarly called), very foolishly interrupted the feast by some exclamation of surprise ; whereas, had he but touched the end of a table with his finger, it would have been impossible for the fairy host to have removed an article, as that which has been touched by mortal fingers becomes to them accursed. As it was, the lovely vision faded before the eyes of the astonished labourer.

BETTY STOGS AND JAN THE MOUNSTER.

I N the " high countries," as the parishes of Morva, Zennor, and Towednack are called, there has long existed a tradition that the children of dirty, lazy, " courseying " women are often taken away by the Small People, carefully cleansed, and then re- turned—of course all the more beautiful for being washed by the fairies in morning-dew. This notion has evidently prevailed for many ages, and, like many an old tradition, it has been remodelled in each generation to adapt it to the conditions of the time. The following is but slightly modified in its principal characteristics from a story somewhat coarsely told, and greatly extended, by an old woman in Morva. A woman, up the higher side, called Betty Stogs, very nearly lost her baby a few months ago. Stogs was only a nickname, but every one knew her by that and no other. It was given to her because she was so untidy about the feet and legs. She could not darn a hole in her stocking—the lazy slut could never knit one. Betty was always pulling the legs of her stockings down under her feet, that the holes in her heels might not be seen—as long as the tops would come under the garter—and she often gartered half-way down the leg to meet the necessities of the case. Betty was reared up in Towednack, at no great distance from Wheal Reeth, at which Bal the old man, her father, worked. He also farmed a few acres of land, and, " out of core," he and his daughter worked on it. The old people used to say—they wouldn't put the poor innocent chield to work to Bal, for fear the great rough heathens from Lelant might overcome her ; so they kept her at home, and the old man would brag how his Betty could cut furze and turf. Instead of staying at home in the evenings, Betty was always racing round the lanes to class-meetings ; for she had been a " professor ever since she was a chield." Betty was an only child, and the old people had saved a little money, and they hoped some one " above the common " would marry her. In Higher Side there lived a man called Jan the Mounster (monster), and, tempted by the bit of money, he resolved to lay himself out to catch Betty. Jan became a converted character—he met in the same class with Betty, and expressed himself as being "so fond of the means of grace." Things went on in this way for some time, and it was found that Betty " had met with a misfortune." The old people were now in a great hurry to marry their daughter, and promised Jan money enough to buy a set of cheene (china), and lots of beautiful clome (earthenware) ; but Mounster required more than this, and fought off. He left the "people," that he mightn't be read out. He said he was heartily sick of the lot, told strange stories about their doings, and became as bad a character as ever. Time advanced, and Betty's mother —who was herself a wretchedly dirty woman, and, as people said, too fond of the " drop of drink "—saw that she must lose no chance of making her daughter an honest woman. So she went to Penzance and bought a new bed—a real four-poster—a new dresser, painted bright lead and liver colour—an eight-day clock, in a painted mahogany case—a mass of beautiful clome—and a glass milk-cup. When all these things were ranged in a cottage, Jan was well enough pleased with them, and hung his " great turnip of a watch " up in the middle of the dresser, to see how it would look. When he had satisfied himself, he told the old woman he would marry Betty out of hand, if she would give them their great pretty, bright, warming-pan to hang opposite the door. This was soon settled, and Jan the Mounster and Betty Stogs were married.

In a little time the voice of a baby was heard in Jan's cottage, but the poor child had no cradle, only a " costan" (a straw and bramble basket) ; and, in addition to the ordinary causes of neglect, another cause was introduced—Betty took to drink. A great, nasty suss of a woman, who went about pretending to sell crochet-work, but in reality to sell gin—which she kept in a bottle under the dirty rags, which she called " the most beautiful croshar-work collars and cuffs, that all the ladies in the towns and up the country wear on Sundays and high holidays "—formed a close acquaintance with Jan's wife. The result was, things went from bad to worse. Jan was discontented, and went to Bal, and returned from Bal always a sullen man. One day Betty had to bake some bread— she had never before done so, as her mother had always attended to that job. Jan had left his watch hanging to the dresser, that Betty might know the time. All went well till the middle of the day; and, just as the bread was ready to put down, in came the crochet-woman. First Betty had a noggin of gin—she then had her fortune told—and because she was promised no end of good luck and the handsomest children in the country, and Jan the best luck in tribute-pitches, the kettle was boiled, and some pork fried for the fortune-teller.

All this time the dough was forgotten, and it was getting sour and heavy. At last, when the woman went away, the lump of sour " leven " was put down to bake. The neglected child got troublesome, and as Jan would be home early to supper, Betty was in a great hurry to get things done. To quiet the child, she gave it Jan's watch; and, that it might be the better pleased, she opened it, " that the dear chield might see the pretty little wheels spinning round." In a short time the " machine " was thrown down in the ashes, and it, of course, stopped. Betty, at last, wished to know the time; she then found the watch clogged full of dirt. To put the thing to rights she washed it out in the kettle of dish-water, which had not been changed for two or three days, and was thick with salt pilchard-bones, and potato-skins. She did her best to clean the watch, for she was now terribly afraid of Jan, and she wiped all the little wheels, as far as she could reach, with the corner of the dishcloth, but the confounded thing would not go. She had to bake the bread by guess; and, therefore, when she took it up, it was as black as soot, and as hard as a stone.

Jan came home; and you may judge the temper he was in at finding things as they were, and his watch stopped. Betty swore to the deepest that she had never taken the thing into her hands. Next morning Jan got up early to go to Bal; and taking the burnt loaf, he tried to cut it with a knife, but it was in vain—as well try to cut a stone; next he tried the dag (axe), and Mounster said it strook fire, and the dag never made the least mark in the crust.

The poor fellow had to go to his work without his breakfast, and to depend upon the share of a comrade's fuggun for dinner.

Next day, Friday, was pay-day, and Jan having got his pay, went to St Ives for bread, and took the precious watch with him to be set to rights.   The watchmaker soon found out the complaint; here was a bit of fish-bone, there a piece of potato-paring ; in one tooth a piece of worsted from a dishcloth, in another a particle of straw, and ashes everywhere.

The murder was out ; and that night Jan, having first drunk to excess in St Ives, went home and nearly murdered his wife.   From this time Jan was drunk every day, and Betty was so as often as she could get gin.   The poor child was left half the day to suck his thumbs, and to tumble and toss on the filthy rags in the old costan, without any one to look after it.

One day Betty was in a " courseying " mood, and went from house to house, wherever she could find a woman idle enough to gossip with her.   Betty stayed away till dark—it was Jan's last core by day—and the poor child was left all alone.

When she came home she was surprised not to hear the child, but she thought it might have cried itself to sleep, and was not concerned.   At last, having lit the candle, she looked in the costan, and there was no child to be seen.   Betty searched about, in and out, every place she could think of ; still there were no signs of the child.   This pretty well sobered Betty, and she remembered that she had to unlock the door to get into the cottage.

While yet full of fear and trembling to meet her husband, Jan came home from Bal.   He was, of course, told that his " croom of a chield was lost."   He didn't believe a word of what Betty told him, but he went about and called up all the neighbours, who joined him in the search.   They spent the night in examining every spot around the house and in the village—all in vain.

After daybreak they were all assembled in deep and earnest consultation, when the cat came running into the house, with her tail on end, and mewing anxiously.   She ran forth and back round a brake of furze, constantly crying, as if she wished the people to follow her.   After a long time some one thought of going after the cat, and in the middle of the furze-brake, on a beautiful green, soft spot of mossy grass, was the baby sleeping, " as sweet as a little nut," wrapped carefully up in some old dry gowns, and all its clothes clean and dry.   When they unwrapped the child, they found he was covered over with bright flowers, as we place them round a babe in the coffin.   He had a bunch of violets in his dear little hands, and there were wallflowers and primroses, and balm and mint spread over his body. The furze was high all around, so that no cold wind could reach the infant. Every one declared that the child never looked so handsome before. It was plain enough, said the old women, that the Small People had taken the child and washed it from top to toe ; that their task of cleansing the babe was a long one, and that the sun arose before they could finish it ; that they had placed the child where it was found, intending to take it away the next night.

They were never known to come for the babe, but every one said that this affair worked a great change in Betty Stogs and in Jan the Mounster. The cottage was kept tidy, the child clean ; and its father and mother drank less, and lived happier, for ever afterwards.

THE FOUR-LEAVED CLOVER.

NOT many years since a farmer lived in Bosfrancan in St Burrien, who had a very fine red-and-white cow called Daisey. The cow was always fat, with her dewlaps and udder sweeping the grass. Daisey held her milk from calf to calf ; had an udder like a bucket, yet she would never yield more than a gallon or so of milk, when one might plainly see that she had still at least two gallons more in her udder. All at once, when the milk was in full flow, she would give a gentle bleat, *cock up* her ears, and the milk would stop at once. If the milkmaid tried to get any more from her after that, she would up foot, kick the bucket, and spill all the milk, yet stand as still as a stock, and keep chewing her cud all the time. Everybody would have thought the cow bewitched, if she hadn't been always fat and held her milk all the year round ; besides, everything prospered with the farmer, and all the other cows had more milk than any of the neighbours'. No one could tell what the deuce could be the matter with Daisey ; and they tried to drive her to Burrien Church-town fair, that they might be rid of her, as she was always fit for the butchers. All the men and boys on the farm couldn't get her to Church-town. As fast as they drove her up Alsie Lane, she would take down Cotneywilley, through by the Crean, down the Bottoms, and up the Gilley, and be in the field again before the men and boys would be half way home.

One midsummer's day in the evening, the maid was later than usual milking, as she had been down to Penberth to the *games*. The stars were beginning to blink when she finished her task. Daisey was the last cow milked, and the bucket was so full she could scarcely lift it to her head. Before rising from the

milking-stool, the maid plucked up a handful of grass and clover
to put in the head of her hat, that she might carry the bucket the
steadier.   She had no sooner placed the hat on her head, than
she saw hundreds and thousands of Small People swarming in all
directions about the cow, and dipping their hands into the milk,
taking it out on the clover blossoms and sucking them.   The grass
and clover, all in blossom, reached to the cow's belly.   Hundreds
of the little creatures ran up the long grass and clover stems, with
buttercups, lady's smocks, convolvuluses, and foxglove flowers,
to catch the milk that Daisey let flow from her four teats, like a
shower, among them.   Right under the cow's udder the maid
saw one much larger than the others lying on his back, with his
heels cocked up to the cow's belly.   She knew he must be a
Piskie, because he was laughing, with his mouth open from ear to
ear.   The little ones were running up and down his legs, filling
their cups, and emptying them into the Piskie's mouth.   Hundreds
of others were on Daisey's back, scratching her rump, and tickling
her round the horns and behind the ears.   Others were smooth-
ing down every hair of her shining coat into its place.

The milkmaid wasn't much startled to see them, as she had
so often heard of fairies, and rather wished to see them.   She
could have stayed for hours, she said, to look at them dancing
about among the clover, which they hardly bent any more than
the dew-drops.

The cows were in the field called Park-an-Ventan, close under
the house.   Her mistress came out into the garden between the
field and the house, and called to know what was keeping the
maid so long.   When the maid told what she had seen, her mistress said she couldn't believe her unless she had found a four-leaved
grass.   Then the maid thought of the handful of grass in the
head of her hat.   In looking it over by the candlelight, she found
a bunch of three-leaved grass, and one stem with four leaves.
They knew that it was nothing strange that she should see the
Small People, but they didn't know what plan to take to get rid
of them, so that they might have the whole of Daisey's milk, till the
mistress told her mother about it.   Her mother was a very notable
old dame, who lived in Church-town.   The old woman knew all
about witches, fairies, and such things ; was noted for being a
sharp, careful old body ; for when she happened to break the eye
of her stocking darning-needle, she would take it to the blacksmith
that he might put a new eye to it.   The smith always charged her
twopence.   She would rather pay that than throw it away.

Our Betty told her daughter that everybody knowed that the

Small People couldn't abide the smell of fish, nor the savour of salt or grease; and advised her to rub the cow's udder with fish brine to drive the Small People away. Well, she did what her mammy told her to do. Better she had let it alone. From that time Daisey would yield all her milk, but she hadn't the half, nor quarter, so much as before, but took up her udder, so that one could hardly see it below her flanks. Every evening, as soon as the stars began to twinkle, the cow would go round the fields bleating and crying as if she had lost her calf; she became hair-pitched, and pined away to skin and bone before the next Burrien fair, when she was driven to Church-town and sold for next to nothing. I don't know what became of her afterwards; but nothing throve with the farmer, after his wife had driven the Small People away, as it did before.

THE FAIRY OINTMENT.

MANY years since, there lived as housekeeper with a celebrated squire, whose name is associated with the history of his native country, one Nancy Tregier. There were many peculiarities about Nancy; and she was, being a favourite with her master, allowed to do much as she pleased. She was in fact a petted, and, consequently, a spoiled servant. Nancy left Pendeen one Saturday afternoon to walk to Penzance, for the purpose of buying a pair of shoes. There was an old woman, Jenny Trayer, living in Pendeen Cove—who had the reputation of being a witch—or, as some people mildly put it, "who had strange dealings;" and with her Nancy desired, for sundry reasons best known to herself, to keep on the closest of terms. So on this Saturday, Nancy first called on the old woman to inquire if she wished to have anything brought home from Penzance. Tom, the husband of Nancy's friend, did no work; but now and then he would go to sea for an hour or two and fish. It is true everybody gave Jenny just what she asked for her fish, out of pure fear. Sometimes they had a "venture" with the smugglers, who, in those days, carried on a roaring trade in Pendeen Cove. The old Squire was a justice; but he winked very hard, and didn't know anything about the smugglers. Indeed, some ill-natured people—and there are always such to be found in any nook or corner—said Nancy often took her master home a choice bottle of Cogniac; even a case of "Hollands" now and then; and, especially when there was to be a particularly "great run," there were some beautiful silk handkerchiefs to be seen at the Squire's. But this is beyond our story. When Nancy went into Jenny's cottage, Tom was there, and right busy was she in preparing some ointment, and touching her husband's eyes with it : this Jenny tried to hide in the mouth of the oven at the side of the chimney. Tom got up and said he must be off, and left the two women together. After a few idle compliments, Jenny said that Nancy must have something to drink before she started for Penzance, and she went to the *spence* for the bottles. Nancy, ever curious, seized the moment, dipped her finger into the pot of green ointment, and, thinking it was good for the eyes, she just touched her right eye with it before Jenny returned. They then took a horn or two together, and being thus spliced, Nancy started for Penzance.

Penzance Market was in those days entirely in the street ; even the old market-house had not yet an existence. Nancy walked about doing a little business and a great deal of gossiping ; when amongst the standings in Market-Jew Street, whom should Nancy see but Tom Trayer, picking off the standings, shoes, stockings, hanks of yarn, and pewter spoons—indeed, some of all the sorts of things which were for sale. Nancy walked up to him, and, taking him by the arm, said, " Tom ! ar'then't ashamed to be here carrying on such a game ? However thee canst have the impudence, I can't think, to be picking the things from the standings and putting them in thy pocket in broad daylight, and the people all around thee." Tom looked very much surprised when Nancy spoke to him. At last he said, " Is that you, Nancy ?—which eye can you see me upon ? " Nancy shut her left eye, this made no difference ; she then shut her right eye, and, greatly to her surprise, she saw all the people, but she no longer saw Tom. She opened her right eye, and there was Tom as before. She winked, and winked, and was surprised, you may be sure, to find that she could not see Tom with either eye. " Now, Nancy," said Tom, " right or left." " Well," said Nancy, " 'tis strange ; but there is something wrong with my left eye." *

" Oh, then, you see me with the right, do you ? "

Then Tom put his finger on her right eye, and from that moment she was blind on that side.

On her way home, Nancy was always going off the road on her blind side ; but the hedges kept her from wandering far away. On the downs near Pendeen there were no hedges, so Nancy wandered into a furze brake,—night came on, she could not find her way out, and she was found in it the next morning fast asleep.

---

* The tale, " Nursing a Fairy," p. 83, where a similar incident occurs, will be remembered.

The old Squire was out hunting in the early morning, according to his usual custom.   In passing along the road leading to Carnyorth, he saw a woman's knitting-work hanging on a bramble, and the yarn from the stocking leading away into the brake.   He took the yarn in his hand and followed it until he came to the old woman, who had the ball in her pocket.   When the Squire awakened the old woman, she told him the story which I have told you.   Her master, however, said that he didn't believe she had been into Penzance at all, but that she had stayed in the Cove and got drunk : that when dark night came, she had endeavoured to find her way home,—lost her road,—fallen down, and probed her eye out on a furze bush, and then gone off in drunken unconsciousness.   Nancy told her master that he was no better than an unbelieving heathen ; and to the day of her death she protested that Tom Trayer put her eye out.   Jenny's ointment is said to have been made with a four-leaved clover, gathered at a certain time of the moon.   This rendered Fairyland visible, and made men invisible.

Another version of this story, varying in a few details, was given me by a gentleman, a native of St Levan.   It is as follows :—

HOW JOAN LOST THE SIGHT OF HER EYE.

JOAN was housekeeper to Squire Lovell, and was celebrated for her beautiful knitting.   One Saturday afternoon Joan wished to go to Penzance to buy a pair of shoes for herself, and some things for the Squire. So the weather being particularly fine, away she trudged.

Joan dearly loved a bit of gossip, and always sought for company.   She knew Betty Trenance was always ready for a jaunt : to be sure, everybody said Betty was a witch ; but, says Joan, "Witch or no witch, she shall go ; bad company is better than none."

Away went Joan to Lemorna, where Betty lived.   Arrived at Betty's cottage, she peeped through the latch-hole (the finger-hole), and saw Betty rubbing some green ointment on the children's eyes.   She watched till Betty Trenance had finished, and noticed that she put the salve on the inner end of the chimney stool, and covered it over with a rag.

Joan went in, and Betty was delighted, sure enough, to see her, and sent the children out of the way.   But Betty couldn't walk to Penzance, she was suffering pain, and she had been taking milk and suet, and brandy and rue, and she must have some more.   So away went Betty to the other room for the bottle.

Joan seized the moment, and taking a very small bit of the ointment on her finger, she touched her right eye with it.   Betty came with the bottle, and Joan had a drink ; when she looked round she was surprised to see the house swarming with small people. They were playing all sorts of pranks on the key-beams and rafters. Some were swinging on cobwebs, some were riding the mice, and others were chasing them into and out of the holes in the thatch. Joan was surprised at the sight, and thought she must have a four-leaved clover about her.

However, without stopping to take much drink, she started alone for Penzance. She had wasted, as it was, so much time, that it was nearly dark when she reached the market.

After having made her purchases, and as she was about to leave the market, who should Joan spy but Betty's husband, Tom Trenance. There he was, stealing about in the shadows, picking from the standings, shoes and stockings from one, hanks of yarn from another, pewter spoons from a third, and so on. He stuffed these things into capacious pockets, and yet no one appeared to notice Tom.

Joan went forth to him.

"Aren't ye ashamed to be here in the dark carrying on such a game ? "

"Is that you, Dame Joan," says Tom ; "which eye can you see me upon ? "

After winking, Joan said she could see Tom plain enough with her right eye.

She had no sooner said the word than Tom Trenance pointed his finger to her eye, and she lost the sight of it from that hour.

"The work of the world" had Joan to find her way out of Penzance. She couldn't keep the road, she was always tumbling into the ditch on her blind side. When near the Fawgan, poor Joan, who was so weary that she could scarcely drag one leg after the other, prayed that she might find a quiet old horse on which she might ride home.

Her desire was instantly granted. There, by the roadside, stood an old, bony white horse, spanned with its halter.

Joan untied the halter from the legs and placed it on the head of the horse ; she got on the hedge, and seated herself on the horse's back.

There she was mounted, "Gee wup, gee wup ; k'up, k'up, k'up." The horse would not budge. Busy were Joan's heels rattling against the ribs of the poor horse, and thwack, thwack went a thorn-stick over his tail, and by and by the old blind brute began to walk. Joan beat, and kicked, and k'uped, and coaxed, the horse went but little faster until it got to the top of the hill.

Then away, away, like the wind it went through Toldava Lanes, and it swelled out until the horse became as high as the tower. Over hedges and ditches, across all the corners that came into the road, on went the horse. Joan held on by the mane with both hands, and shouted, "Woa ! woa ! woey !" until she could shout no longer.

At length they came to Toldava Moor ; the "ugly brute" took right away down towards the fowling-pool, when Joan, fearing he might plunge in and drown her, let go her hold.

The wind was blowing so strong, and the pair were going so fast against it, that Joan was lifted off, over the hindquarters of the horse, and by luck she fell soft on the rushes at the very edge of the fowling-pool.

When she looked up, Joan saw whatever she had been riding going down the " bottom " in a blaze of fire, and the devil riding after, with lots of men, horses, and hounds, all without heads. All the marketing was lost ; and in getting through the bogs, Joan had her shoes dragged from her feet. At last she got to Trove Bottoms, and seeing the Bougé (sheep-house), she clambered over the hedge as she best could ; got into it, and laying herself down amongst the sheep, she soon fell fast asleep, thoroughly wearied out.

She would have slept for a week, I believe, if she had not been disturbed. But, according to custom on Sunday morning, the Squire and his boys came out to the Downs to span the sheep, and there, greatly to their surprise, they found her.

They got the miserable woman home between them. The Squire charged her with having got drunk, and said her eye had been scratched out by a furze-bush ; but Joan never wandered from her story, and to the day of her death she told it to all young women, warning them never to meddle with " Fairy Salve."

THE OLD WOMAN WHO TURNED HER SHIFT.

IN a lone house—situated not far from the hill on which now stands Knill's Steeple, as it is called—which was then known as Chyanwheal, or the *House on the Mine*, lived a lone woman, the widow of a miner, said to have been killed in one of the very ancient " coffens," as the open mine-workings existing in this hill are termed. A village now bears this name, but it has derived it from this lone house. Whether it was that they presumed upon her solitude, or whether the old lady had given them some inducement, is not now known, but the spriggans of Trencrom Hill were in the habit of meeting almost every night in her cottage to divide their plunder. The old woman usually slept, or at least she pretended to sleep, during the visit of the spriggans. When they left, they always placed a small coin on the table by her bedside, and with this indeed the old woman was enabled to provide herself with not merely the necessaries of life, but to add thereto a few of those things which were luxuries to one in her position. The old lady, however, was not satisfied with this. She resolved to bide her time, and when the spriggans had an unusually large amount of plunder, to make herself rich at once and for ever at their expense. Such a time at last arrived. The spriggans had gathered, we know not how much valuable gold and jewellery. It gleamed and glistened on the floor, and the old woman in bed looked on with a most covetous eye. After a while, it appears, the spriggans were not able to settle the question of division with their usual amicability. The little thieves began to quarrel amongst themselves.

Now, thought the old woman, is my time. Therefore huddling herself up under the bedclothes, she very adroitly contrived to turn her shift, and having completed the unfailing charm, she jumped from her bed, placed her hand on a gold cup, and exclaimed, " Thee shusn't hae one on 'em ! "

In affright the spriggans all scampered away, leaving their stolen treasure behind them. The last and boldest of the spriggans, however, swept his hand over the old woman's only garment as he left the house. The old woman, now wealthy, removed in a little time from Chyanwheal to St Ives, and, to the surprise of every one, purchased property and lived like a gentlewoman. Whenever, however, she put on the shift which had secured her her wealth, she was tortured beyond endurance. The doctors and all the learned people used hard names to describe her pains, but the wise women knew all along that they came of the spriggans.

THE FAIRY WIDOWER.

NOT many years since a very pretty girl called Jenny Permuen lived in Towednack. She was of poor parents, and lived in service. There was a good deal of romance, or what the old people called nonsense, in Jenny. She was always smartly dressed, and she would arrange wildflowers very gracefully in her hair. As a consequence, Jenny attracted much of the attention of the young men, and again, as a consequence, a great deal of envy from the young women. Jenny was, no doubt, vain ; and her vanity, which most vain persons will say is not usual, was accompanied by a considerable amount of weakness on any point connected with her person. Jenny loved flattery, and being a poor, uneducated girl, she had not the genius necessary to disguise her frailty. When any man told her she was lovely, she quite admitted the truth of the assertion by her pleased looks. When any woman told her not to be such a fool as to believe such nonsense, her lips, and eyes too, seemed to say you are only jealous of me, and if there was a pool of water near, nature's mirror was speedily consulted to prove to herself that she was really the best-looking girl in the parish. Well, one day Jenny, who had been for some time out of a situation, was sent by her mother down to the lower parishes to " look for a place." Jenny went on merrily enough until she came to the four cross roads on the Lady Downs, when she discovered that she knew not which road to take. She looked first one way and then another, and she felt fairly puzzled, so she sat down on a boulder of granite, and began, in pure want of thought, to break off the beautiful fronds of ferns which grew abundantly around the spot she had chosen. It is hard to say what her intentions were, whether to go on, to return, or to remain where she was, so utterly indifferent did Jenny appear. Some say she was entirely lost in wild dreams of self-glorification. However, she had not sat long on this granite stone, when hearing a voice near her, she turned round and saw a young man.

" Well, young woman," says he, " and what are you after ? "

" I am after a place, sir," says she.

" And what kind of a place do you want, my pretty young woman ? " says he, with the most winning smile in the world.

" I am not particular, sir," says Jenny ; " I can make myself generally useful."

" Indeed," says the stranger ; " do you think you could look after a widower with one little boy ? "

" I am very fond of children," says Jenny.

" Well, then," says the widower, " I wish to hire for a year and a day a young woman of your age, to take charge of my little boy."

" And where do you live ? " inquired Jenny.

" Not far from here," said the man ; " will you go with me and see ? "

" An it please you to show me," said Jenny.

" But first, Jenny Permuen,"—Jenny stared when she found the stranger knew her name. He was evidently an entire stranger in the parish, and how could he have learnt her name, she thought. So she looked at him somewhat astonished. " Oh ! I see, you suppose I didn't know you ; but do you think a young widower could pass through Towednack and not be struck with such a pretty girl ? Beside," he said, " I watched you one day dressing your hair in one of my ponds, and stealing some of my sweet-scented violets to put in those lovely tresses. Now, Jenny Permuen, will you take the place ? "

" For a year and a day ? " asked Jenny.

" Yes, and if we are pleased with each other then, we can renew the engagement."

"Wages," said Jenny.

The widower rattled the gold in his breeches-pocket.

"Wages ! well, whatever you like to ask," said the man.

Jenny was charmed ; all sorts of visions rose before her eyes, and without hesitation she said—

"Well, I 'll take the place, sir ; when must I come ? "

" I require you now—my little boy is very unhappy, and I think you can make him happy again. You 'll come at once ? "

"But mother"——

"Never mind mother, I 'll send word to her."

"But my clothes"——

" The clothes you have will be all you require, and I 'll put you in a much gayer livery soon."

"Well, then," says Jane, "'tis a bargain "——

" Not yet," says the man ; I 've got a way of my own, and you must swear my oath."

Jenny looked frightened.

" You need not be alarmed," said the man, very kindly ; " I only wish you to kiss that fern-leaf which you have in your hand, and say, ' For a year and a day I promise to stay.' "

" Is that all ? " said Jenny ; so she kissed the fern-leaf and said—

> " For a year and a day
> I promise to stay."

Without another word he walked forward on the road leading eastward. Jenny followed him—she thought it strange that her new master never opened his lips to her all the way, and she grew very tired with walking. Still onward and onward he went, and Jenny was sadly weary and her feet dreadfully sore. At last poor Jenny began to cry. He heard her sob and looked round.

" Tired are you, poor girl ? Sit down—sit down," says the man, and he took her by the hand and led her to a mossy bank. His kindness completely overcame her, and she burst into a flood of tears. He allowed her to cry for a few minutes, then taking a bunch of leaves from the bottom of the bank, he said, " Now I must dry your eyes, Jenny."

He passed the bunch of leaves rapidly first over one and then over the other eye.

The tears were gone. Her weariness had departed. She felt herself moving, yet she did not know that she had moved from the bank. The ground appeared to open, and they were passing very rapidly under the earth. At last there was a pause.

"Here we are, Jenny," said he, "there is yet a tear of sorrow on your eyelids, and no human tears can enter our homes, let me wipe them away." Again Jenny's eyes were brushed with the small leaves as before, and, lo! before her was such a country as she had never seen previously. Hill and valley were covered with flowers, strangely varied in colour, but combining into a most harmonious whole; so that the region appeared sown with gems which glittered in a light as brilliant as that of the summer sun, yet as mild as the moonlight. There were rivers clearer than any water she had ever seen on the granite hills, and waterfalls and fountains; while everywhere ladies and gentlemen dressed in green and gold were walking, or sporting, or reposing on banks of flowers, singing songs or telling stories. Oh! it was a beautiful world.

"Here we are at home," said Jenny's master; and strangely enough he too was changed; he was the most beautiful little man she had ever seen, and he wore a green silken coat covered with ornaments of gold. "Now," said he again, "I must introduce you to your little charge." He led Jenny into a noble mansion in which all the furniture was of pearl and ivory, inlaid with gold and silver, and studded with emeralds. After passing through many rooms, they came at length to one which was hung all over with lace, as fine as the finest cobweb, most beautifully worked with flowers; and, in the middle of this room was a little cot made out of some beautiful sea-shell, which reflected so many colours that Jenny could scarcely bear to look at it. She was led to the side of this, and she saw, as she said, "One of God's sweetest angels sleeping there." The little boy was so beautiful that she was ravished with delight.

"This is your charge," said the father; "I am the king in this land, and I have my own reasons for wishing my boy to know something of human nature. Now you have nothing to do but to wash and dress the boy when he wakes, to take him to walk in the garden, and to put him to bed when he is weary."

Jenny entered on her duties, and gave, and continued to give, satisfaction. She loved the darling little boy, and he appeared to love her, and the time passed away with astonishing rapidity.

Somehow or other she had never thought of her mother. She had never thought of her home at all. She was happy and in luxury, and never reckoned the passing of time.

Howsoever happiness may blind us to the fact, the hours and days move onward. The period for which Jenny had bound herself was gone, and one morning she awoke and all was changed. She was sleeping in her own bed in her mother's cottage. Everything was strange to her, and she appeared strange to everybody. Numerous old gossips were called in to see Jenny, and to all Jenny told her strange tale alike. One day, old Mary Calineck of Zennor came, and she heard, as all the others had done, the story of the widower, and the baby, and the beautiful country. Some of the old crones who were there at the time said the girl was " gone clean daft." Mary looked very wise—" Crook your arm, Jenny," said she.

Jenny sat up in the bed and bent her arm, resting her hand on her hip.

" Now say, I hope my arm may never come uncrooked if I have told ye a word of a lie."

" I hope my arm may never come uncrooked if I have told ye a word of a lie," repeated Jenny.

" Uncrook your arm," said Mary.

Jenny stretched out her arm.

" It is truth the girl is telling," said Mary; " and she has been carried by the Small People to some of their countries under the hills."

" Will the girl ever come right in her mind ? " asked her mother.

" All in good time," said Mary; " and if she will but be honest, I have no doubt but her master will take care that she never wants."

Howbeit, Jenny did not get on very well in the world. She married and was discontented and far from happy. Some said she always pined after the fairy widower. Others said they were sure she had misbehaved herself, or she would have brought back lots of gold. If Jenny had not dreamt all this, while she was sitting picking ferns on the granite boulder, she had certainly had a very strange adventure.

THE SMALL PEOPLE'S GARDENS.

IF the adventurous traveller who visits the Land's End district will go down as far as he can on the south-west side of the Logan Rock Cairn, and look over, he will see, in little sheltered places between the cairns, close down to the water's edge, beautifully green spots, with here and there some ferns and cliff-pinks. These are the gardens of the Small People, or, as they are called by the natives, Small Folk. They are beautiful little creatures, who appear to pass a life of constant enjoyment amongst their own favourite flowers. They are harmless : and if man does not meddle with them when they are holding their fairs—which are indeed high festivals—the Small Folk never interfere with man or anything belonging to him. They are known to do much good, especially when they discover a case of oppressed poverty; but they do it in their own way. They love to do good for its own sake, and the publication of it in any way draws down their censure, and sometimes severe anger, on the object whom it was their purpose to serve. To prove that those lovely little creatures are no dream, I may quote the words of a native of St Levan :—

"As I was saying, when I have been to sea close under the cliffs, of a fine summer's night, I have heard the sweetest of music, and seen hundreds of little lights moving about amongst what looked like flowers. Ay! and they are flowers too, for you may smell the sweet scent far out at sea. Indeed, I have heard many of the old men say, that they have smelt the sweet perfume, and heard the music from the fairy gardens of the Castle, when more than a mile from the shore." Strangely enough, you can find no flowers but the sea-pinks in these lovely green places by day, yet they have been described by those who have seen them in the midsummer moonlight as being covered with flowers of every colour, all of them far more brilliant than any blossoms seen in any mortal garden.

ST LEVAN FAIRIES.

YEARS since—the time is past now—the green outside the gate at the end of Trezidder Lane was a favourite place with the Small Folks on which to hold their fairs. One might often see the rings in the grass which they made in dancing, where they footed it. Mr Trezillian was returning late one night from Penzance ; when he came near the gate, he saw a number of little creatures spinning round and round. The sight made him light-headed, but he could not resist the desire to be amongst them, so he got off his horse. In a moment they were all over him like a swarm of bees, and he felt as if they were sticking needles and pins into him. His horse ran off, and he didn't know what to do, till, by good luck, he thought of what he had often heard, so he turned his glove inside out, threw it amongst the Small Folk, and ere the glove reached the ground they were all gone. Mr Trezillian had now to find his horse, and the Small Folk, still determining to lead him a dance, bewildered him. He was piskie-led, and he could not find out where he was until broad daylight. Then he saw he was not a hundred yards from the place at which he had left his horse. On looking round the spot where he had seen the Small Folk dancing, he found a pair of very small silver knee-buckles of a most ancient shape, which, no doubt, some little gentleman must have lost when he was punishing the farmer. Those who knew the families will well remember the little silver buckles, which were kept for some time at Trezidder and some time at Raftra.

Down in Penberth Cove lived an old woman who was an especial favourite with these little people. She was a good old creature, and had been for many years bedridden. These Small Folk were her only company. Her relations dropped in once a day, rendered her the little aid she required, and left food by the bedside. But day by day, and all the day long, the Small Folk vied with each other to amuse her. The men, she related, were for the most part dressed in green, with a red or a blue cap and a feather—" They look for all the world like little sodgers." As for the ladies—you should have heard the old woman tell of the gay ladies, with their feathers, hooped petticoats with furbelows, trains, and fans, and what saucy little creatures they were with the men! No sooner was the old woman left alone than in they came and began their frolics, dancing over the rafters and key-beams, swinging by the cobwebs like rope-dancers, catching the mice and riding them in and out through the holes in the thatch. When one party got tired another party came, and by daylight, and even by moonlight, the old bedridden creature never wanted amusement.

THE ADVENTURE OF CHERRY OF ZENNOR.

THIS may be regarded as another version of the story of the Fairy Widower:—Old Honey lived with his wife and family in a little hut of two rooms and a " talfat," * on the cliff side of Trereen in Zennor. The old couple had half-a-score of children, who were all reared in this place. They lived as they best could on the produce of a few acres of ground, which were too poor to keep even a goat in good heart. The heaps of crogans (limpet-shells) about the hut, led one to believe that their chief food was limpets and gweans (periwinkles). They had, however, fish and potatoes most days, and pork and broth now and then of a Sunday. At Christmas and the Feast they had white bread. There was not a healthier nor a handsomer family in the parish than Old Honey's. We are, however, only concerned with one of them—his

* *Talfat* is a half-floor at one end of a cottage on which a bed is placed.

daughter Cherry. Cherry could run as fast as a hare, and was ever full of frolic and mischief.

Whenever the miller's boy came into the "town," tied his horse to the furze-rick and called in to see if any one desired to send corn to the mill, Cherry would jump on to its back and gallop off to the cliff. When the miller's boy gave chase, and she could ride no further over the edge of that rocky coast, she would take to the cairns, and the swiftest dog could not catch her, much less the miller's boy.

Soon after Cherry got into her teens she became very discontented, because year after year her mother had been promising her a new frock that she might go off as smart as the rest, "three on one horse to Morva Fair." * As certain as the time came round the money was wanting, so Cherry had nothing decent. She could neither go to fair, nor to church, nor to meeting.

Cherry was sixteen. One of her playmates had a new dress smartly trimmed with ribbons, and she told Cherry how she had been to Nancledry to the preaching, and how she had ever so many sweethearts who brought her home. This put the volatile Cherry in a fever of desire. She declared to her mother she would go off to the "low countries" † to seek for service, that she might get some clothes like other girls.

Her mother wished her to go to Towednack, that she might have the chance of seeing her now and then of a Sunday.

" No, no ! " said Cherry, " I 'll never go to live in the parish where the cow ate the bell-rope, and where they have fish and taties (potatoes) every day, and conger-pie of a Sunday for a change."

One fine morning Cherry tied up a few things in a bundle and prepared to start. She promised her father that she would get service as near home as she could, and come home at the earliest opportunity. The old man said she was bewitched, charged her to take care she wasn't carried away by either the sailors or pirates, and allowed her to depart. Cherry took the road leading to Ludgvan and Gulval. When she lost sight of the chimneys of Trereen, she go out of heart, and had a great mind to go home again. But she went on.

At length she came to the four cross roads on the Lady Downs, sat herself down on a stone by the roadside, and cried to think of her home, which she might never see again.

* A Cornish proverb.

† The terms "high" and "low countries," are applied respectively to the hills and the valleys of the country about Towednack and Zennor.

Her crying at last came to an end, and she resolved to go home and make the best of it.

When she dried her eyes and held up her head she was surprised to see a gentleman coming towards her ;—for she couldn't think where he came from ; no one was to be seen on the Downs a few minutes before.

The gentleman wished her " Good morning," inquired the road to Towednack, and asked Cherry where she was going.

Cherry told the gentleman that she had left home that morning to look for service, but that her heart had failed her, and she was going back over the hills to Zennor again.

"I never expected to meet with such luck as this," said the gentleman.   " I left home this morning to seek for a nice clean girl to keep house for me, and here you are."

He then told Cherry that he had been recently left a widower, and that he had one dear little boy, of whom Cherry might have charge.   Cherry was the very girl that would suit him.   She was handsome and cleanly.   He could see that her clothes were so mended that the first piece could not be discovered ; yet she was as sweet as a rose, and all the water in the sea could not make her cleaner.   Poor Cherry said " Yes, sir," to everything, yet she did not understand one quarter part of what the gentleman said.   Her mother had instructed her to say " Yes, sir," to the parson, or any gentleman, when, like herself, she did not understand them.   The gentleman told her he lived but a short way off, down in the low countries ; that she would have very little to do but milk the cow and look after the baby ; so Cherry consented to go with him.

Away they went, he talking so kindly that Cherry had no notion how time was moving, and she quite forgot the distance she had walked.

At length they were in lanes, so shaded with trees that a checker of sunshine scarcely gleamed on the road.   As far as she could see, all was trees and flowers.   Sweetbriars and honeysuckles perfumed the air, and the reddest of ripe apples hung from the trees over the lane.

Then they came to a steam of water as clear as crystal, which ran across the lane.   It was, however, very dark, and Cherry paused to see how she should cross the river.   The gentleman put his arm around her waist and carried her over, so that she did not wet her feet.

The lane was getting darker and darker, and narrower and narrower, and they seemed to be going rapidly down-hill.

Cherry took firm hold of the gentleman's arm, and thought, as he had been so kind to her, she could go with him to the world's end.

After walking a little farther, the gentleman opened a gate which led into a beautiful garden, and said, " Cherry, my dear, this is the place we live in."

Cherry could scarcely believe her eyes. She had never seen anything approaching this place for beauty. Flowers of every dye were around her ; fruits of all kinds hung above her ; and the birds, sweeter of song than any she had ever heard, burst out into a chorus of rejoicing. She had heard granny tell of enchanted places. Could this be one of them ? No. The gentleman was as big as the parson ; and now a little boy came running down the garden-walk shouting, " Papa, papa."

The child appeared, from his size, to be about two or three years of age ; but there was a singular look of age about him. His eyes were brilliant and piercing, and he had a crafty expression. As Cherry said, " He could look anybody down."

Before Cherry could speak to the child, a very old, dry-boned, ugly-looking woman made her appearance, and seizing the child by the arm, dragged him into the house, mumbling and scolding. Before, however, she was lost sight of, the old hag cast one look at Cherry, which shot through her heart " like a gimblet."

Seeing Cherry somewhat disconcerted, the master explained that the old woman was his late wife's grandmother ; that she would remain with them until Cherry knew her work, and no longer, for she was old and ill-tempered, and must go. At length, having feasted her eyes on the garden, Cherry was taken into the house, and this was yet more beautiful. Flowers of every kind grew everywhere, and the sun seemed to shine everywhere, and yet she did not see the sun.

Aunt Prudence—so was the old woman named—spread a table in a moment with a great variety of nice things, and Cherry made a hearty supper. She was now directed to go to bed, in a chamber at the top of the house, in which the child was to sleep also. Prudence directed Cherry to keep her eyes closed, whether she could sleep or not, as she might, perchance, see things which she would not like. She was not to speak to the child all night. She was to rise at break of day; then take the boy to a spring in the garden, wash him, and anoint his eyes with an ointment, which she would find in a crystal box in a cleft of the rock, but she was not, on any account, to touch her own eyes with it. Then Cherry was to call the cow : and having taken a bucket full of milk, to draw a bowl of the last milk for the boy's breakfast. Cherry was dying with curiosity. She several times began to question the child, but he always stopped her with, " I 'll tell Aunt Prudence." According to her orders, Cherry was up in the morning early. The little boy conducted the girl to the spring, which flowed in crystal purity from a granite rock, which was covered with ivy and beautiful mosses. The child was duly washed, and his eyes duly anointed. Cherry saw no cow, but her little charge said she must call the cow.

" Pruit ! pruit ! pruit !" called Cherry, just as she would call the cows at home ; when, lo ! a beautiful great cow came from amongst the trees, and stood on the bank beside Cherry.

Cherry had no sooner placed her hands on the cow's teats than four streams of milk flowed down and soon filled the bucket. The boy's bowl was then filled, and he drank it. This being done, the cow quietly walked away, and Cherry returned to the house to be instructed in her daily work.

The old woman, Prudence, gave Cherry a capital breakfast, and then informed her that she must keep to the kitchen, and attend to her work there—to scald the milk, make the butter, and clean all the platters and bowls with water and gard (gravel sand). Cherry was charged to avoid curiosity. She was not to go into any other part of the house ; she was not to try and open any locked doors.

After her ordinary work was done on the second day, her master required Cherry to help him in the garden, to pick the apples and pears, and to weed the leeks and onions.

Glad was Cherry to get out of the old woman's sight. Aunt Prudence always sat with one eye on her knitting, and the other boring through poor Cherry. Now and then she 'd grumble, " I knew Robin would bring down some fool from Zennor—better for both that she had tarried away."

Cherry and her master got on famously, and whenever Cherry had finished weeding a bed, her master would give her a kiss to show her how pleased he was.

After a few days, old Aunt Prudence took Cherry into those parts of the house which she had never seen. They passed through a long dark passage. Cherry was then made to take off her shoes ; and they entered a room, the floor of which was like glass, and all round, perched on the shelves, and on the floor, were people, big and small, turned to stone. Of some, there were only the head and shoulders, the arms being cut off ; others were perfect. Cherry told the old woman she " wouldn't cum any furder for the wurld." She thought from the first she was got into a land of Small People underground, only master was like other men; but now she know'd she was with the conjurors, who had turned all these people to stone. She had heard talk on 'em up in Zennor, and she knew they might at any moment wake up and eat her.

Old Prudence laughed at Cherry, and drove her on, insisted upon her rubbing up a box, "like a coffin on six legs," until she could see her face in it. Well, Cherry did not want for courage, so she began to rub with a will; the old woman standing by, knitting all the time, calling out every now and then, "Rub! rub! rub! harder and faster!" At length Cherry got desperate, and giving a violent rub at one of the corners, she nearly upset the box. When, O Lor! it gave out such a doleful, unearthly sound, that Cherry thought all the stone-people were coming to life, and with her fright she fell down in a fit. The master heard all this noise, and came in to inquire into the cause of the hubbub. He was in great wrath, kicked old Prudence out of the house for taking Cherry into that shut-up room, carried Cherry into the kitchen, and soon, with some cordial, recovered her senses. Cherry could not remember what had happened; but she knew there was something fearful in the other part of the house. But Cherry was mistress now—old Aunt Prudence was gone. Her master was so kind and loving that a year passed by like a summer day. Occasionally her master left home for a season; then he would return and spend much time in the enchanted apartments, and Cherry was certain she had heard him talking to the stone-people. Cherry had everything the human heart could desire, but she was not happy; she would know more of the place and the people. Cherry had discovered that the ointment made the little boy's eyes bright and strange, and she thought often that he saw more than she did; she would try; yes, she would!

Well, next morning the child was washed, his eyes anointed, and the cow milked; she sent the boy to gather her some flowers in the garden, and taking a "crum" of ointment, she put it into her eye. Oh, her eye would be burned out of her head! Cherry ran to the pool beneath the rock to wash her burning eye; when lo! she saw at the bottom of the water, hundreds of little people, mostly ladies, playing,—and there was her master, as small as the others, playing with them. Everything now looked different about the place. Small people were everywhere, hiding in the flowers sparkling with diamonds, swinging in the trees, and run-

ning and leaping under and over the blades of grass.   The master
never showed himself above the water all day ; but at night he rode
up to the house like the handsome gentleman she had seen before.
He went to the enchanted chamber and Cherry soon heard the
most beautiful music.

In the morning, her master was off, dressed as if to follow the
hounds.   He returned at night, left Cherry to herself, and proceeded at once to his private apartments.   Thus it was day after
day, until Cherry could stand it no longer.   So she peeped through
the keyhole, and saw her master with lots of ladies, singing ;
while one dressed like a queen was playing on the coffin.   Oh,
how madly jealous Cherry became when she saw her master kiss
this lovely lady !   However, the next day, the master remained at
home to gather fruit.   Cherry was to help him, and when, as usual,
he looked to kiss her, she slapped his face, and told him to kiss
the Small People, like himself, with whom he played under the
water.   So he found out that Cherry had used the ointment.
With much sorrow he told her she must go home,—that he would
have no spy on his actions, and that Aunt Prudence must come
back.   Long before day, Cherry was called by her master.   He
gave her lots of clothes and other things ;—took her bundle in one
hand, and a lantern in the other, and bade her follow him.   They
went on for miles on miles, all the time going up hill, through
lanes, and narrow passages.   When they came at last on level
ground, it was near daybreak.   He kissed Cherry, told her she
was punished for her idle curiosity ; but that he would, if she behaved well, come sometimes on the Lady Downs to see her.   Saying this, he disappeared.   The sun rose, and there was Cherry
seated on a granite stone, without a soul within miles of her,—a
desolate moor having taken the place of a smiling garden.   Long,
long did Cherry sit in sorrow, but at last she thought she would
go home.

Her parents had supposed her dead, and when they saw her,
they believed her to be her own ghost.   Cherry told her story,
which every one doubted, but Cherry never varied her tale, and
at last every one believed it.   They say Cherry was never afterwards right in her head, and on moonlight nights, until she died,
she would wander on to the Lady Downs to look for her master.

ANNE JEFFERIES AND THE FAIRIES.

ANNE JEFFERIES was the daughter of a poor labouring man, who lived in the parish of St Teath. She was born in 1626, and is supposed to have died in 1698.

When she was nineteen years old, Anne, who was a remarkably sharp and clever girl, went to live as a servant in the family of Mr Moses Pitt. Anne was an unusually bold girl, and would do things which even boys feared to attempt. Of course, in those days every one believed in fairies, and everybody feared those little airy beings. They were constantly the talk of the people, and this set Anne longing anxiously to have an interview with some of them. So Anne was often abroad after sundown, turning up the fern leaves, and looking into the bells of the foxglove to find a fairy, singing all the time—

> " Fairy fair and fairy bright ;
> Come and be my chosen sprite."

She never allowed a moonlight night to pass without going down into the valley, and walking against the stream, singing—

> " Moon shines bright, waters run clear,
> I am here, but where 's my fairy dear ? "

The fairies were a long time trying this poor girl ; for, as they told her afterwards, they never lost sight of her ; but there they would be, looking on when she was seeking them, and they would run from frond to frond of the ferns, when she was turning them up in her anxious search.

One day Anne, having finished her morning's work, was sitting in the arbour in her master's garden, when she fancied she heard some one moving aside the branches, as though endeavouring to look in upon her ; and she thought it must be her sweetheart, so she resolved to take no notice. Anne went on steadily with her work, no sound was heard but the regular beat of the knitting-needles one upon the other. Presently she heard a suppressed laugh, and then again a rustle amidst the branches. The back of the arbour was towards the lane, and to enter the garden it was necessary to walk down the lane to the gate, which was, however, not many yards off.

Click, click went the needles, click, click, click. At last Anne began to feel vexed that the intruder did not show himself, and she pettishly said, half aloud—

" You may stay there till the kueney * grows on the gate, ere I 'll come to 'ee."

There was immediately a peculiar ringing and very musical laugh. Anne knew this was not her lover's laugh, and she felt afraid. But it was bright day, and she assured herself that no one would do her any mischief, as she knew herself to be a general favourite in the parish. Presently Anne felt assured that the garden gate had been carefully opened and again closed, so she waited anxiously the result. In a few moments she perceived at the entrance of the arbour six little men, all clothed very handsomely in green. They were beautiful little figures, and had very charming faces, and such bright eyes. The grandest of these little visitors, who wore a red feather in his cap, advanced in front of the others, and, making a most polite bow to Anne, addressed her familiarly in the kindest words.

This gentleman looked so sweetly on Anne that she was charmed beyond measure, and she put down her hand as if to shake hands with her little friend, when he jumped into her palm, and she lifted him into her lap. He then, without any more ado, clambered upon her bosom and neck, and began kissing her. Anne never felt so charmed in her life as while this one little gentleman was playing with her ; but presently he called his companions, and they all clambered up by her dress as best they could, and kissed her neck, her lips, and her eyes. One of them ran his fingers over her eyes, and she felt as if they had been pricked with a pin. Suddenly Anne became blind, and she felt herself whirled through the air at a great rate. By and by, one of her little companions said something which sounded like " Tear away," and lo ! Anne had her sight at once restored. She was in one of the most beautiful places—temples and palaces of gold and silver. Trees laden with fruits and flowers. Lakes full of gold and silver fish, and the air full of birds of the sweetest song, and the most brilliant colours. Hundreds of ladies and gentlemen were walking about. Hundreds more were idling in the most luxuriant bowers, the fragrance of the flowers oppressing them with a sense of delicious repose. Hundreds were also dancing, or engaged in sports of various kinds. Anne was, however, surprised to find that these happy people were no longer the small people she had previously seen. There was now no more than the difference usually seen in a crowd, between their height and her own. Anne found herself arrayed in the most highly-decorated clothes. So grand, indeed, did she appear, that she doubted her

* Moss, or mildew ; properly, *cuzney.*

identity. Anne was constantly attended by her six friends ; but the finest gentleman, who was the first to address her, continued her favourite, at which the others appeared to be very jealous. Eventually Anne and her favourite contrived to separate themselves, and they retired into some most lovely gardens, where they were hidden by the luxuriance of the flowers. Lovingly did they pass the time, and Anne desired that this should continue for ever. However, when they were at the happiest, there was heard a great noise, and presently the five other fairies at the head of a great crowd came after them in a violent rage. Her lover drew his sword to defend her, but this was soon beaten down, and he lay wounded at her feet. Then the fairy who had blinded her again placed his hands upon her eyes, and all was dark. She heard strange noises, and felt herself whirled about and about, and as if a thousand flies were buzzing around her.

At length her eyes were opened, and Anne found herself on the ground in the arbour where she had been sitting in the morning, and many anxious faces were around her, all conceiving that she was recovering from a convulsion fit.*

THE PISKIE THRESHERS.

MANY an industrious farmer can speak of the assistance which he has received from the piskies. Mr T. Q. Couch tells a story of this kind so well that no other is required.† Long, long ago, before threshing-machines were thought of, the farmer who resided at C———, in going to his barn one day, was surprised at the extraordinary quantity of corn that had been threshed the previous night, as well as to discover the mysterious agency by which it was effected. His curiosity led him to inquire into the matter ; so at night, when the moon was up, he crept stealthily to the barn-door, and looking through a chink, saw a little fellow, clad in a tattered suit of green, wielding the " dreshel " (flail) with astonishing vigour, and beating the floor with blows so rapid that the eye could not follow the motion of the implement. The farmer slunk away unperceived, and went to bed, where he lay a long while awake, thinking in what way he could best show his gratitude to the piskie for such an important service. He came to the conclusion at length, that, as the little fellow's clothes were getting very old and ragged, the gift of a new suit would be a proper way to lessen the obligation ; and, accordingly, on the morrow he had a suit of green made, of what was supposed to be the proper

* See Moses Pitt's Letter, Appendix K   † See *Notes and Queries.*

size, which he carried early in the evening to the barn, and left
for the piskie's acceptance.   At night the farmer stole to the door
again to see how his gift was taken.   He was just in time to see
the elf put on the suit, which was no sooner accomplished than,
looking down on himself admiringly, he sung—

> " Piskie fine, and piskie gay,
> Piskie now will fly away."

THE MURYANS' BANK.*

THE ant is called by the peasantry a Muryan.   Believing that
they are the Small People in their state of decay from off the
earth, it is deemed most unlucky to destroy a colony of ants.   If
you place a piece of tin in a bank of Muryans at a certain age of
the moon, it will be turned into silver.

* *Murrian*, Welsh, " Crig-murrian," the hill of ants.

TREGEAGLE.

"In Cornwaile's fair land, bye the poole on the moore,
Tregeagle the wicked did dwell."
                    —*Tregeagle; or, Dozmare Pool.*
                        By JOHN PENWARNE.

ROMANCES OF TREGEAGLE.

THE DEMON TREGEAGLE.

" Thrice he began to tell his doleful tale,
And thrice the sighs did swallow up his voice."
—THOMAS SACKVILLE.

WHO has not heard of the wild spirit Tregeagle? He haunts equally the moor, the rocky coasts, and the blown sand-hills of Cornwall. From north to south, from east to west, this doomed spirit is heard of, and to the day of judgment he is doomed to wander, pursued by avenging fiends. For ever endeavouring to perform some task by which he hopes to secure repose, and being for ever defeated. Who has not heard the howling of Tregeagle? When the storms come with all their strength from the Atlantic, and urge themselves upon the rocks around the Land's End, the howls of the spirit are louder than the roaring of the winds. When calms rest upon the ocean, and the waves can scarcely form upon the resting waters, low wail-ings creep along the coast. These are the wailings of this wander-ing soul. When midnight is on the moor or on the mountains, and the night winds whistle amidst the rugged cairns, the shrieks of Tregeagle are distinctly heard. We know, then, that he is pursued by the demon dogs, and that till daybreak he must fly with all speed before them. The voice of Tregeagle is every-where, and yet he is unseen by human eye. Every reader will at once perceive that Tregeagle belongs to the mythologies of the oldest nations, and that the traditions of this wandering spirit in Cornwall, which centre upon one tyrannical magistrate, are but the appropriation of stories which belong to every age and country. Tradition thus tells Tregeagle's tale.

There are some men who appear to be from their births given over to the will of tormenting demons. Such a man was Tre-geagle. He is as old as the hills, yet there are many circum-stances in the story of his life which *appear* to remove him from this remote antiquity. Modern legends assert him to belong to comparatively modern times, and say that, without doubt, he was one of the Tregeagles who once owned Trevorder near Bodmin. We have not, however, much occasion to trouble ourselves with the man or his life ; it is with the death and the subsequent existence of a myth that we are concerned.

Certain it is that the man Tregeagle was diabolically wicked. He seems to have been urged on from one crime to another until the cup of sin was overflowing.

Tregeagle was wealthy beyond most men of his time, and his wealth purchased for him that immunity, which the Church, in her degenerate days, too often accorded to those who could aid, with their gold or power, the sensual priesthood. As a magistrate, he was tyrannical and unjust, and many an innocent man was wantonly sacrificed by him for the purpose of hiding his own dark deeds. As a landlord, he was rapacious and unscrupulous, and frequently so involved his tenants in his toils, that they could not escape his grasp. The stain of secret murder clings to his memory, and he is said to have sacrificed a sister whose goodness stood between him and his demon passions ; his wife and children perished victims to his cruelties. At length death drew near to relieve the land of a monster whose name was a terror to all who heard it. Devils waited to secure the soul they had won, and Tregeagle in terror gave to the priesthood wealth, that they might fight with them and save his soul from eternal fire. Desperate was the struggle, but the powerful exorcisms of the banded brotherhood of a neighbouring monastery, drove back the evil ones, and Tregeagle slept with his fathers, safe in the custody of the churchmen, who buried him with high honours in St Breock Church. They sang chants and read prayers above his grave, to secure the soul which they thought they had saved. But Tregeagle was not fated to rest. Satan desired still to gain possession of such a gigantic sinner, and we can only refer what ensued to the influence of the wicked spiritings of his ministers.

A dispute arose between two wealthy families respecting the ownership of extensive lands around Bodmin. The question had been rendered more difficult by the nefarious conduct of Tregeagle, who had acted as steward to one of the claimants, and who had destroyed ancient deeds, forged others, and indeed made it appear that he was the real proprietor of the domain. Large portions of the land Tregeagle had sold, and other parts were leased upon long terms, he having received all the money and appropriated it. His death led to inquiries, and then the transactions were gradually brought to light. Involving, as this did, large sums of money—and indeed it was a question upon which turned the future well-doing or ruin of a family—it was fought by the lawyers with great pertinacity. The legal questions had been argued several times before the judges at the assizes. The trials had been deferred, new trials had been sought for and granted, and every possible plan known to the lawyers for postponing the settlement of a suit had been tried. A day was at length fixed, upon which a final decision must be come to, and a special jury was sworn to administer justice between the contending parties. Witnesses innumerable were examined as to the validity of a certain deed, and the balance of evidence was equally suspended. The judge was about to sum up the case and refer the question to the jury, when the defendant in the case, coming into court, proclaimed aloud that he had yet another witness to produce. There was a strange silence in the judgment-hall. It was felt that something chilling to the soul was amongst them, and there was a simultaneous throb of terror as Tregeagle was led into the witness-box.

When the awe-struck assembly had recovered, the lawyers for the defendant commenced their examination, which was long and terrible. The result, however, was the disclosure of an involved system of fraud, of which the honest defendant had been the victim, and the jury unhesitatingly gave a verdict in his favour.

The trial over, every one expected to see the spectre-witness removed. There, however, he stood, powerless to fly, although he evidently desired to do so. Spirits of darkness were waiting to bear him away, but some spell of holiness prevented them from touching him. There was a struggle with the good and the evil angels for this sinner's soul, and the assembled court appeared frozen with horror. At length the judge with dignity commanded the defendant to remove his witness.

"To bring him from the grave has been to me so dreadful a task, that I leave him to your care, and that of the Prior's, by whom he was so beloved." Having said this, the defendant left the court.

The churchmen were called in, and long were the deliberations between them and the lawyers, as to the best mode of disposing of Tregeagle.

They could resign him to the devil at once, but by long trial the worst of crimes might be absolved, and as good churchmen they could not sacrifice a human soul. The only thing was to give the spirit some task, difficult beyond the power of human nature, which might be extended far into eternity. Time might thus gradually soften the obdurate soul, which still retained all the black dyes of the sins done in the flesh, that by infinitely slow degrees repentance might exert its softening power. The spell therefore put upon Tregeagle was, that as long as he was employed on some endless assigned task, there should be hope of salvation, and that he should be secure from the assaults of the devil as long as he laboured steadily. A moment's rest was fatal—labour unresting, and for ever, was his doom.

One of the lawyers, remembering that Dosmery Pool* was bottomless, and that a thorn-bush which had been flung into it, but a few weeks before, had made its appearance in Falmouth Harbour, proposed that Tregeagle might be employed to empty this profound lake. Then one of the churchmen, to make the task yet more enduring, proposed that it should be performed by the aid of a limpet-shell having a hole in it.

This was agreed to, and the required incantations were duly made. Bound by mystical spells, Tregeagle was removed to the dark moors and duly set to work. Year after year passed by, and there, day and night, summer and winter, storm and shine, Tregeagle was bending over the dark water, working hard with his perforated shell ; yet the pool remained at the same level.

His old enemy the devil kept a careful eye on the doomed one, resolving, if possible, to secure so choice an example of evil. Often did he raise tempests sufficiently wild, as he supposed, to drive Tregeagle from his work, knowing that if he failed for a season to labour, he could seize and secure him. These were long tried in vain ; but at length an auspicious hour presented itself.

Nature was at war with herself, the elements had lost their balance, and there was a terrific struggle to recover it. Lightnings flashed and coiled like fiery snakes around the rocks of Roughtor. Fire-balls fell on the desert moors and hissed in the accursed lake. Thunders peeled through the heavens, and echoed from hill to hill ; an earthquake shook the solid earth, and terror was on all living. The winds arose and raged with a fury which was irresistible, and hail beat so mercilessly on all things, that it spread death around. Long did Tregeagle stand the " pelting of the pitiless storm," but at length he yielded to its force and fled. The demons in crowds were at his heels. He doubled, however, on his pursuers, and returned to the lake ; but so rapid were they, that he could not rest the required moment to dip his shell in the now seething waters.

* Or *Dozmare.* Unfortunately for its bottomless character, in a recent hot and rainless summer, this little lake became dry.

Three times he fled round the lake, and the evil ones pursued him. Then, feeling that there was no safety for him near Dosmery Pool, he sprang swifter than the wind across it, shrieking with agony, and thus,—since the devils cannot cross water, and were obliged to go round the lake,—he gained on them and fled over the moor.

Away, away went Tregeagle, faster and faster the dark spirits pursuing, and they had nearly overtaken him, when he saw Roach Rock and its chapel before him. He rushed up the rocks, with giant power clambered to the eastern window, and dashed his head through it, thus securing the shelter of its sanctity. The defeated demons retired, and long and loud were their wild wailings in the air. The inhabitants of the moors and of the neighbouring towns slept not a wink that night.

Tregeagle was safe, his head was within the holy church, though his body was exposed on a bare rock to the storm. Earnest were the prayers of the blessed hermit in his cell on the rock to be relieved from his nocturnal and sinful visitor.

In vain were the recluse's prayers. Day after day, as he knelt at the altar, the ghastly head of the doomed sinner grinned horridly down upon him. Every holy ejaculation fell upon Tregeagle's ear like molten iron. He writhed and shrieked under the torture; but legions of devils filled the air, ready to seize him, if for a moment he withdrew his head from the sanctuary. Sabbath after Sabbath the little chapel on the rock was rendered a scene of sad confusion by the interruptions which Tregeagle caused. Men trembled with fear at his agonising cries, and women swooned. At length the place was deserted, and even the saint of the rock was wasting to death by the constant perturbation in which he was kept by the unholy spirit, and the demons who, like carrion birds, swarmed around the holy cairn. Things could not go on thus. The monks of Bodmin and the priests from the neighbouring churches gathered together, and the result of their long and anxious deliberations was, that Tregeagle, guarded by two saints, should be taken to the north coast, near Padstow, and employed in making trusses of sand, and ropes of sand with which to bind them. By powerful spell, Tregeagle was removed from Roach, and fixed upon the sandy shores of the Padstow district. Sinners are seldom permitted to enjoy any peace of soul. As the ball of sand grew into form, the tides rose, and the breakers spread out the sands again a level sheet; again was it packed together and again washed away. Toil! toil! toil! day and night unrestingly, sand on sand grew with each hour, and ruthlessly the ball was swept, by one blow of a sea wave, along the shore.

The cries of Tregeagle were dreadful; and as the destruction of the sand heap was constantly recurring, a constantly increasing despair gained the mastery over hope, and the ravings of the baffled soul were louder than the roarings of the winter tempest.

Baffled in making trusses of sand, Tregeagle seized upon the loose particles and began to spin them into a rope. Long and patiently did he pursue his task, and hope once more rose like a star out of the midnight darkness of despair. A rope was forming, when a storm came up with all its fury from the Atlantic, and swept the particles of sand away over the hills.

The inhabitants of Padstow had seldom any rest. At every tide the howlings of Tregeagle banished sleep from each eye. But now so fearful were the sounds of the doomed soul, in the madness of the struggle between hope and despair, that the people fled the town, and clustered upon the neighbouring plains, praying, as with one voice, to be relieved from the sad presence of this monster.

St Petroc, moved by the tears and petitions of the people, resolved to remove the spirit; and by the intense earnestness of his prayers, after long wrestling, he subdued Tregeagle to his will. Having chained him with the bonds which the saint had forged with his own hands, every link of which had been welded with a prayer, St Petroc led the spirit away from the north coast, and stealthily placed him on the southern shores.

In those days Ella's Town, now Helston, was a flourishing port. Ships sailed into the estuary, up to the town, and they brought all sorts of merchandise, and returned with cargoes of tin from the mines of Breage and Wendron.

The wily monk placed his charge at Bareppa, and there condemned him to carry sacks of sand across the estuary of the Loo, and to empty them at Porthleven, until the beach was clean down to the rocks. The priest was a good observer. He knew that the sweep of the tide was from Trewavas Head round the coast towards the Lizard, and that the sand would be carried back steadily and speedily as fast as the spirit could remove it.

Long did Tregeagle labour; and, of course, in vain. His struggles were giant-like to perform his task, but he saw the sands return as regularly as he removed them. The sufferings of the poor fishermen who inhabited the coast around Porthleven were great. As the howlings of Tregeagle disturbed the dwellers in Padstow, so did they now distress those toil-worn men.

> " When sorrow is highest.
> Relief is nighest."

And a mischievous demon-watcher, in pure wantonness, brought that relief to those fishers of the sea.

Tregeagle was laden with a sack of sand of enormous size, and was wading across the mouth of the estuary, when one of those wicked devils, who were kept ever near Tregeagle, in very idleness tripped up the heavily-laden spirit. The sea was raging with the irritation of a passing storm; and as Tregeagle fell, the sack was seized by the waves, and its contents poured out across this arm of the sea.

There, to this day, it rests a bar of sand, fatally destroying the harbour of Ella's Town. The rage of the inhabitants of this sea-port,—now destroyed,—was great; and with all their priests, away they went to the Loo Bar, and assailed their destroyer. Against human anger Tregeagle was proof. The shock of tongues fell harmlessly on his ear, and the assault of human weapons was unavailing.

By the aid of the priests, and faith-inspired prayers, the bonds were once more placed upon Tregeagle; and he was, by the force of bell, book, and candle, sent to the Land's End. There he would find no harbour to destroy, and but few people to terrify. His task was to sweep the sands from Porthcurnow Cove round the headland called Tol-Peden-Penwith, into Nanjisal Cove. Those who know that rugged headland, with its cubical masses of granite, piled in Titanic grandeur one upon another, will appreciate the task; and when to all the difficulties are added the strong sweep of the Atlantic current,—that portion of the Gulf-stream which washes our southern shores,—it will be evident that the melancholy spirit has, indeed, a task which must endure until the world shall end.

Even until to-day is Tregeagle labouring at his task. In calms his wailing is heard; and those sounds which some call the "soughing of the wind," are known to be the moanings of Tregeagle; while the coming storms are predicated by the fearful roarings of this condemned mortal.

JAHN TERGAGLE THE STEWARD.

THERE are numerous versions of this legend, and sundry statements made as to the man who is supposed to have achieved the no very envious immortality which he enjoys.

One or two of these may interest the reader.

The following very characteristic narrative, from a much-esteemed correspondent, gives several incidents which have not a place in the legend as I have related it, which comprehends the explanation given for the appearance of Tregeagle at so many different parts of the county.

The Tregeagle, of whom mention occurs in the writings of Cornish legendary authors, was a real person: a member of a respectable family, resident during the seventeenth century at Trevorder, in the parish of St Breock, and identical probably with a John Tregeagle whose tombstone may yet be seen in the parish church there, close to the chancel.

Lingering one day amid the venerable arches of that same church, the narrator, a native of the parish, encountered, near a small transept called the Trevorder aisle, the sexton, a man then perhaps of about eighty years of age. The conversation turning not unnaturally on the "illustrious dead," the narrator was gratified in receiving from the lips of the old man the following characteristic specimen of folk-lore, the greater part of which has remained clearly imprinted in his memory after a lapse of many years; though [he thinks he has had to supply the very last sentence of all from the general popular tradition] here and there he may have had to supply a few expressions :—

"Theess Jahn Tergagle, I've a heerd mun tell, sir, he was a steward to a lord.*

"And a man came fore to the court and paid az rent: and Jahn Tergagle didn't put no cross to az name in the books.

"And after that Tergagle daied: and the lord came down to look after az rents: and when he zeed the books, he zeed this man's name that there wasn't no cross to ut.

"And he zent for the man, and axed 'n for az rent: and the man zaid he'd apaid az rent: and the lord said he hadn't, there warn't no cross to az name in the books, and he tould 'n that he'd have the law for 'n if he didn't pay.

"And the man, he didn't know what to do: and he went vore to the minister of Simonward; † and the minister axed 'n if he'd a got faith: and the man, he hadn't got faith, and he was obliged for to come homewards again.

"And after that the 'Zaizes was coming naigh, and he was becoming afeerd, sure enough: and he went vore to the minister again, and tould 'n he'd a got faith; the minister might do whatever a laiked.

"And the minister draed a ring out on the floor: and he caaled out dree times, Jahn Tergagle, Jahn Tergagle, Jahn Tergagle! and (I've a heerd the ould men tell ut, sir) theess Jahn Tergagle stood before mun in the middle of the ring.

"And he went vore wi' mun to the Ezaizes, and gave az evidence and tould how this man had a paid az rent; and the lord he was cast.

"And after that they was come back to their own house, theess Jahn

---

* Lord—*i.e.*, a landlord.   † St Breward.

Tergagle he gave mun a brave deal of trouble ; he was knackin' about the place, and wouldn't laive mun alone at all.

"And they went vore to the minister, and axed he for to lay un.

" And the minister zaid, thicky * was their look-out ; they'd a brought'n up, and they was to gett'n down again the best way they could. And I've a heerd the ould men tell ut, sir. The minister he got dree hunderd pound for a layin' of un again.

"And first, a was bound to the old epping-stock † up to Churchtown ; ‡ and after that a was bound to the ould oven in T'evurder ; James Wyatt down to Wadebridge, he was there when they did open ut.

"And after that a was bound to Dozmary Pool ; and they do say that there he ez now emptying of it out with a lampet-shell, with a hole in the bottom of ut."

This is a very ancient idea, and was one of the torments of the classical Tartarus. The treacherous daughters of Danaus being condemned therein to empty Lethe with a bottomless vessel :—

> " Et Danai proles Veneris quæ numma læsit,
> In cava Lethæas solia portat aquas."

Dosmare Pool is a small lake or tarn on the Bodmin Moors, a fit representative of Lethe, with its black water and desolate environs.—J. C. H.

Another correspondent to whom I am much indebted for valuable notes on the folk-lore of the Land's End district, sends me the following version :—

You may know the story better than I do ; however, I'll give you the west-country version. A man in the neighbourhood of Redruth, I think (I have almost forgotten the story), lent a sum of money to another without receiving bond or note, and the transaction was witnessed by Tregagle, who died before the money was paid back. When the lender demanded the money, the borrower denied having received it. He was brought into a court of justice, when the man denied on oath that he ever borrowed the money, and declared that if Tregagle saw any such thing take place, he wished that Tregagle would come and declare it. The words were no sooner out of his mouth than Tregagle stood before him, and told him that it was easy to bring him, but that he should not find it so easy to put him away. Tregagle followed the man day and night, wouldn't let him have a moment's rest, until he got all the parsons, conjurors, and other wise men together, to lay him. The wise ones accomplished this for a short time by binding the spirit to empty Dosmery (or Dorsmery) Pool with a crogan (limpet-shell). He soon finished the job and came to the man

---

* Thicky, correctly written thilke—*i.e.*, the ilka, a true word frequent in Chaucer.

† Perhaps Uppingstock, an erection of stone steps for the farmers' wives to get on their horses by.

‡ Not Chúrchtown, but Churchtówn.

again, who sent for Parson Corker, of Burrian, who was a noted hand for laying spirits, driving the devil from the bedside of old villains, and other kinds of jobs of the same kind. When the parson came into the room with the spirit and the man, the first thing the parson did was to draw a circle and place the man to stand within it ; the spirit took the form of a black bull, and (roared as you may still hear Tregagle roar in Genvor Cove before a northerly storm) did all he could to get at the man with his horns and hoofs. The parson continued reading all the time. At first the reading seemed to make him more furious, but little by little he became as gentle as a lamb, and allowed the parson to do what he would with him, and consented at last to go to Genvor Cove (in Escols Cliff), and make a truss of sand, which he was to carry above a certain rock in Escols Cliff. He was many years trying, without being able to accomplish this piece of work, until it came to a very cold winter, when Tregagle, by taking water from the stream near by, and pouring over the sand, caused it to freeze together, so that he finished the task, came back to the man, and would have torn him in pieces, but the man happened to have a child in his arms, so the spirit couldn't harm him. The man sent for the parson without delay ; Parson Corker couldn't manage him alone, this time ; had to get some more parsons to help,—very difficult job ;—bound Tregagle at last to the same task, and not to go near the fresh water. He is still there, making his truss of sand and spinning sand ropes to bind it. What some people take to be the "*calling of the northern cleves*" (cliffs) is the roaring of Tregagle because there is a storm coming from the north to scatter his sand.*   W. B.

* In connection with the incident given of Tregeagle and the child, the following is interesting :—

I find in the *Temple Bar Magazine* for January 1862, "The Autobiography of an Evil Spirit," professing to be an examination of a strange story related by Dr Justinus Kerner. In this a woman is possessed by a devil or sometimes by devils. " Sometimes a legion of fiends appeared to take possession of her, and the clamour on such occasions is compared to that of a pack of hounds. Amid all these horrors her confinement occurred, which was the means of procuring her some respite, as the demon appeared to have no power over her while her innocent babe was in her arms." To this the author adds the following note :—

This ancient general and beautiful superstition is graphically illustrated in the legend of Swardowski, the Polish Faust. Satan, weary of the services the magician is continually requiring at his hands, decoys him to a house in Cracow, where, for some unexplained reason, he expects to have him at a disadvantage. Put on his guard by the indiscretion of a flock of ravens and owls, who cannot suppress their satisfaction at seeing him enter the house, Swardowski snatches a new-born child from the cradle and paces the room with it in his arms. In rushes the devil, as terrible as horns, tail, and hoofs can make him : but confronted with the infant, recoils and collapses *instanter*. This suggests to him the propriety of resorting to "moral suasion ;" and after a while he thus addresses the magician,—"Thou art a gentleman and knowest that *verbum nobile debet esse stabile*." Swardowski feels that he cannot break his word of honour as a gentleman, replaces the child in the cradle, and flies up the chimney with his companion. In the confusion of his faculties, however, the demon would seem to have mistaken the way ;

DOSMERY POOL.

M R BOND, in his "Topographical and Historical Sketches of the Boroughs of East and West Looe," writes— " This pool is distant from Looe about twelve miles off.　Mr Carew says :—

> ' Dosmery Pool amid the moores,
>   On top stands of a hill ;
>   More than a mile about, no streams
>   It empt, nor any fill.'

It is a lake of fresh water about a mile in circumference, the only one in Cornwall (unless the Loe Pool near Helston may be deemed such), and probably takes its name from *Dome-Mer*, sweet or fresh-water sea.　It is about eight or ten feet deep in many parts. The notion entertained by some, of there being a whirlpool in its middle, I can contradict, having, some years ago, passed all over in a boat then kept there."

Such is Mr Bond's evidence ; but this is nothing compared with the popular belief, which declares the pool to be bottomless ; and beyond this, is it not known to every man of faith, that a thorn-bush thrown into Dosmery Pool has sunk in the middle of it, and after some time has come up in Falmouth Harbour ?

Notwithstanding that Carew says that " no streams it empt, nor any fill," James Michell, in his parochial history of St Neot's, says,—" It is situate on a small stream called St Neot's River, a branch of the Fowey, which rises in Dosmare Pool."

There is a ballad, " *Tregeagle; or, Dozmaré Poole: an Anciente Cornishe Legende, in two parts,*" by John Penwarne.　He has given a somewhat different version of the legend from any I have heard, and in the ballad very considerable liberties have been taken. It must, however, be admitted, that nearly all the incidents intro-duced in the poem are to be found in some of the many stories current amongst the peasantry.

Speaking of Dozmaré Pool, Mr Penwarne says :—

" There is a popular story attached to this lake, ridiculous enough, as most of those tales are.　It is, that a person of the name of Tregeagle, who had been a rich and powerful man, but very

at all events, the pair fly upwards instead of downwards,—Swardowski lustily intoning a hymn till suddenly he finds his companion gone, and himself fixed at an immeasurable height in the air, and hears a voice above him saying, " Thus shalt thou hang until the day of judgment !"　He has, however, changed one of his disciples into a spider, and is in the habit of letting him down to collect the news of earth.　When, therefore, we see any floating threads of gossamer, we may suspect that " a chiel's amang us taking notes," though it is not equally probable that he will ever " prent them."

wicked, guilty of murder and other heinous crimes, lived near this place ; and that, after his death, his spirit haunted the neighbourhood, but was at length exorcised and laid to rest in Dozmaré Pool. But having in his lifetime, in order to enjoy the good things of this world, disposed of his soul and body to the devil, his infernal majesty takes great pleasure in tormenting him, by imposing on him difficult tasks ; such as spinning a rope of sand, dipping out the pool with a limpet-shell, &c., and at times amuses himself with hunting him over the moors with his hell-hounds, at which time Tregeagle is heard to roar and howl in a most dreadful manner, so that 'roaring or howling like Tregeagle,' is a common expression amongst the vulgar in Cornwall. Such is the foundation on which is built the following tale. The author has given it an ancient dress, as best suited to the subject."

Tregeagle, in the ballad, is a shepherd dwelling "by the poole on the moore." He was ambitious and unscrupulous. "I wish for all that I see !" was his exclamation, when "a figure gigantick" is seen "midst the gloom of the night."

This spirit offers Tregeagle, in exchange for his soul, all that he desires for one hundred years. Tregeagle does not hesitate :—

> "'A bargaine ! a bargaine !' he said aloude ;
> 'At my lot I will never repine ;
> I sweare to observe it, I sweare by the roode.
> And am readye to seale and to sygne with my bloode,
> Both my soul and my body are thine.'"

Tregeagle is thrown into a trance, from which he awakes to find himself "cloathed in gorgeous attyre," and master of a wide domain of great beauty :—

> "Where Dozmare lake its darke waters did roll,
> A castle now reared its heade,
> Wythe manye a turrete soe statelye and talle ;
> And many a warden dyd walke on its walle,
> All splendidly cloathed in redde."

Surrounded with all that is supposed to minister to the enjoyment of a sensual life, time passes on, and "Tregeagle ne'er notyc'd its flyghte." Yet we are told "he marked each day with some damnable deed." In the midst of his vicious career he is returning home through a violent storm, and he is accosted by a damsel on a white horse and a little page by her side, who craves his protection. Tregeagle takes this beautiful maiden to his castle. The page is made to tell the lady's story ; she is called Goonhylda, and is the daughter of " Earl Cornwaill," living in Launceston, or, as it was then called, " Dunevyd Castle." Engaged in the plea- sures of the hunt, the lady and her page are lost and overtaken by the storm. Tregeagle, as the storm rages savagely, makes them his " guests for the nyghte," promising to send a " quicke messenger " to inform her father of her whereabouts. At the same time—

> " If that the countenance speaketh the mynde,
>   Dark deeds he revolved in hys breaste."

The earl hears nothing of his daughter; and having passed a miserable night, he sets forth in the morning, "wyth hys knyghtes, and esquyers, and serving-men all," in search of his child; and—

> " At length to the plaine he emerged from the woode,
>   For a father, alas, what a syghte !
> There lay her fayre garments all drenched in blood,
> Her palfreye all torn in the dark crimson floode,
>   By the ravenous beasts of the nyghte."

This is a delusion caused by enchantment; Goonhylda still lives. Tregeagle offers himself to Goonhylda, who rejects his suit with scorn, and desires to leave the castle. Tregeagle coolly informs her that she cannot quit the place; Goonhylda threatens him with her father's vengeance. She is a prisoner, but her page contrives to make his escape, and in the evening arrives at Launceston Castle gate. The Earl of Cornwall, hearing from the page that his daughter lives and is a prisoner, arms himself and all his re- tainers—

> " And ere the greye morne peep'd the eastern hills o'er,
>   At Tregeagle's gate sounded hys horne."

Tregeagle will not obey the summons, but suddenly " they hearde the Black Hunter's dread voyce in the wynde ! "

> " They heard hys curste hell-houndes runn yelping behynde,
>   And his steede thundered loude on the eare ! "

This gentleman in black shakes the castle with his cry, " Come forth, Sir Tregeagle ! come forth and submit to thy fate !" Of course he comes forth, and " the rede bolte of vengeaunce shot forth wyth a glare, and strooke him a corpse to the grounde ! "

> " Then from the black corpse a pale spectre appear'd,
>   And hyed him away through the night."

Goonhylda is of course found uninjured, and taken home by the earl. The castle disappears and Dozmare Pool re-appears; but—

" Stylle as the traveller pursues hys lone waye,
    In horroure at nyghte o'er the waste,
IIe hears Syr Tregeagle with shrieks rushe awaye,
IIe hears the Black Hunter pursuing his preye,
    And shrynkes at hys bugle's dread blaste."

THE WISH HOUNDS.

THE tradition of the Midnight Hunter and his headless hounds
—always, in Cornwall, associated with Tregeagle—prevails
everywhere.

The Abbot's Way on Dartmoor, an ancient road which extends
into Cornwall, is said to be the favourite coursing ground of "the
wish or wisked hounds of Dartmoor," called also the "yell-
hounds," and the "yeth-hounds." The valley of the Dewerstone is
also the place of their midnight meetings. Once I was told at
Jump, that Sir Francis Drake drove a hearse into Plymouth at
night with headless horses, and that he was followed by a pack of
"yelling hounds" without heads. If dogs hear the cry of the
wish hounds they all die. May it not be that "wish" is connected
with the west-country word "whist," meaning more than ordinary
melancholy, a sorrow which has something weird surrounding it?

" And then he sought the dark-green lane,
    Whose willows mourn'd the faded year,
Sighing (I heard the love-lorn swain),
    '*Wishness!* oh, *wishness!* walketh here.'"
    — *The Wishful Swain of Devon.*   By POLWHELE.

The author adds in a note, "An expression used by the vulgar
in the north of Devon to express local melancholy. There is
something sublime in this impersonation of *wishness.*" The expression is as common in Cornwall as it is in Devonshire.

Mr Kemble has the following incorrect remarks on this word:—
" In Devonshire to this day all magical or supernatural dealings go
under the common name of wishtness. Can this have any
reference to Woden's name 'wyse?'" Mr Polwhele's note gives
the true meaning of the word. Still Mr Kemble's idea is supported
by the fact that "there are *Wishanger* (Wisehangre or Woden's
Meadow), one about four miles south-west of Wanborough in
Surrey, and another near Gloucester." *   And we find also, "south-

* Kemble's "Saxons in England," vol. i., p. 346. Wistman's Wood on Dartmoor, no

K

east of Pixhill in Tedstone, Delamere, there are *Wishmoor* and Inksmoor near Sapey Bridge in Whitbourn." *

CHENEY'S HOUNDS.

IN the parish of St Teath, a pack of hounds was once kept by an old squire named Cheney. How he or they died I cannot learn ; but on " Cheney Downs " the ghosts of the dogs are sometimes seen, and often heard, in rough weather.

In the western parishes of the county, I can name several places which are said to be haunted by the " wish hounds." †

doubt derives it name from its extraordinary character. Carrington, in his " Dartmoor," well describes its oaks :—

> " But of this grove,
> This pigmy grove, not one has climb'd the air,
> So emulously that its loftiest branch
> May brush the traveller's brow. The twisted roots
> Have clasp'd, in search of nourishment, the rocks,
> And straggled wide, and pierced the stony soil."
> " Around the boughs.
> Hoary and feebly, and around the trunks
> With grasp destructive feeding on the life
> That lingers yet, the ivy winds, and moss
> Of growth enormous."
>
> —*Dartmoor, a descriptive poem.*
> By N. T. CARRINGTON, 1826. Murray.

* " The British, Roman, and Saxon Antiquities and Folk-lore of Worcestershire." By Jabez Allies.

† See *Athenæum.* No. 1013, March 27, 1847. See Appendix L for Notes on the BARGEST.

THE MERMAIDS.

" One Friday morning we set sail,
　　And when not far from land,
We all espied a fair mermaid
　　With a comb and glass in her hand.
The stormy winds they did blow," &c.
　　　　　　　　　　　　　—*Old Song.*

ROMANCES OF THE MERMAIDS.

MORVA OR MORVETH (*Sea-daughters*).

" You dwell not on land, but in the flood,
Which would not with me agree."
—Duke Magnus and the Mermaid.—SMALAND.

THE parish of this name is situated on the north-west coast of Cornwall,—the parish of St Just being on its western borders, and that of Zennor on the east, between it and St Ives. The Cornish historian Tonkin says, "*Morva* signifies Locus Maritimus, a place near the sea, as this parish is. The name is sometimes written *Morveth*, implying much the same sense."

The similarity of this name to " Morgan," *sea-women*, and " Morverch," *sea-daughters*, which Mr Keightley has shown us is applied to the mermaids of the Breton ballads, is not a little curious. There are several stories current in this parish of *ladies seen on the rocks*, of *ladies going off from the shore to peculiar isolated rocks. at special seasons*, and of *ladies sitting weeping and wailing on the shore*. Mr Blight, in his " Week at the Land's End," speaking of the church in the adjoining parish, Zennor, which still remains in nearly its primitive condition, whereas Morva church is a modern structure, says—" Some of the bench ends were carved ; on one is a strange figure of a *mermaid*, which to many might seem out of character in a church." (Mr Blight gives a drawing of this bench end.) This is followed by a quotation bearing the initials R. S. H., which, it is presumed, are those of the Rev. R. S. Hawker, of Morwenstow :—

" The fishermen who were the ancestors of the Church, came from the Galilean waters to haul for men. We, born to God at the font, are children of the water. Therefore, all the early symbolism of the Church was of and from the sea. The carvure of the early arches was taken from the sea and its creatures. Fish, dolphins, mermen, and mermaids abound in the early types, transferred to wood and stone."

Surely the poet of "the Western Shore" might have explained the fact of the figures of mermaids being carved on the bench ends of some of the old churches with less difficulty, had he remembered that nearly all the churches on the coast of Cornwall were built by and for fishermen, to whom the superstitions of mermen and mermaidens had the familiarity of a creed.

The intimate connection between the inhabitants of Brittany, of Cornwall, and of Wales, would appear to lead to the conclusion that the Breton word *Morverch*, or mermaid, had much to do with the name of this parish, Morva,—of Morvel, near Liskeard,—and probably of Morwenstow, of which the vicar, Mr Hawker, writes— " My glebe occupies a position of wild and singular beauty. Its western boundary is the sea, skirted by tall and tremendous cliffs, and near their brink, with the exquisite taste of ecclesiastical antiquity, is placed the church. The original and proper designation of the parish is *Morwen*-stow—that is, Morwenna's Stow, or station ; but it has been corrupted by recent usage, like many other local names."

MERRYMAIDS AND MERRYMEN.

THE "merry-maids" of the Cornish fishermen and sailors possess the well-recognised features of the mermaid. The Breton ballad, quoted by Mr Keightley, relating to the Morgan (*sea-women*) and the Morverch (sea-daughters), peculiarly adapts itself to the Cornish merry-maid.

" Fisher, hast thou seen the mermaid combing her hair, yellow as gold, by the noontide sun, at the edge of the water ? "

" I have seen the fair mermaid ; I have also heard her singing her songs plaintive as the waves."

The Irish legends make us acquainted with the amours of men with those sea-sirens. We learn that the Merrows, or Moruachs, came occasionally from the sea, and interested themselves in the affairs of man. Amongst the fragments which have been gathered, here a pebble and there a pebble, along the Western coast, will be found similar narratives.

The sirens of the Ægean Sea—probably the parents of the mediæval mermaid—possess in a pre-eminent degree the beauty and the falsehood of all the race. Like all other things, even those mythical creations take colour from that they work in, like the dyer's hand. The Italian mermaid is the true creature of the romance of the sunny South ; while the lady of our own southern seas, although she possesses much in common with her Mediterranean sister, has less poetry, but more human sympathy. The following stories, read in connection with those given by Mr Keightley and by Mr Croker, will show this.*

When, five-and-thirty years since, I spent several nights in a fisherman's cottage on a south-western coast, I was treated to many a "long yarn" respecting mermaids seen by the father and his sons in the southern ocean. The appearance of those creatures on our own shores, they said, was rare; but still they knew they had been seen. From them I learned of more than one family who have received mysterious powers from the sea-nymphs; and I have since heard that members of those families still live, and that they intimate to their credulous friends their firm belief that this power, which they say has been transmitted to them, was derived, by some one of their ancestors, from merman or mer-maiden.

Usually those creatures are associated with some catastrophe; but they are now and then spoken of as the benefactors of man.

One word more. The story of "*The Mermaid's Vengeance*" has been produced from three versions of evidently the same legend, which differed in many respects one from the other, yet agreeing in the main with each other. The first I heard at the Lizard, or rather at Coverach; the second in Sennen Cove, near the Land's End; the third at Perranzabaloe. I have preferred the last locality, as being peculiarly fitted for the home of a mermaid story, and because the old man who told the tale there was far more graphic in his incidents; and these were strung more closely together than either of the other stories.†

* See "The Fairy Family: a Series of Ballads and Metrical Tales Illustrating the Fairy Mythology of Europe," Longman, 1857; "The Fairy Mythology, Illustrative of the Romance and Superstitions of Various Countries," by Thomas Keightley; and "Irish Fairy Legends," by Crofton Croker.

† The following extract from a letter from an esteemed correspondent shows the exist-ence of a belief in those fabled creations of the ocean amongst an extensive class of the labouring population of Cornwall. There is so much that is characteristic in my corre-spondent's letter that it is worth preserving as supporting the evidence of the existing belief:—

"I had the chance of seeing what many of our natives firmly believed to be that family. Some fourteen years ago I found myself, with about fifty emigrants, in the Gulf of St Lawrence, on board the old tub *Resolution*, Captain Davies, commander. We were shrouded in a fog so thick that you might cut it like a cheese, almost all the way from the Banks to Anticosti. One morning, soon after sunrise, when near that island, the fog as thick as night overhead, at times would rise and fall on the shore like the tantalising stage curtain. All at once there was a clear opening right through the dense clouds which rested on the water, that gave us a glimpse of the shore, with the rocks covered with what to us appeared very strange creatures. In a minute, the hue and cry from

THE MERMAID OF PADSTOW.

THE port of Padstow has a good natural harbour, so far as rocky area goes, but it is so choked up with drifting sands as to be nearly useless. A peasant recently thus explained the cause. He told how " it was once deep water for the largest vessel, and under the care of a *merry-maid*—as he called her ; but one day, as she was sporting on the surface, a fellow with a gun shot at her. " She dived for a moment ; but re-appearing, raised her right arm, and vowed that henceforth the harbour should be desolate." " And," added the old man, " it always will be so. We have had commissions, and I know not what, about converting this place into a harbour of refuge. A harbour of refuge would be a great blessing, but not all the Government commissions in the world could keep the sand out, or make the harbour deep enough to swim a frigate, unless the parsons can find out the way to take up the merry-maid's curse."

Another tale refers the choking up of this harbour to the bad spirit Tregeagle.

THE MERMAID'S ROCK.

TO the westward of the beautiful Cove of Lemorna is a rock which has through all time borne the above name. I have never been enabled to learn any special story in connection with this rock. There exists the popular fancy of a lady showing herself here previous to a storm—with, of course, the invariable comb and glass. She is said to have been heard singing most plaintively before a wreck, and that, all along the shore, the spirits have echoed her in low moaning voices.* Young men are

stem to stern, among all the cousin Johnnys, was 'What are they, you? What are they, you ?' Somebody gave the word mermaids. Old men, women, and children, that hadn't been out of their bunks for weeks, tore on deck to see the mermaids, when, alas! the curtain dropped, or rather closed, and the fair were lost to sight, but to memory dear; for, all the way to Quebec, those not lucky enough to see the sight bothered the others out of their lives to know how they looked, and if we saw the comb and glass in their hands. The captain might as well save his breath as tell them that the creatures they saw on the rocks were seals, walruses, and sea-calves. 'Not *yet*, *Captain* dear, you won't come that over me at all ; no, not by a long chalk ! no, not at all, I can tell 'e ! I know there are mermaids in the sea ; have heard many say so who have seen them too ! but as for sea-calves, I ain't such a calf nor donkey neither as to believe ut. There may be a few of what we call soils (seals) for all I know ; perhaps so, but the rest were mermaidens.' No doubt, centuries hence, this story of the mermaidens will be handed down with many additions, in the log-huts of the Western States."

* The undulations of the air, travelling with more rapidity than the currents, reach our shores long before the tempest by which they have been established in the centre of

said to have swam off to the rock, lured by the songs which they heard, but they have never returned. Have we not in this a dim shadow of the story of the Sirens?

THE MERMAID OF SEATON.

NEAR Looe,—that is, between Down Derry and Looe,—there is a little sand-beach called " Seaton."

Tradition tells us that here once stood a goodly commercial town bearing this name, and that when it was in its pride, Plymouth was but a small fishing-village.

The town of Seaton is said to have been overwhelmed with sand at an early period, the catastrophe having been brought about,—as in the case of the filling up of Padstow harbour,—by the curse of a mermaid, who had suffered some injury from the sailors who belonged to this port. Beyond this I have been unable to glean any story worth preserving.

THE OLD MAN OF CURY.

MORE than a hundred years since, on a fine summer day, when the sun shone brilliantly from a cloudless sky, an old man from the parish of Cury, or, as it was called in olden time, Corantyn, was walking on the sands in one of the coves near the Lizard Point. The old man was meditating, or at least he was walking onward, either thinking deeply, or not thinking at all—that is, he was " lost in thought "—when suddenly he came upon a rock on which was sitting a beautiful girl with fair hair, so long that it covered her entire person. On the in-shore side of the rock was a pool of the most transparent water, which had been left by the receding tide in the sandy hollow the waters had scooped out. This young creature was so absorbed in her occupation,—arranging her hair in the watery mirror, or in admiration of her own lovely face, that she was unconscious of an intruder.

The old man stood looking at her for some time ere he made up his mind how to act. At length he resolved to speak to the maiden. " What cheer, young one ? " he said ; " what art thee doing there by thyself, then, this time o' day ? " As soon as she heard the voice, she slid off the rock entirely under the water.

the Atlantic, and by producing a low moaning sound, " the soughing of the wind," predicates the storms. The "moans of Tregeagle " is another expression indicatin the same phenomenon.

The old man could not tell what to make of it. He thought the girl would drown herself, so he ran on to the rock to render her assistance, conceiving that in her fright at being found naked by a man she had fallen into the pool, and possibly it was deep enough to drown her. He looked into the water, and, sure enough, he could make out the head and shoulders of a woman, and long hair floating like fine sea-weeds all over the pond, hiding what appeared to him to be a fish's tail. He could not, however, see anything distinctly, owing to the abundance of hair floating around the figure. The old man had heard of mermaids from the fishermen of Gunwalloe ; so he conceived this lady must be one, and he was at first very much frightened. He saw that the young lady was quite as much terrified as he was, and that, from shame or fear, she endeavoured to hide herself in the crevices of the rock, and bury herself under the sea-weeds.

Summoning courage, at last the old man addressed her, " Don't 'e be afraid, my dear. You needn't mind me. I wouldn't do ye any harm. I'm an old man, and wouldn't hurt ye any more than your grandfather."

After he had talked in this soothing strain for some time, the young lady took courage, and raised her head above the water. She was crying bitterly, and, as soon as she could speak, she begged the old man to go away.

" I must know, my dearie, something about ye, now I have caught ye. It is not every day that an old man catches a merry-maid, and I have heard some strange tales of you water-ladies. Now, my dear, don't 'e be afraid, I would not hurt a single hair of that beautiful head. How came ye here ? " After some further coaxing she told the old man the following story :—She and her husband and little ones had been busy at sea all the morning, and they were very tired with swimming in the hot sun ; so the merman proposed that they should retire to a cavern, which they were in the habit of visiting in Kynance Cove. Away they all swam, and entered the cavern at mid-tide. As there was some nice soft weed, and the cave was deliciously cool, the merman was disposed to sleep, and told them not to wake him until the rise of the tide. He was soon fast asleep, snoring most lustily. The children crept out and were playing on the lovely sands ; so the mermaid thought she should like to look at the world a little. She looked with delight on the children rolling to and fro in the shallow waves, and she laughed heartily at the crabs fighting in their own funny way. " The scent from the flowers came down over the cliffs so sweetly," said she, " that I longed to get nearer the lovely things which yielded those rich odours, and I floated on from rock to rock until I came to this one ; and finding that I could not proceed any further, I thought I would seize the opportunity of dressing my hair." She passed her fingers through those beautiful locks, and shook out a number of small crabs, and much broken sea-weed. She went on to say that she had sat on the rock amusing herself, until the voice of a mortal terrified her, and until then she had no idea that the sea was so far out, and a long dry bar of sand between her and it. "What shall I do? what shall I do? Oh! I'd give the world to get out to sea! Oh! oh! what shall I do?"

The old man endeavoured to console her ; but his attempts were in vain. She told him her husband would "carry on" most dreadfully if he awoke and found her absent, and he would be certain of awaking at the turn of the tide, as that was his dinner-time. He was very savage when he was hungry, and would as soon eat the children as not, if there was no other food at hand. He was also dreadfully jealous, and if she was not at his side when he awoke, he would at once suspect her of having run off with some other merman. She begged the old man to bear her out to sea. If he would but do so, she would procure him any three things he would wish for. Her entreaties at length pre-vailed ; and, according to her desire, the old man knelt down on the rock with his back towards her. She clasped her fair arms around his neck, and locked her long finny fingers together on his throat. He got up from the rock with his burthen, and carried the mermaid thus across the sands. As she rode in this way, she asked the old man to tell her what he desired.

"I will not wish," said he, "for silver and gold, but give me the power to do good to my neighbours : first, to break the spells of witchcraft ; next, to charm away diseases ; and thirdly, to dis-cover thieves, and restore stolen goods."

All this she promised he should possess ; but he must come to a half-tide rock on another day, and she would instruct him how to accomplish the three things he desired. They had reached the water, and taking her comb from her hair, she gave it to the old man, telling him he had but to comb the water and call her at any time, and she would come to him. The mermaid loosened her grasp, and sliding off the old man's back into the sea, she waved him a kiss and disappeared. At the appointed time the old man was at the half-tide rock,—known to the present time as the Mermaid's Rock,—and duly was he instructed in many mys-teries. Amongst others, he learned to break the spells of witches from man or beast ; to prepare a vessel of water, in which to show to any one who had property stolen the face of the thief ; to charm shingles, tetters, St Antony's fire, and St Vitus's dance ; and he learnt also all the mysteries of bramble leaves, and the like.

The mermaid had a woman's curiosity, and she persuaded her old friend to take her to some secret place, from which she could see more of the dry land, and of the funny people who lived on it, "and had their tails split, so that they could walk." On taking the mermaid back to the sea, she wished her friend to visit her abode, and promised even to make him young if he would do so, which favour the old gentleman respectfully declined. A family, well known in Cornwall, have for some generations exercised the power of charming, &c. They account for the possession of this power in the manner related. Some remote great-grandfather was the individual who received the mermaid's comb, which they retain to the present day, and show us evidence of the truth of their being supernaturally endowed. Some people are unbelieving enough to say the comb is only a part of a shark's jaw. Sceptical people are never lovable people.

THE MERMAID'S VENGEANCE.*

IN one of the deep valleys of the parish of Perranzabuloe, which are remarkable for their fertility, and especially for the abundance of fruit which the orchards produce, lived in days long ago, amidst a rudely-civilised people, a farmer's labourer, his wife, with one child, a daughter. The man and woman were equally industrious. The neatly white-washed walls of their mud-built cottage, the well-kept gravelled paths, and carefully-weeded beds of their small garden, in which flowers were cultivated for ornament, and vegetables for use, proclaimed at once the character of the inmates. In contrast with the neighbouring cottages, this one, although smaller than many others, had a superior aspect, and the occupiers of it exhibited a strong contrast to those peasants and miners amidst whom they dwelt.

Pennaluna, as the man was called, or Penna the Proud, as he was, in no very friendly spirit, named by his less thoughtful and more impulsive fellows, was, as we have said, a farmer's labourer.

* Several versions of the following story have been given me. The general idea of the tale belongs to the north coast ; but the fact of mermaidens taking innocents under their charge was common around the Lizard, and in some of the coves near the Land's End.

His master was a wealthy yeoman, and he, after many years' experience, was so convinced of the exceeding industry and sterling honesty of Penna, that he made him the manager of an outlying farm in this parish, under the hind (or hine—the Saxon pronunciation is still retained in the West of England), or general supervisor of this and numerous other extensive farms.

Penna was too great a favourite with the Squire to be a favourite of the hind's ; he was evidently jealous of him, and from not being himself a man of very strict principles, he hated the unobtrusive goodness of his underling, and was constantly on the watch to discover some cause of complaint. It was not, however, often that he was successful in this. Every task committed to the care of Penna, —and he was often purposely overtasked,—was executed with great care and despatch. With the wife of Penna, however, the case was unfortunately different. Honour Penna was as industrious as her husband, and to him she was in all respects a helpmate. She had, however, naturally a proud spirit, and this had been encouraged in her youth by her parents. Honour was very pretty as a girl, and, indeed, she retained much beauty as a woman. The only education she received was the wild one of experience, and this within a very narrow circle. She grew an ignorant girl, amongst ignorant men and women, few of them being able to write their names, and scarcely any of them to read. There was much native grace about her, and she was flattered by the young men, and envied by the young women, of the village,—the envy and the flattery being equally pleasant to her. In the same village was born, and brought up, Tom Chenalls, who had, in the course of years, become hind to the Squire. Tom, as a young man, had often expressed himself fond of Honour, but he was always distasteful to the village maiden, and eventually, while yet young, she was married to Pennaluna, who came from the southern coast, bringing with him the recommendation of being a stranger, and an exceedingly hard-working man, who was certain to earn bread, and something more, for his wife and family. In the relations in which these people were now placed towards each other, Chenalls had the opportunity of acting ungenerously towards the Pennas. The man bore this uncomplainingly, but the woman frequently quarrelled with him whom she felt was an enemy, and whom she still regarded but as her equal. Chenalls was a skilled farmer, and hence was of considerable value to the Squire ; but although he was endured for his farming knowledge and his business habits, he was never a favourite with his employer. Penna, on the contrary, was an especial favourite, and the evidences of this were so often brought strikingly under the observation of Chenalls, that it increased the irritation of his hate, for it amounted to that. For years things went on thus. There was the tranquil suffering of an oppressed spirit manifested in Penna—the angry words and actions of his wife towards the oppressor,—and, at the same time, as she with much fondness studied to make their humble home comfortable for her husband, she reviled him not unfrequently for the meek spirit with which he endured his petty, but still trying, wrongs. The hind dared not venture on any positive act of wrong towards those people, yet he lost no chance of annoying them, knowing that the Squire's partiality for Penna would not allow him to venture beyond certain bounds, even in this direction.

Penna's solace was his daughter. She had now reached her eighteenth year, and with the well-developed form of a woman, she united the simplicity of a child. Selina, as she was named, was in many respects beautiful. Her features were regular, and had they been lighted up with more mental fire, they would have been beautiful ; but the constant repose, the want of animation, left her face merely a pretty one. Her skin was beautifully white, and transparent to the blue veins which traced their ways beneath it, to the verge of that delicacy which indicates disease ; but it did not pass that verge. Selina was full of health, as her well-moulded form at once showed, and her clear blue eye distinctly told. At times there was a lovely tint upon the cheek—not the hectic of consumptive beauty,—but a pure rosy dye, suffused by the healthy life stream, when it flowed the fastest.

The village gossips, who were always busy with their neighbours, said strange things of this girl. Indeed, it was commonly reported that the real child of the Pennas was a remarkably plain child, in every respect a different being from Selina. The striking difference between the infant and the woman was variously explained by the knowing ones. Two stories were, however, current for miles around the country. One was, that Selina's mother was constantly seen gathering dew in the morning, with which to wash her child, and that the fairies on the Towens had, in pure malice, aided her in giving a temporary beauty to the girl, that it might lead to her betrayal into crime. Why this malice, was never clearly made out.

The other story was, that Honour Penna constantly bathed the child in a certain pool, amidst the arched rocks of Perran, which was a favourite resort of the mermaids ; that on one occasion the child, as if in a paroxysm of joy, leapt from her arms into the water, and disappeared.   The mother, as may well be supposed, suffered a momentary agony of terror ; but presently the babe swam up to the surface of the water, its little face more bright and beautiful than it had ever been before.   Great was the mother's joy, and also—as the gossips say—great her surprise at the sudden change in the appearance of her offspring.   The mother knew no difference in the child whom she pressed lovingly to her bosom, but all the aged crones in the parish declared it to be a change-ling.   This tale lived its day ; but, as the girl grew on to woman-hood, and showed none of the special qualifications belonging either to fairies or mermaids, it was almost forgotten.   The un-complaining father had solace for all his sufferings in wandering over the beautiful sands with his daughter.   Whether it was when the summer seas fell in musical undulations on the shore, or when, stirred by the winter tempests, the great Atlantic waves came up in grandeur, and lashed the resisting sands in giant rage, those two enjoyed the solitude.   Hour after hour, from the setting sun time, until the clear cold moon flooded the ocean with her smiles of light, would the father and child walk these sands.   They seemed never to weary of them and the ocean.

Almost every morning, throughout the milder seasons, Selina was in the habit of bathing, and wild tales were told of the frantic joy with which she would play with the breaking billows.   Some-times floating over, and almost dancing on the crests of the waves, at other times rushing under them, and allowing the breaking waters to beat her to the sands, as though they were loving arms, endeav-ouring to encircle her form.   Certain it is, that Selina greatly enjoyed her bath, but all the rest must be regarded as the creations of the imagination.   The most eager to give a construction unfav-ourable to the simple mortality of the maiden was, however, com-pelled to acknowledge that there was no evidence in her general con-duct to support their surmises. Selina, as an only child, fared the fate of others who are unfortunately so placed, and was, as the phrase is, spoiled.   She certainly was allowed to follow her own inclinations without any check.   Still her inclinations were bounded to work-ing in the garden, and to leading her father to the sea-shore. Honour Penna, sometimes, it is true, did complain that Selina could not be trusted with the most ordinary domestic duty.   Be-yond this, there was one other cause of grief, that was, the increas-ing dislike which Selina exhibited towards entering a church.   The girl, notwithstanding the constant excuses of being sick, suffering from headache, having a pain in her side, and the like, was often taken, notwithstanding, by her mother to the church.   It is said that she always shuddered as she passed the church-stile, and again on stepping from the porch into the church itself. When once within the house of prayer she evinced no peculiar liking or disliking, observing respectfully all the rules during the performance of the church-service, and generally sleeping, or seeming to sleep, during the sermon. Selina Pennaluna had reached her eighteenth year; she was admired by many of the young men of the parish, but, as if surrounded by a spell, she appeared to keep them all at a distance from her. About this time, a nephew to the Squire, a young soldier,—who had been wounded in the wars,—came into Cornwall to heal his wounds, and recover health, which had suffered in a trying campaign.

This young man, Walter Trewoofe, was a rare specimen of manhood. Even now, shattered as he was by the combined influences of wounds, an unhealthy climate, and dissipation, he could not but be admired for fineness of form, dignity of carriage, and masculine beauty. It was, however, but too evident, that this young man was his own idol, and that he expected every one to bow down with him, and worship it. His uncle was proud of Walter, and although the old gentleman could not fail to see many faults, yet he regarded them as the follies of youth, and trusted to their correction with the increase of years and experience. Walter, who was really suffering severely, was ordered by his surgeon, at first, to take short walks on the sea-shore, and, as he gained strength, to bathe. He was usually driven in his uncle's pony-carriage to the edge of the sands. Then dismounting he would walk for a short time, and quickly wearing, return in his carriage to the luxuriant couches at the manor-house.

On some of those occasions Walter had observed the father and daughter taking their solitary ramble. He was struck with the quiet beauty of the girl, and seized an early opportunity of stopping Penna to make some general inquiry respecting the bold and beautiful coast. From time to time they thus met, and it would have been evident to any observer that Walter did not so soon weary of the sands as formerly, and that Selina was not displeased with the flattering things he said to her. Although the young soldier had hitherto led a wild life, it would appear as if for a considerable period the presence of goodness had repressed every tendency to evil in his ill-regulated heart. He continued, therefore, for some time playing with his own feelings and those of the childlike being who presented so much of romance, combined with the most homely tameness, of character. Selina, it is true, had never yet seen Walter except in the presence of her father, and it is questionable if she had ever for one moment had a warmer feeling than that of the mere pleasure—a silent pride—that a gentleman, at once so handsome, so refined, and the nephew of her father's master, should pay her any attention.   Evil eyes were watching with wicked earnestness the growth of passion, and designing hearts were beating quicker with a consciousness that they should eventually rejoice in the downfall of innocence.   Tom Chenalls hoped that he might achieve a triumph, if he could but once asperse the character of Selina.   He took his measures accordingly.   Having noticed the change in the general conduct of his master's nephew, he argued that this was due to the refining influence of a pure mind, acting on one more than ordinarily impressionable to either evil or good.

Walter rapidly recovered health, and with renewed strength the manly energy of his character began to develop itself.   He delighted in horse-exercise, and Chenalls had always the best horse on the farms at his disposal.   He was a good shot, and Chenalls was his guide to the best shooting-grounds.   He sometimes fished, and Chenalls knew exactly where the choicest trout and the richest salmon were to be found.   In fact, Chenalls entered so fully into the tastes of the young man, that Walter found him absolutely necessary to him to secure the enjoyments of a country life.

Having established this close intimacy, Chenalls never lost an opportunity of talking with Walter respecting Selina Penna.   He soon satisfied himself that Walter, like most other young men who had led a dissipated life, had but a very low estimate of women generally.   Acting upon this, he at first insinuated that Selina's innocence was but a mask, and at length he boldly assured Walter that the cottage girl was to be won by him with a few words, and that then he might put her aside at any time as a prize to some low-born peasant.   Chenalls never failed to impress on Walter the necessity of keeping his uncle in the most perfect darkness, and of blinding the eyes of Selina's parents.   Penna was,—so thought Chenalls,—easily managed, but there was more to be feared from the wife.   Walter, however, with much artifice, having introduced himself to Honour Penna, employed the magic of that flattery, which, being properly applied, seldom fails to work its way to the heart of a weak-minded woman.   He became an especial favourite with Honour, and the blinded mother was ever pleased at the attention bestowed with so little assumption,—as she thought,—of pride, on her daughter, by one so much above them.   Walter eventually succeeded in separating occasionally, though not often, Penna and his daughter.   The witching whispers of unholy love were poured into the trusting ear. Guileless herself, this child-woman suspected no guile in others, least of all in one whom she had been taught to look upon as a superior being to herself. Amongst the villagers, the constant attention of Walter Trewoofe was the subject of gossip, and many an old proverb was quoted by the elder women, ill-naturedly, and implying that evil must come of this intimacy. Tom Chenalls was now employed by Walter to contrive some means by which he could remove Penna for a period from home. He was not long in doing this. He lent every power of his wicked nature to aid the evil designs of the young soldier, and thus he brought about that separation of father and child which ended in her ruin.

Near the Land's End the squire possessed some farms, and one of them was reported to be in such a state of extreme neglect, through the drunkenness and consequent idleness of the tenant, that Chenalls soon obtained permission to take the farm from this occupier, which he did in the most unscrupulous disregard for law or right. It was then suggested that the only plan by which a desirable occupier could be found, would be to get the farm and farm-buildings into good condition, and that Penna, of all men, would be the man to bring this quickly about. The squire was pleased with the plan. Penna was sent for by him, and was proud of the confidence which his master reposed in him. There was some sorrow on his leaving home. He subsequently said that he had had many warnings not to go, but he felt that he dared not disoblige a master who had trusted him so far—so he went.

Walter needed not any urging on the part of Chenalls, though he was always ready to apply the spur when there was the least evidence of the sense of right asserting itself in the young man's bosom. Week after week passed on. Walter had rendered himself a necessity to Selina. Without her admirer the world was cold and colourless. With him all was sunshine and glowing tints.

Three months passed thus away, and during that period it had only been possible for Penna to visit his home twice. The father felt that something like a spirit of evil stood between him and his daughter. There was no outward evidence of any change, but there was an inward sense—undefined, yet deeply felt—like an overpowering fear—that some wrong had been done. On parting, Penna silently but earnestly prayed that the deep dread might be removed from his mind. There was an aged fisherman, who resided in a small cottage built on the sands, who possessed all the superstitions of his class. This old man had formed a father's liking for the simple-hearted maiden, and he had persuaded

L

himself that there really was some foundation for the tales which the gossips told.   To the fisherman, Walter Trewoofe was an evil genius.   He declared that no good ever came to him, if he met Walter when he was about to go to sea.   With this feeling he curiously watched the young man and maiden, and he, in after days, stated his conviction that he had seen "merry maidens" rising from the depth of the waters, and floating under the billows, to watch Selina and her lover.   He has also been heard to say, that on more than one occasion Walter himself had been terrified by sights and sounds.   Certain, however, it is, these were insufficient, and the might of evil passions were more powerful than any of the protecting influences of the unseen world.

Another three months had gone by, and Walter Trewoofe had disappeared from Perranzabuloe.   He had launched into the gay world of the metropolis, and rarely, if ever, dreamed of the deep sorrow which was weighing down the heart he had betrayed. Penna returned home—his task was done—and Chenalls had no reason for keeping him any longer from his wife and daughter. Clouds gathered slowly but unremittingly around him.   His daughter retired into herself, no longer as of old reposing her whole soul on her father's heart.   His wife was somewhat changed too—she had some secret in her heart which she feared to tell. The home he had left was not the home to which he had returned. It soon became evident that some shock had shaken the delicate frame of his daughter.   She pined rapidly ; and Penna was awakened to a knowledge of the cause by the rude rejoicing of Chenalls, who declared "that all people who kept themselves so much above other people were sure to be pulled down."   On one occasion he so far tempted Penna with sneers, at his having hoped to secure the young squire for a son-in-law, that the long-enduring man broke forth and administered a severe blow upon his tormentor.   This was duly reported to the squire, and added thereto was a magnified story of a trap which had been set by the Pennas to catch young Walter ; it was represented that even now they intended to press their claims, on account of grievous wrongs upon them, whereas it could be proved that Walter was guiltless—that he was indeed the innocent victim of designing people, who thought to make money out of their assumed misfortune.   The squire made his inquiries, and there were not a few who eagerly seized the opportunity to gain the friendship of Chenalls by representing this family to have been hypocrites of the deepest dye ; and the poor girl especially was now loaded with a weight of iniquities of which she had no knowledge.   All this ended in the dismissal of Penna from the Squire's service, and in his being deprived of the cottage in which he had taken so much pride. Although thrown out upon the world a disgraced man, Penna faced his difficulties manfully. He cast off, as it were, the primitive simplicity of his character, and evidently worked with a firm resolve to beat down his sorrows. He was too good a workman to remain long unemployed; and although his new home was not his happy home as of old, there was no repining heard from his lips. Weaker and weaker grew Selina, and it soon became evident to all, that if she came from a spirit-world, to a spirit-world she must soon return. Grief filled the hearts of her parents—it prostrated her mother, but the effects of severe labour, and the efforts of a settled mind, appeared to tranquillise the breast of her father. Time passed on, the wounds of the soul grew deeper, and there lay, on a low bed, from which she had not strength to move, the fragile form of youth with the countenance of age. The body was almost powerless, but there beamed from the eye the evidences of a spirit getting free from the chains of clay.

The dying girl was sensible of the presence of creations other than mortal, and with these she appeared to hold converse, and to derive solace from the communion. Penna and his wife alternately watched through the night hours by the side of their loved child, and anxiously did they mark the moment when the tide turned, in the full belief that she would be taken from them when the waters of the ocean began to recede from the shore. Thus days passed on, and eventually the sunlight of a summer morning shone in through the small window of this humble cottage,—on a dead mother—and a living babe.

The dead was buried in the churchyard on the sands, and the living went on their ways, some rejoicingly and some in sorrow.

Once more Walter Trewoofe appeared in Perran-on-the-sands. Penna would have sacrificed him to his hatred; he emphatically protested that he had lived only to do so; but the good priest of the Oratory contrived to lay the devil who had possession, and to convince Penna that the Lord would, in His own good time, and in His own way, avenge the bitter wrong. Tom Chenalls had his hour of triumph; but from the day on which Selina died everything went wrong. The crops failed, the cattle died, hay-stacks and corn-ricks caught fire, cows slipped their calves, horses fell lame, or stumbled and broke their knees,—a succession of evils steadily pursued him. Trials find but a short resting-place with the good; they may be bowed to the earth with the weight of a sudden sorrow, but they look to heaven, and their elasticity is restored. The evil-minded are crushed at once, and grovel on the ground in irremediable misery. That Chenalls fled to drink in his troubles appeared but the natural result to a man of his character. This unfitted him for his duties, and he was eventually dismissed from his situation. Notwithstanding that the Squire refused to listen to the appeals in favour of Chenalls, which were urged upon him by Walter, and that indeed he forbade his nephew to countenance "the scoundrel" in any way, Walter still continued his friend. By his means Tom Chenalls secured a small cottage on the cliff, and around it a little cultivated ground, the produce of which was his only visible means of support. That lonely cottage was the scene, however, of drunken carousals, and there the vicious young men, and the no less vicious young women, of the district, went after nightfall, and kept "high carnival" of sin. Walter Trewoofe came frequently amongst them; and as his purse usually defrayed the costs of a debauch, he was regarded by all with especial favour.

One midnight, Walter, who had been dancing and drinking for some hours, left the cottage wearied with his excesses, and although not drunk, he was much excited with wine. His pathway lay along the edge of the cliffs, amidst bushes of furze and heath, and through several irregular, zigzag ways. There were lateral paths striking off from one side of the main path, and leading down to the sea-shore. Although it was moonlight, without being actually aware of the error, Walter wandered into one of those; and before he was awake to his mistake, he found himself on the sands. He cursed his stupidity, and, uttering a blasphemous oath, he turned to retrace his steps.

The most exquisite music which ever flowed from human lips fell on his ear; he paused to listen, and collecting his unbalanced thoughts, he discovered that it was the voice of a woman singing a melancholy dirge :—

> " The stars are beautiful, when bright
>   They are mirror'd in the sea ;
>   But they are pale beside that light
>   Which was so beautiful to me.
>   My angel child, my earth-born girl,
>   From all your kindred riven,
>   By the base deeds of a selfish churl,
>   And to a sand-grave driven !
>   How shall I win thee back to ocean?
>   How canst thou quit thy grave,
>   To share again the sweet emotion
>   Of gliding through the wave ?"

Walter, led by the melancholy song, advanced slowly along the sands. He discovered that the sweet, soft sounds proceeded from the other side of a mass of rocks, which project far out over the sands, and that now, at low-water, there was no difficulty in walking around it. Without hesitation he did so, and he beheld, sitting at the mouth of a cavern, one of the most beautiful women he had ever beheld. She continued her song, looking upwards to the stars, not appearing to notice the intrusion of a stranger. Walter stopped, and gazed on the lovely image before him with admiration and wonder, mingled with something of terror. He dared not speak, but fixed, as if by magic, he stood gazing on. After a few minutes, the maiden, suddenly perceiving that a man was near her, uttered a piercing shriek, and made as if to fly into the cavern. Walter sprang forward and seized her by the arm, exclaiming, " Not yet, my pretty maiden, not yet."

She stood still in the position of flight, with one arm behind her, grasped by Walter, and turning round her head, her dark eyes beamed with unnatural lustre upon him. Impressionable he had ever been, but never had he experienced anything so entrancing, and at the same time so painful, as that gaze. It was Selina's face looking lovingly upon him, but it seemed to possess some new power—a might of mind from which he felt it was impossible for him to escape. Walter slackened his hold, and slowly allowed the arm to fall from his hand. The maiden turned fully round upon him. " Go ! " she said. He could not move. " Go, man ! " she repeated. He was powerless.

> " Go to the grave where the sinless one sleepeth !
> Bring her cold corse where her guarding one weepeth ;
> Look on her, love her again, ay ! betray her,
> And wreath with false smiles the pale face of her slayer !
> Go, go ! now, and feel the full force of my sorrow !
> For the glut of my vengeance there cometh a morrow."

Walter was statue-like, and he awoke from this trance-like state only when the waves washed his feet, and he became aware that even now it was only by wading through the waters that he could return around the point of rocks. He was alone. He called ; no one answered. He sought wildly, as far as he now dared, amidst the rocks, but the lovely woman was nowhere to be discovered.

There was no real danger on such a night as this ; therefore Walter walked fearlessly through the gentle waves, and recovered the pathway up from the sands. More than once he thought he heard a rejoicing laugh, which was echoed in the rocks, but no one was to be seen. Walter reached his home and bed, but he found no sleep; and in the morning he arose with a sense of wretchedness which was entirely new to him. He feared to make any one of his rough companions a confidant, although he felt this would have relieved his heart. He therefore nursed the wound which he now felt, until a bitter remorse clouded his existence. After some days, he was impelled to visit the grave of the lost one, and in the fulness of the most selfish sorrow, he sat on the sands and shed tears. The priest of the Oratory observed him, and knowing Walter Trewoofe, hesitated not to inquire into his cause of sorrow. His heart was opened to the holy man, and the strange tale was told—the only result being, that the priest felt satisfied it was but a vivid dream, which had resulted from a brain over-excited by drink. He, however, counselled the young man, giving him some religious instruction, and dismissed him with his blessing. There was relief in this. For some days Walter did not venture to visit his old haunt, the cottage of Chenalls. Since he could not be lost to his companions without greatly curtailing their vicious enjoyments, he was hunted up by Chenalls, and again enticed within the circle. His absence was explained on the plea of illness. Walter was, however, an altered man; there was not the same boisterous hilarity as formerly. He no longer abandoned himself without restraint to the enjoyments of the time. If he ever, led on by his thoughtless and rough-natured friends, assumed for a moment his usual mirth, it was checked by some invisible power. On such occasions he would turn deadly pale, look anxiously around, and fall back, as if ready to faint, on the nearest seat. Under these influences, he lost health. His uncle, who was really attached to his nephew, although he regretted his dissolute conduct, became now seriously alarmed. Physicians were consulted in vain; the young man pined, and the old gossips came to the conclusion that Walter Trewoofe was ill-wished, and there was a general feeling that Penna or his wife was at the bottom of it. Walter, living really on one idea, and that one the beautiful face which was, and yet was not, that of Selina, resolved again to explore the spot on which he had met this strange being, of whom nothing could be learned by any of the covert inquiries he made. He lingered long ere he could resolve on the task; but wearied, worn by the oppression of one undefined idea, in which an intensity of love was mixed with a shuddering fear, he at last gathered sufficient courage to seize an opportunity for again going to the cavern. On this occasion, there being no moon, the night was dark, but the stars shone brightly from a sky, cloudless, save a dark mist which hung heavily over the western horizon. Every spot of ground being familiar to him, who, boy and man, had traced it over many times, the partial darkness presented no difficulty. Walter had scarcely reached the level sands, which were left hard by the retiring tide, than he heard again the same magical voice as before. But now the song was a joyous one, the burthen of it being—

> " Join all hands—
>   Might and main,
> Weave the sands,
>   Form a chain,
> He, my lover,
>   Comes again ! "

He could not entirely dissuade himself but that he heard this repeated by many voices ; but he put the thought aside, referring it, as well he might, to the numerous echoes from the cavernous openings in the cliffs.

He reached the eastern side of the dark mass of rocks, from the point of which the tide was slowly subsiding. The song had ceased, and a low moaning sound—the soughing of the wind—passed along the shore. Walter trembled with fear, and was on the point of returning, when a most flute-like murmur rose from the other side of the rocky barrier, which was presently moulded into words :—

> " From your couch of glistering pearl,
>   Slowly, softly, come away ;
> Our sweet earth-child, lovely girl,
>   Died this day,—died this day."

Memory told Walter that truly was it the anniversary of Selina Pennaluna's death, and to him every gentle wave falling on the shore sang, or murmured—

> " Died this day,—died this day."

The sand was left dry around the point of the rocks, and Walter, impelled by a power which he could not control, walked onward. The moment he appeared on the western side of the rock, a wild laugh burst into the air, as if from the deep cavern before him, at the entrance of which sat the same beautiful being whom he had formerly met. There was now an expression of rare joy on her face, her eyes glistened with delight, and she extended her arms, as if to welcome him.

" Was it ever your wont to move so slowly towards your loved one ? "

Walter heard it was Selina's voice.   He saw it was Selina's features ; but he was conscious it was not Selina's form.

" Come, sit beside me, Walter, and let us talk of love."   He sat down without a word, and looked into the maiden's face with a vacant expression of fondness.   Presently she placed her hand upon his heart ; a shudder passed through his frame ; but having passed, he felt no more pain, but a rare intensity of delight.   The maiden wreathed her arm around his neck, drew Walter towards her, and then he remembered how often he had acted thus towards Selina.   She bent over him and looked into his eyes.   In his mind's mirror he saw himself looking thus into the eyes of his be-trayed one.

" You loved her once ? " said the maiden.

" I did indeed," answered Walter, with a sigh.

" As you loved her, so I love you," said the maiden, with a smile which shot like a poisoned dart through Walter's heart. She lifted the young man's head lovingly between her hands, and bending over him, pressed her lips upon and kissed his forehead, Walter curiously felt that although he was the kissed, yet that he was the kisser.

" Kisses," she said, " are as true at sea as they are false on land. You men kiss the earth-born maidens to betray them.   The kiss of a sea-child is the seal of constancy.   You are mine till death."

" Death ! " almost shrieked Walter.

A full consciousness of his situation now broke upon Walter. He had heard the tales of the gossips respecting the mermaid origin of Selina ; but he had laughed at them as an idle fancy. He now felt they were true.   For hours Walter was compelled to sit by the side of his beautiful tormentor, every word of assumed love and rapture being a torture of the most exquisite kind to him. He could not escape from the arms which were wound around him. He saw the tide rising rapidly.   He heard the deep voice of the winds coming over the sea from the far west.   He saw that which appeared at first as a dark mist, shape itself into a dense black mass of cloud, and rise rapidly over the star-bedecked space above him.   He saw by the brilliant edge of light which occasionally fringed the clouds that they were deeply charged with thunder. There was something sublime in the steady motion of the storm ; and now the roll of the waves, which had been disturbed in the Atlantic, reached our shores, and the breakers fell thunderingly within a few feet of Walter and his companion.   Paroxysms of terror shook him, and with each convulsion he felt himself grasped with still more ardour, and pressed so closely to the maiden's bosom, that he heard her heart dancing of joy.

At length his terrors gave birth to words, and he implored her to let him go.

"The kiss of the sea-child is the seal of constancy." Walter vehemently implored forgiveness. He confessed his deep iniquity. He promised a life of penitence.

"Give me back the dead," said the maiden bitterly, and she planted another kiss, which seemed to pierce his brain by its coldness, upon his forehead.

The waves rolled around the rock on which they sat; they washed their seat. Walter was still in the female's grasp, and she lifted him to a higher ledge. The storm approached. Lightnings struck down from the heavens into the sands, and thunders roared along the iron cliffs. The mighty waves grew yet more rash, and washed up to this strange pair, who now sat on the highest pinnacle of the pile of rocks. Walter's terrors nearly overcame him; but he was roused by a liquid stream of fire, which positively hissed by him, followed immediately by a crash of thunder, which shook the solid earth. Tom Chenall's cottage on the cliff burst into a blaze, and Walter saw, from his place amidst the raging waters, a crowd of male and female roisterers rush terrified out upon the heath, to be driven back by the pelting storm. The climax of horrors appeared to surround Walter. He longed to end it in death, but he could not die. His senses were quickened. He saw his wicked companion and evil adviser struck to the ground, a blasted heap of ashes, by a lightning stroke, and at the same moment he and his companion were borne off the rock on the top of a mountainous wave, on which he floated; the woman holding him by the hair of his head, and singing in a rejoicing voice, which was like a silver bell heard amidst the deep base bellowings of the storm—

> " Come away, come away,
>   O'er the waters wild !
>   Our earth-born child
> Died this day, died this day.

> " Come away, come away !
>   The tempest loud
>   Weaves the shroud
> For him who did betray.

> " Come away, come away !
>   Beneath the wave
>   Lieth the grave
> Of him we slay, him we slay.

" Come away, come away !
        He shall not rest
        In earth's own breast
    For many a day, many a day.

" Come away, come away !
        By billows tost
        From coast to coast,
        Like deserted boat
        His corse shall float
    Around the bay, around the bay."

Myriads of voices on that wretched night were heard amidst the roar of the storm. The waves were seen covered with a multitudinous host, who were tossing from one to the other the dying Walter Trewoofe, whose false heart thus endured the vengeance of the mermaid, who had, in the fondness of her soul, made the innocent child of humble parents the child of her adoption. Appendix M.

THE ROCKS.

" Among these rocks and stones, methinks I see
More than the heedless impress that belongs
To lonely nature's casual work : they bear
A semblance strange of power intelligent,
And of design not wholly worn away."
    —*The Excursion.*—WORDSWORTH.

ROMANCES OF THE ROCKS.

CROMLECH AND DRUID STONES.

" Surely there is a hidden power that reigns
'Mid the lone majesty of untamed nature,
Controlling sober reason."
—*Caractacus.*—WILLIAM MASON.

IT is a common belief amongst the peasantry over every part of Cornwall, that no human power can remove any of those stones which have been rendered sacred to them by traditionary romance. Many a time have I been told that certain stones had been removed by day, but that they always returned by night to their original positions, and that the parties who had dared to tamper with those sacred stones were punished in some way. When the rash commander of a revenue cutter landed with a party of his men and overturned the Logan Rock, to prove the folly of the prevalent superstition, he did but little service in dispelling an old belief, but proved himself to be a fool for his pains.

I could desire, for the preservation of many of our Celtic remains, that we could impress the educated classes with a similar reverence for the few relics which are left to us of an ancient and a peculiar people, of whose history we know so little, and from whose remains we might, by careful study, learn so much. Those poised stones and perforated rocks must be of high antiquity, for we find the Anglo-Saxons making laws to prevent the British people from pursuing their old pagan practices.*

The geologist, looking upon the Logan stones and other curiously-formed rock masses, dismisses at once from his mind the idea of their having been formed by the hand of man, and hastily sets aside the tradition that the Druid ever employed them, or that the old Celt ever regarded them with reverence. There

---

* " Perforated stones must once have been common in England, and probably in Scotland also, as the Anglo-Saxon laws repeatedly denounce similar superstitious practices."—*The Archæology and Prehistoric Annals of Scotland*, p. 97. DANIEL WILSON.

cannot be a doubt but that many huge masses of granite are, by atmospheric causes, now slowly passing into the condition required for the formation of a Logan rock. It is *possible* that in some cases the "weathering" may have gone on so uniformly around the stone, as to poise it so exactly that the thrust of a child will shake a mass many tons in weight.

The result, however, of my own observations, made with much curiosity and considerable care, has been to convince me, that in by far the greatest number of instances the disintegration, though general around the line of a "bed-way" or horizontal joint, has gone on rapidly on the side exposed to the beat of the weather, while the opposite extremity has been but slightly worn ; consequently, the stones have a tendency to be depressed on the sheltered side. With a little labour man could correct this natural defect, and with a little skill make a poised stone. We have incontrovertible evidence that certain poised stones have been regarded, through long periods of time, as of a sacred character. Whether these stones were used by the Druids, or merely that the ignorant people supposed them to have some peculiar virtue, I care not. The earliest inhabitants of Cornwall, probably Celts,* were possessed with some idea that these stones were connected with the mysteries of existence ; and from father to son, for centuries, notwithstanding the introduction of Christianity, these stones have maintained their *sacred character.* Therefore, may we not infer that the leaders of the people availed themselves of this feeling ; and finding many rocks of a gigantic size, upon which nature had begun the work, they completed them, and used the mighty moving masses to impress with terror—the principle by which they ruled—the untaught, but poetically constituted, minds of the people. Dr Borlase has been laughed at for finding rock-basins, the works of the Druids, in every granitic mass. At the same time, those who laugh have failed to examine those rock-masses with unprejudiced care, and hence they have erred as wildly as did the Cornish antiquary, but in a contrary direction. Hundreds of depressions are being formed by the winds and rains upon the faces of the granite rocks. With these no Druid ever perplexed himself or his people. But there are numerous hollows to be found in large flat rocks which have unmistakably been formed, if not entirely, partly by the hands of man. The Sacrificing Rock, or Carn Brea, is a remarkable example. The larger

* "A Celtic race, however, continued to occupy the primeval districts of Cornwall, and preserved, almost to our own day, a distinct dialect of the Celtic tongue."—*Prehistoric Annals of Scotland*, p. 195. DANIEL WILSON. *See* Appendix N, *The Celts.*

hollows on the Men-rock, in Constantine, several basins in the Logan Rock group, and at Carn Boscawen, may be referred to as other examples. With these remarks, I proceed to notice a few of the most remarkable rock-masses with which tradition has associated some tale.

THE LOGAN OR LOGING ROCK.*

MODRED, in Mason's "Caractacus," addressing Vellinus and Elidurus, says—

> "Thither, youths,
> Turn your astonish'd eyes ; behold yon huge
> And unhewn sphere of living adamant,
> Which, poised by magic, rests its central weight
> On yonder pointed rock : firm as it seems,
> Such is the strange and virtuous property,
> It moves obsequious to the gentlest touch
> Of him whose breath is pure ; but to a traitor,
> Though even a giant's prowess nerved his arm,
> It stands as fixed as Snowdon."

This faithfully preserves the traditionary idea of the purposes to which this in every way remarkable rock was devoted.

Up to the time when Lieutenant Goldsmith, on the 8th of April 1824, slid the rock off from its support, to prove the falsehood of Dr Borlase's statement, that " it is morally impossible that any lever, or, indeed, force, however applied in a mechanical way, can remove it from its present position," the Logan Rock was believed to cure children, who were rocked upon it at certain seasons, of several diseases ; but the charm is broken, although the rock is restored.†

---

* " It may be observed that I have always used the words Loging Rock for the celebrated stone at Trereen Dinas. Much learned research seems to have been idly expended on the supposed name, ' Logan Rock.' *To log* is a verb in general use throughout Cornwall for vibrating or rolling like a drunken man ; and *an* is frequently heard in provincial pronunciation for *ing*, characteristic of the modern present participle. The Loging Rock is, therefore, strictly descriptive of its peculiar motion."—*Davies Gilbert.*

† When this great natural curiosity was, as it was thought, destroyed, the public wrath was excited, and appeased only by the conciliatory spirit manifested by Mr Davies Gilbert, who persuaded the Lords of the Admiralty to lend Lieutenant Goldsmith the required apparatus for replacing it. Mr D. Gilbert found the money ; and after making the necessary arrangements, on the 2d of November 1824, Goldsmith "had the glory of replacing this immense rock in its natural position." The glory of Goldsmith and of Shrubsall, who overturned another large Logan Rock, is certainly one not to be desired.

MINCAMBER, MAIN-AMBER, OR AMBROSE'S STONE.

A MIGHTY Logan Stone was poised and blessed by Ambrose Merlin, not far from Penzance. " So great," says Drayton, in his " Polyalbion," " that many men's united strength cannot remove it, yet with one finger you may wag it."

Merlin proclaimed that this stone should stand until England had no king ; and Scawen tells us—

" Here, too, we may add what wrong another sort of strangers have done to us, especially in the civil wars, and in particular by the destroying of Mincamber, a famous monument, being a rock of infinite weight, which, as a burden, was laid upon other great stones, and yet so equally thereon poised up by nature only, that a little child could instantly move it, but no one man, or many, remove it. This natural monument all travellers that came that way desired to behold ; but in the time of Oliver's usurpation, when all monumental things became despicable, one Shrubsall, one of Oliver's heroes, then Governor of Pendennes, by labour and much ado, caused to be undermined and thrown down, to the great grief of the country, but to his own great glory, as he thought ; doing it, as he said, with a small cane in his hand. I myself have heard him to boast of this act, being a prisoner under him." *

So was Merlin's prophecy fulfilled.

ZENNOR COITS.

C. TAYLOR STEPHENS, lately deceased, who was for some time the rural postman of Zennor, sought, in his poem, " The Chief of Barat-Anac," to embody in a story some descriptions of the Zennor coits and other rock curiosities.

I employed this man for some weeks to gather up for me all that remained of legendary lore in Zennor and Morva. He did his work well ; and from his knowledge of the people, he learned more from them than any other man could have done. The results of his labours are scattered through these volumes.

C. Taylor Stephens wrote me on the subject of the cromlechs as follows :—

---

* " *Ambers* or *Main Ambers*, which signify anointed or consecrated stones."—*C. S Gilbert, Historical Survey.* See also Scawen's " Dissertation on the Cornish Language," Stukeley's " Stonehenge," and Jabez Allies's " Worcestershire." Appendix O, *Ambrosiæ Petræ.*

Superstitious Belief respecting the Quoits.

" I was in the neighbourhood of Zennor in 1859, and by accident came across the Zennor cromlech, and was struck with the mode of its construction (not having heard of its existence before), and thinking it bore some resemblance to the Druidical altars I had read of, I inquired of a group of persons who were gathered round the village smithery, whether any one could tell me anything respecting the heap of stones on the top of the hill. Several were in total ignorance of their existence. One said, ' Tes caal'd the gient's kite ; thas all I knaw.' At last, one more thoughtful, and one who, I found out, was considered the wiseacre and oracle of the village, looked up and gave me this important piece of information, — ' Them ere rocks were put there afore you nor me was boern or thoft ov ; but who don it es a puzler to everybody in *Sunnur* (Zennor). I de bleve theze put up theer wen thes ere wurld wus maade ; but wether they wus or no don't very much mattur by hal akounts. Thes I'd knaw, that nobody caant take car em awa ; if anybody was too, they'd be brot there agin. Hees an ef they wus tuk'd awa wone nite, theys shur to be hal rite up top o' th hil fust thing in morenin. But I caant tel ee s' much as Passen can ; ef you 'd zea he, he 'd tel he hal about et.' "

In one of the notes received from the poet and postman he gives a curious instance of the many parts a man played in those remote districts but a few years since :—

" My venerable grandpapa was well known by all the old people, for he was not only a local preacher, but a charmer, a botanist, a veterinary surgeon, a secretary to a burial and sick benefit society, and, moreover, the blacksmith of the neighbourhood."

THE MÊN-AN-TOL.

NOT more than two miles from Penzance stands the celebrated cromlech of Lanyon—often pronounced Lanine. This, like all the other cromlechs, marks, no doubt, the resting-place of a British chieftain, many of whose followers repose within a short distance of this, the principal monument.

Beyond the village of Lanyon, on a " furzy down," stands the Mên-an-tol, or the " holed stone." For some purpose—it is in vain to speculate on it now—the bardic priesthood employed this stone, and probably the superstition which attaches to it may indicate its ancient uses.

If scrofulous children are passed *naked* through the Mên-an-tol three times, and then drawn on the grass three times *against the sun*, it is felt by the faithful that much has been done towards insuring a speedy cure. Even men and women who have been afflicted with spinal diseases, or who have suffered from scrofulous taint, have been drawn through this magic stone, which all declare still retains its ancient virtues.

If two brass pins are carefully laid across each other on the top edge of this stone, any question put to the rock will be answered, by the pins acquiring, through some unknown agency, a peculiar motion.

THE CRICK STONE IN MORVA.

I F any one suffering from a " crick in the back " can pass through this forked rock, on the borders of Zennor and Morva, without touching the stone, he is certain of being cured. This is but a substitute for the holed stone, which, it is admitted, has much more virtue than the forked stone.

In various parts of the county there are, amongst the granitic masses, rocks which have fallen across each other, leaving small openings, or there are holes, low and narrow, extending under a pile of rocks. In nearly every case of this kind, we find it is popularly stated, that any one suffering from rheumatism or lumbago would be cured if he crawled through the openings. In some cases, nine times are insisted on " to make the charm complete."

Mrs Bray, in her " Traditions of Devonshire," gives several examples of the prevalence of this superstition over the granitic district of Dartmoor.*

THE DANCING STONES, THE HURLERS, &c.

I N many parts of Cornwall we find, more or less perfect, circles of stones, which the learned ascribe to the Druids. Tradition, and the common people, who have faith in all that their fathers have taught them, tell us another tale. These stones are everlasting marks of the Divine displeasure, being maidens or men, who were changed into stone for some wicked profanation of the Sabbath-day. These monuments of impiety are scattered over the county ; they are to be found, indeed, to the extremity of *Old* Cornwall, many of those circles being upon Dartmoor. It is not necessary to name them all. Every purpose will be served if the tourist is directed to those which lie more directly in the route which is usually prescribed. In the parish of Burian are the " *Dawns Myin* " or *Mên*—the dancing stones—commonly called " The Merry Maidens ; " and near them are two granite pillars, named the " Pipers." One Sabbath evening some of the thoughtless maidens of the neighbouring village, instead of attending

* " Creeping under tolmens for the cure of diseases is still practised in Ireland, and also in the East, as is shown by Mrs Colonel Elwood in her Travels."—*Gentleman's Magazine*, July 1831.

vespers, strayed into the fields, and two evil spirits, assuming the guise of pipers, began to play some dance tunes. The young people yielded to the temptation ; and, forgetting the holy day, commenced dancing. The excitement increased with the exercise, and soon the music and the dance became extremely wild ; when, lo ! a flash of lightning from the clear sky transfixed them all, the tempters and the tempted, and there in stone they stand.

The celebrated circle of nineteen stones,—which is seen on the road to the Land's End,—known as the " Boscawen-ûn Circle," is another example. The " Nine Maids," or the " Virgin Sisters," in Stithians, and other " Nine Maids," or, as called in Cornish, Naw-whoors, in St Colomb-Major parish, should also be seen, in the hope of impressing the moral lesson they convey yet more strongly on the mind.*

The three circles, which are seen on the moors not far from the Cheesewring, in the parish of St Cleer, are also notable examples of the punishment of Sabbath-breaking. These are called the " Hurlers," and they preserve the position in which the several parties stood in the full excitement of the game of hurling, when, for the crime of profaning the Sabbath, they were changed into stone.†

* The following quotations are from Davies Gilbert. It must not be forgotten that this gentleman was President of the Royal Society, and *therefore* a sceptic in local traditionary story :—

"On the south-west part of the parish of Stithians, towards Gwendron, are still to be seen nine stones set perpendicularly erect in the earth, in a direct manner, about ten feet apart, called the Nine Maids, probably set up there in memory of nine religious sisters or nuns in that place before the fifth century ; not women turned into stone, as the English name implies, and as the country people thereabout will tell you."

"The Nine Maids—in Cornish, Naw-voz, *alias* the nine sisters—in Cornish, Naw-whoors—which very name informs us that they were sepulchral stones, erected in memory either of nine natural or spiritual sisters of some religious house, and not so many maids turned into stones for dancing on the Sabbath-day, as the country people will tell you. Those stones are set in order by a line, as is such another monument, also called the Nine Maids, in Gwendron, by the highway, about twenty-five feet distance from each other."

† " With respect to the stones called the 'Hurlers' being once men, I will say with Hals, ' Did but the ball which these Hurlers used when flesh and blood appear directly over them, immovably pendant in the air, one might be apt to credit some little of the tale ;' but as this is not the case, I must add my belief of their being erected by the Druids for some purpose or other—probably a court of justice ; long subsequent to which erection, however, they may have served as a goal for hurl-players."—*Topographical and Historical Sketches of the Boroughs of East and West Love, by Thomas Bond.*

May we not address Mr Bond, "O ye of little faith ?" A very small amount of which would have found the ball, fixed as a boulder of granite, not as it passed through the air, but as it rolled along the ground.

That an ancient priesthood, endeavouring to reach the minds of an ignorant people through their sensations, should endeavour to persuade the old Celtic population that

THE NINE MAIDS, OR VIRGIN SISTERS.

NINE " Moor Stones " are set up near the road in the parish of Gwendron, or Wendron, to which the above name is given. The perpendicular blocks of granite have evidently been placed with much labour in their present position. Tradition says they indicate the graves of nine sisters. Hals appears to think some nuns were buried here. From one person only I heard the old story of the stones having been metamorphosed maidens. Other groups of stone might be named, as Rosemedery, Tregaseal, Boskednan, Botallack, Tredinek, and Crowlas, in the west, to which the same story extends, and many others in the eastern parts of the county ; but it cannot be necessary.

THE TWELVE-O'CLOCK STONE.

NUMBERS of people would formerly visit a remarkable Logan stone, near Nancledrea, which had been, by supernatural power, impressed with some peculiar sense at midnight. Although it was quite impossible to move this stone during daylight, or indeed by human power at any other time, it would rock like a cradle exactly at midnight. Many a child has been cured of rickets by being placed naked at this hour on the twelve-o'clock stone. If, however, the child was " misbegotten," or, if it was the offspring of dissolute parents, the stone would not move, and consequently no cure was effected. On the Cuckoo Hill, eastward of Nancledrea, there stood, but a few years since, two piles of rock about eight feet apart, and these were united by a large flat-stone carefully placed upon them,—thus forming a doorway which was, as my informant told me, " large and high enough to drive a horse and cart through." It was formerly the custom to march in procession through this " doorway" in going to the twelve-o'clock stone.

The stone-mason has, however, been busy hereabout ; and every mass of granite, whether rendered notorious by the Giants or holy by the Druids, if found to be of the size required, has been removed.*

God's vengeance had fallen on the Sabbath-breaker, is not to be wondered at. Up to a very recent period, hurling matches usually came off on the Sunday.—See " Hurling," in the chapter on Cornish Customs.

* The following are a few of the interesting remains of old Cornwall which have entirely disappeared from this neighbourhood within a few years :—

Between St Ives and Zennor, on the lower road over Tregarthen Downs, stood a Logan

THE MEN-SCRYFA.

A T the entrance to Penzance rises, rather abruptly, a hill, crowned with a very remarkable earthwork. It is known as Castle Lesgudzhek, or, the " Castle of the Bloody Field," to this day.

Tradition, our only guide, tells us that this castle was one of the strong places of a British king, in the third or fourth century ; that a rival chieftain, from the eastern part of Danmonium, besieged him. The defence was long and desperate. The besiegers, wearying of the unsuccessful toil, retired at length to the plains of Gulval ; and that the besieged left his castle, and gave his enemies battle on the plain which extends from Penzance to Marazion. The " bloody field " remained in possession of the chieftain of Lesgudzhek, and the leader of the eastern men was killed near where he was buried. The *Men-Scryfa*, or inscribed stone, was raised over his grave,—its height, nine feet, being the exact height of the defeated warrior ?

RIALOBRAN CUNOVAL FIL

is engraven on the block ; thus handing to us the name of the unfortunate warrior, who was probably the son of the hero from whom Gulval draws its name ; and if so, may we not suppose that he was but endeavouring to recover the possessions which once belonged to his parent.

TABLE-MÊN.

THE SAXON KINGS' VISIT TO THE LAND'S END.

A T a short distance from Sennen church, and near the end of a cottage, is a block of granite, nearly eight feet long, and about three feet high. This rock is known as the Table-mên, or

---

rock. An old man, perhaps ninety years of age, told me he had often logged it, and that it would make a noise which could be heard for miles.

At Balnoon, between Nancledrea and Knill's Steeple, some miners came upon "two slabs of granite cemented together," which covered a walled grave three feet square—an ancient kistvean. In it they found an earthenware vessel containing some black earth, and a leaden spoon. The spoon was given to Mr Praed of Trevetha, and may possibly be in the possession of the present proprietor. The kistvean was utterly destroyed.

At Brunnion, not far from St Ives, in the garden attached to the house which is occupied by the Hoskings, is an arched doorway of carefully-worked granite. Tradition saith this doorway belonged to an ancient church, and that the present garden was the burial-ground. Close by, at Treverrack, is a field known as the " Chapel Field," in which the plough is constantly turning up stones which have been carefully chiselled.

In Bosprenis Croft there was a very large coit or cromlech. It is said to have been fifteen feet square, and not more than one foot thick in any part. This was broken in two parts some years since, and taken to Penzance to form the beds for two ovens.

Table-*main*, which appears to signify the stone-table. At Bosavern, in St Just, is a somewhat similar flat stone ; and the same story attaches to each.

It is to the effect that some Saxon kings used the stone as a dining-table. The number has been variously stated ; some traditions fixing on three kings, others on seven. Hals is far more explicit ; for, as he says, on the authority of the chronicle of Samuel Daniell, they were—

Ethelbert, 5th king of Kent ;
Cissa, 2d king of the South Saxons ;
Kingills, 6th king of the West Saxons ;
Sebert, 3d king of the East Saxons ;
Ethelfred, 7th king of the Northumbers ;
Penda, 5th king of the Mercians ;
Sigebert, 5th king of the East Angles,—who all flourished about the year 600.

At a point where the four parishes of Zennor, Morvah, Gulval, and Madron meet, is a flat stone with a cross cut on it. The Saxon kings are also said to have dined on this.

The only tradition which is known amongst the peasantry of Sennen is, that Prince Arthur and the kings who aided him against the Danes, in the great battle fought near Vellan-Drucher, dined on the Table-mên, after which they defeated the Danes.

MERLYN'S PROPHECIES.

PROPHECIES by Merlyn are tolerably prevalent in Cornwall. The character of these may be known by one or two examples—

" Aga syth tyer, war and meyne Merlyn
Ara neb syth Leskey Paul, Penzance hag Newlyn. "

This has been translated—

" There shall land on the stone of Merlyn,
Those who shall burn Paul, Penzance, and Newlyn. "

This prophecy is supposed to have been accomplished when the Spaniards, in the reign of Elizabeth, landed at Mousehole, a fishing village in the Mount's Bay. Near the pier at Mousehole is still a rock called " Merlyn Car," or " Merlyn's Rock," and not far from it another, called " the Spaniard."

THE LEVAN STONE.

This bisected mass of granite has been already noticed in connection with St Levan.

> " When, with panniers astride,
>   A pack-horse can ride
>   Through the Levan Stone,
>   The world will be done."

THE RAME HEAD AND THE DODMAN.

Merlyn is said to have pronounced the following prophecy, standing near St German's Grotto on the shores of Whitsand Bay :—

> " When the Rame Head and Dodman meet,
>   Man and woman will have cause to greet."

THE ARMED KNIGHT.

" A T low water there is to be seen, off the Land's End, towards the Scilly Island (probably so called from the abundance of eel or conger fishes caught there, which are called sillys, or lillis), for a mile or more, a dangerous strag of ragged rocks, amongst which the Atlantic Sea and the waves of St George's and the British Channel meeting, make a dreadful bellowing and rumbling noise at half-ebb and half-flood, which let seamen take notice of to avoid them.

" Of old, there was one of those rocks more notable than the rest, which tradition saith was ninety feet above the flux and reflux of the sea, with an iron spire at the top thereof, which was over-turned or thrown down in a violent storm, 1647, and the rock was broken in three pieces. This iron spire, as the additions to Camden's " Britannia " inform us, was thought to have been erected by the Romans, or set up as a trophy there by King Athelstan, when he first conquered the Scilly Islands (which was in those parts) ; but it is not very probable such a piece of iron, in this salt sea and air, without being consumed by rust, could endure so long a time. However, it is or was, certain I am it commonly was called in Cornish, An Marogeth Arvowed, *i.e.*, the Armed Knight ; for what reason I know not, except erected by or in memory of some armed knight ; as also Carne-an-peul, *i.e.*, the spile, spire, or javelin rock. Again, remember silly lilly, is in Cornish and Armoric language a conger fish or fishes, from whence Scilly Islands is probably denominated, as elsewhere noted." * Mr Blight says this rock is also called *Guela*, or *Guelaz*,—the " rock easily seen."

---

* Hals, in Gilbert's " History of Cornwall," vol. iii. p. 43.

THE IRISH LADY.

NEAR *Pedn-men-dw*, the " *Headland of Black Rock*," is a curiously-shaped rock, known as the *Irish Lady*. In days long ago some adventurous sailors from Ireland were shipwrecked at night on this rock, and every soul perished, save a lady, who was seen in the morning sitting on the top of the rock. The storm was still raging, and it was quite impossible to render this solitary sufferer any assistance. Days and nights passed away; the people watched the dying woman from the shore, but they could not reach her. At length they saw that her sufferings were at an end; and at last the dead body was washed into the sea. Often, when the winds and waves are high, the fishermen see a lady tranquilly sitting on this rock, *with a rose in her mouth;* to show, it may be presumed, her perfect indifference to the ragings of tempests.*

Sir Humphrey Davy wrote a poem on this tradition. The following is an extract from it :—

" Where yon dark cliff † o'ershadows the blue main,
Theora died amidst the stormy waves,
And on its feet the sea-dews wash'd her corpse,
And the wild breath of storms shook her black locks.
Young was Theora ; bluer was her eye
Than the bright azure of the moonlight night ;
Fair was her cheek, as is the ocean cloud
Red with the morning ray.

" Amidst the groves,
And greens, and nodding rocks that overhang
The gray Killarney pass'd her morning days,
Bright with the beams of joy.

---

* This kind of tradition is not uncommon. The following is a Welsh form of it :—

GWENNO'S STEEPLE.

Among the numerous irregular caves at the western end of Ogofau is one which has derived the name of Ffynnon Gwenno (the Well of Gwenno), from the following tradition, kindly given to us by Mr Johnes. The water which still occupies its lower part, was, in days of yore, reputed to possess medicinal qualities, which attracted numerous bathers from the surrounding districts. Among these a fair maid, named Gweullian, or, for brevity, Gwenno, was induced, on an unfortunate day, to explore the recesses of the cavern beyond a frowning rock, which had always been the prescribed limit to the progress of the bathers. She passed beneath it, and was no more seen. She had been seized by some superhuman power, as a warning to others not to invade those mysterious penetralia. And still, on stormy nights, the spirit of Gweullian is seen to hover over a lofty crag which rises near the entrance of the now deserted cave, and bears the name of Cloch ty Gwenno, or Gwenno's Steeple.—*Note on the Gogofau, or Ogofau Mine.* Memoirs of Geological Survey, vol. i. p. 482.

† A rock near the Land's End called the " Irish Lady."

" To solitude,
To nature, and to God, she gave her youth ;
Hence were her passions tuned to harmony.
Her azure eye oft glisten'd with the tear
Of sensibility, and her soft cheek
Glow'd with the blush of rapture.   Hence she loved
To wander 'midst the green wood silver'd o'er
By the bright moonbeam.   Hence she loved the rocks,
Crown'd with the nodding ivy, and the lake
Fair with the purple morning, and the sea
Expansive, mingling with the arched sky.

" Dark in the midnight cloud,
When the wild blast upon its pinions bore
The dying shrieks of Erin's injured sons,
She scaped the murderer's arm.*

"' The British bark
Bore her across the ocean.   From the west
The whirlwind rose, the fire-fraught clouds of heaven
Were mingled with the wave   The shatter'd bark
Sunk at thy feet, Bolerium, and the white surge
Closed on green Erin's daughter.
                    —PARIS'S *Life of Sir Humphrey Davy*, p. 38.

THE DEVIL'S DOORWAY.

IN the slate (Killas) formations behind Polperro is a good
example of a *fault*.   The geologist, in the pride of his knowledge, refers this to some movement of the solid mass—a rending
of the rocks, produced either by the action of some subterranean
force lifting the earth-crust, or by a depression of one division of
the rocks.   The gray-bearded wisdom of our grandfathers led
them to a conclusion widely different from this.

The mighty ruler of the realms of darkness, who is known to
have an especial fondness for rides at midnight, " to see how his
little ones thrive," ascending from his subterranean country, chose
this spot as his point of egress.

As he rose from below in his fiery car, drawn by a gigantic jet
black steed, the rocks gave way before him, and the rent at Polperro remains to this day to convince all unbelievers.   Not only
this, as his Satanic majesty burst through the slate rocks, his
horse, delighted with the airs of this upper world, reared in wild
triumph, and, planting again his hoof upon the ground, made these

---

* The Irish lady was shipwrecked at the Land's End about the time of the massacre
of the Irish Protestants by the Catholics, in the reign of Charles the First. So says Davy
—the tradition is very old.

islands shake as with an earthquake; and he left the deep impression of his burning foot behind. There, any unbeliever may see the hoof-shaped pool, unmistakable evidence of the wisdom of the days gone by.

PIPER'S HOLE, SCILLY.

O N the banks of Peninnis, in St Mary's, is Piper's Hole, which communicates, as tradition saith, with the island of Tresco, where another orifice known by the same name is seen. Going in at the orifice at Peninnis Banks in St Mary's, it is above man's height, and of as much space in its breadth, but grows lower and narrower farther in : a little beyond which entrance appear rocky basins, or reservoirs, continually running over with fresh water, descending as it distils from the sides of the rocky passage. By the fall of water heard further in, it is probable there may be rocky descents in the passage. The drippings from the sides have worn the passage, as far as it can be seen, into very various angular surfaces. Strange stories are related of this passage, of men going so far in that they never returned ; of dogs going quite through, and coming out at Tresco, with most of their hair off, and such like incredibles. But its retired situation, where lovers retreat to indulge their mutual passion, has made it almost as famous as the cave wherein Dido and Æneas met of old. Its water is exceeding good.*

THE DEVIL'S COITS, &c.

I N St Columb Major, not far from the ruins of what is generally considered to be a British fortification, Castele-an-Dinas, stands a tumulus known as the Devil's Coit. It is curious to find one tradition directly contradicting another. We are told, on the one hand, that—

The devil never came into Cornwall.

Because, when he crossed the Tamar, and made Torpoint for a brief space his resting-place, he could not but observe that everything, vegetable or animal, was put by the Cornish people into a pie.

He saw and heard of fishy pie, star-gazy pie, conger pie, and

---

* Heath's "Scilly Isles." These stories of Piper's Hole are still told, and many of the ignorant inhabitants regard it with superstitious dread. The Fugoe Hole, at the Land's End, has yet to be spoken of in the Witch stories. Several who have attempted to penetrate this hole have escaped only by great luck—"by the skin of their teeth," as the saying is.

indeed pies of all the fishes in the sea.   Of parsley pie, and herby pie, of lamy pie, and piggy pie, and pies without number.   Therefore, fearing they might take a fancy to a " devily pie," he took himself back again into Devonshire.

On the other hand we find, amidst the rocks of the shore and the hills, numerous devil's coits, plenty of devil's footsteps, with devil's bellows, devil's frying-pans, devil's ovens, and devil's caves in abundance.   Of course, on Dartmoor, since the devil remained in Devonshire, we might expect to find such evidences of his presence.   The devil's frying-pan at Mistor is well known, and nearly every granite Tor preserves some impression of this melancholy, wandering wicked one.

KING ARTHUR'S STONE.

IN the western part of Cornwall, all the marks of any peculiar kind found on the rocks are referred either to the giants or the devil.   In the eastern part of the county such markings are almost always attributed to Arthur.   Not far from the Devil's Coit in St Columb, on the edge of the Gossmoor, there is a large stone, upon which are deeply-impressed marks, which a little fancy may convert into the marks of four horse-shoes.   This is " King Arthur's Stone," and these marks were made by the horse upon which the British king rode when he resided at *Castle Denis*, and hunted on these moors.   King Arthur's beds, and chairs, and caves, are frequently to be met with.   The Giant's Coits,—and many traditions of these will be found in the section devoted to the giant romances—are probably monuments of the earliest types of rock mythology.   Those of Arthur belong to the period when the Britons were so far advanced in civilisation as to war under experienced rulers ; and those which are appropriated by the devil are evidently instances of the influence of priestcraft on the minds of an impressible people.*

---

* Another example of like stories in Wales may be interesting :—

"Five juvenile saints, on their pilgrimage to the celebrated shrine of St David, emaciated with hunger, and exhausted with fatigue, here reclined themselves to rest, and reposed their weary heads on this ponderous pillow ; their eyes were soon closed by the powerful hand of sleep, and they were no longer able to resist, by the force of prayer, the artifices of their foes.   The sky was suddenly overwhelmed with clouds—the thunder rolled—the lightning flashed, and the rain poured in torrents.   The storm increased in vehemence ; all nature became chilled with cold, and even Piety and Charity felt its effects.   The drops of rain were soon congealed into enormous hailstones, which, by the force of the wind, were driven with so much violence against the heads of the weary pilgrims as to affix them to their pillow, and the vestiges they left are still discernible. Being borne away in triumph by the malignant sorcerer who inhabits the hollows of

THE COCK-CROW STONE.

A ROCK of white marble (?) with many rock basins on its surface lies in Looe harbour, under Saunder's Lane, and is now
covered by every tide. This stone once stood on the top of an
elevated rock near it, and when in this position, whenever it heard
a cock crow in the neighbouring farmyard of Hay, it turned round
three times.

The topmost stone of that curious pile of rocks in the parish of
St Cleer known as the Cheesewring is gifted in like manner.
Even now the poultry-yards are very distant, but in ancient days
the cocks must have crowed most lustily, to have produced vibra-
tions on either the sensitive rock or the tympanum of man.

these hills, they were concealed in the innermost recesses of his cavern, where they are
destined to remain asleep, bound in the irrefragable chain of enchantment until that
happy period shall arrive when the diocese shall be blessed with a pious bishop, for when
that happens, no doubt Merlin himself, the enemy of malignant sorcerers, will be disenchanted, and he will come and restore to liberty the dormant saints, when they will
immediately engage in the patriotic work of reforming the Welsh."—*From the English
Works of the late Rev. Eleazor Williams,* quoted by **Warington W. Smyth, M.A.**
Memoirs of the Geological Survey, vol. i. p. 480.

LOST CITIES.

" Between Land's End and Scilly rocks
Sunk lies a town that ocean mocks.

.   .   .   .   .   .

Where breathes the man that would not weep
O'er such fine climes beneath the deep?"
Historical Records of Ancient Cornwall.
—THOMAS HOGG.

ROMANCES OF LOST CITIES.

LOST LANDS.

"And oh! how short are human schemes!
Here ended all our golden dreams."
—JONATHAN SWIFT.

THE notion of cities and extensive tracts of cultivated country being under the waters of the ocean and of lakes appears to have existed from all time. In the "Arabian Nights," we have constant references to lands under the sea; and in the traditionary stories of all Celtic people the same idea presents itself in some form or other. Mr Campbell appears to confound stories of mermaids with those traditions which have their origin in actual physical changes. They appear to me to have little relation to each other.*

In addition to the traditions given of large tracts of land which have been lost in the sea, I have given those which relate to cities, or towns, or churches which have been buried in the sands. These traditions are of the same general character.

This subject deserves a much more careful investigation than it has yet received. I hope simply to draw attention to the subject, and to show that those dim traditions point to some buried truth. They are like the buried lights which are supposed to indicate the resting-places of the dead.

THE TRADITION OF THE LYONESSE OR LETHOWSOW.

THOSE who may stand on the extreme point of the Land's End, and, looking over that space where the waters of the Atlantic mix with those of the British Channel, see in the far distance the Scilly Islands, will have to call upon their imagina-

* See West Highland Tales, by J. F. Campbell. Vol. iii. p. 410

tion to conceive that these broad waters roll over a country which has existed within historic time.

A region of extreme fertility, we are told, once united the Scilly Islands with Western Cornwall. A people, known as the Silures, inhabited this tract,—which has been called the Lyonesse, or sometimes Lethowsow,—who were remarkable for their industry and their piety. No less than 140 churches stood over that region, which is now a waste of waters ; and the rocks called the Seven Stones are said to mark the place of a large city. Even tradition is silent on the character of this great cataclysm. We have only one hint—and we know not its value—which appears to show that the deluge was comparatively gradual. One of the ancestors of the Trevilians is said to have had time to remove his family and his cattle ; but at last he had to fly himself with all the speed which a fleet horse could give him. From this it might appear that, though gradual at first, the waters, having broken down the barriers, burst over the whole at last with uncontrolled fury. A small, but very ancient, oratory, " Chapel Idne," or the " Narrow Chapel," formerly stood in Sennen Cove. It is said to have been founded by one Lord of Goonhilly, who owned a portion of the Lyonesse, on the occasion of his escape from the flood. By this war of waters several large towns were destroyed, and an immense number of the inhabitants perished.

In the absence of full traditional evidence, it will not be uninteresting to gather together the fragmentary statements which exist in the writings of historians and others :—

" The number of parish churches lost is so astonishingly great as to baffle the power of evidence, to preclude the possibility of conviction. I, therefore, take upon me to reduce the number from 140 to 40,—to cut off what any dash of Worcester's pen might casually have created, the first figure."—*Whitaker's Supplement to Polwhele's History of Cornwall.*

The Saxon Chronicle says the Lionesse was destroyed on the 11th of November 1099.

" On the third of the Nones of November (1099) the sea overflowed the shore, destroying towns and drowning many persons and innumerable oxen and sheep."—*The Chronicle of Florence of Worcester, translated by Thomas Forester, A.M.* Bohn, 1854.

Solinus (cap 22) applies Siluria to the country lying west of the Land's End. His words are, " Siluram quoque insulam ab ora quam gens Britanna Dunmonii tenent, terbidum fretum distinguit."

" There is a tradition that there formerly existed a large track of land between the Land's End and the Scilly Islands, called the Lioness, which was destroyed by an inundation of the sea. One of the family of Trevilian, now residing in Somerset, but originally Cornish, saved himself by the assistance of his horse at the time of this inundation ; and it is reported that the arms of this family were taken from his fortunate escape, to commemorate his providential preservation."—*Drew and Hitchin's Cornwall.*

"A cave is pointed out in Perranuthnoe, where the ancestor of the Trevelyans is said to have been borne on shore, by the strength of his horse, from the destruction of the Lionesse country west of the Land's End. The Trevelyan family are too old, too honourable, and now too much distinguished by science, for them to covet any addition of honour through the medium of fabulous history.

"It is recorded in the *Saxon Chronicle* that, in the year 1099, there was so very high a tide, and the damage so great in consequence, that men remembered not the like to have ever happened before, and the same day was the first of the new moon. Stow, who wrote his History of England about the year 1580, notices the great tide of 1099, when he says, ' The sea brake in over the banks of the Thames and other ryvers, drowning many towns and much people, with innumerable numbers of oxen and sheepe ; at which time the lands in Kent, that sometime belonged to Duke Godwyne, Earle of Kent, were covered with sandes and drowned, which'are to this day called Godwyne Sandes.' On the slender foundation of these alluvial catastrophes, Florence of Worcester either invented, or, with more than monkish credulity, received the tale of a whole district being engulfed, not at some remote geological period, but in what may be considered as the recent times of authentic history, after the existence of systematic registers and records ; a district covered, as he states, by a city and by a hundred and forty churches, with their accompanying villages, farms, &c., an event that must have shaken the whole of Europe ; and, to increase the wonder, a gentleman, accidentally on horseback, is carried by this animal to the neighbouring shore of Whitsand Bay, or twenty miles further off, to Perranuthnoe, through a sea which had swallowed an entire country, and from which the largest of modern vessels could not possibly have escaped. This idle tale, related by one writer after another, has almost reached our own times. The editor remembers a female relation of a former vicar of St Erth who, instructed by a dream, prepared decoctions of various herbs, and, repairing to the Land's End, poured them into the sea, with certain incantations, expecting to see the Lionesse country rise immediately out of the water, having all its inhabitants alive, notwithstanding their long submersion. But

> ' Perchance some form was unobserved,
> Perchance in prayer or faith she swerved.'

No country appeared, and although the love of marvellous events, and of tales exciting the passions, seems not to have diminished in recent times, yet the editor is unaware of any subsequent attempt having been made to rescue those unfortunate people from their protracted state of suspended animation."—*The Parochial History of Cornwall, by Davies Gilbert*, vol. iii. pp. 109, 110.

"Although a sweep of ocean, twenty-seven miles in breadth, separates at present the Land's End from the Scilly Islands, there can yet be little doubt of their having been heretofore united to each other by the mainland. The records of history indeed do not rise so high as the era when this disjunction was first effected ; but we have documents yet remaining which prove to us that this strait must have been considerably widened, and the number of the Scilly Islands greatly increased within the last sixteen or seventeen centuries, by the waters of the Atlantic (receding probably from the coast of America) pressing towards this coast of Britain, accumulating upon Bolerium, and overwhelming part of the western shores of Cornwall.

"Strabo expressly tells us that the Cassiterides (so called from the Greek name of *tin*, there produced) were in his time only ten in number; whereas they are now divided into a hundred and forty rocky islets. Solinus also makes mention of a large and respectable island, called *Silura*, evidently the Scilly of present times, lying on Damnonian or Cornish coast, and separated from the mainland by a strait turbulent and dangerous—a character which sufficiently marks the compression of its waters. And William of Worcester, an author of our own country, thirteen centuries after Solinus, states, with a degree of positive exactness, stamping authenticity upon its recital, that between Mount's Bay and the Scilly Islands there had been woods, and meadows, and arable lands, and a hundred and forty parish churches, which before his time were submerged by the ocean. Uninterrupted tradition since this period, which subsists to the present day vigorous and particular, authenticates his account, and leaves no doubt upon the mind that a vast track of land, which stretched anciently from the eastern shore of Mount's Bay to the north-western rock of Scilly (with the exception of the narrow strait flowing between the Long-ships and Land's End), has, since the age of Strabo and Solinus, and previous to that of William of Worcester, been overwhelmed and usurped by the waves of the sea. . . . The depth of the water at the Land's End is about eleven fathoms; at the Long-ships, eight; to the north of them, twenty; to the south, thirty; and twenty-five, twenty, and fifteen fathoms between them and the north-west of Scilly. The shallowest water occurs in the midspace between Cornwall and the Isles."—*A Tour through Cornwall in the Autumn of* 1808, *by the Rev. Richard Warner.*

"Yet the cause of that inundation, which destroyed much of these Islands (the Scilly Islands), might reach also to the Cornish shores, is extremely probable, there being several evidences of a like subsidence of the land in the Mount's Bay. The principal anchoring-place, called a lake, is now a haven, or open harbour. The Mount, from its Cornish name, we must conclude to have stood formerly in a wood, but now, at full tide, is half a mile from the sea, and not a tree near it; and in the sandy beach betwixt the Mount and Penzance, where the sands have been dispersed by violent high tides, I have seen the trunks of several large trees in their natural position."—*Borlase, Phil. Trans.*, vol. xlviii. part I.

"That Cornwall once extended further west may be inferred from hence, that about midway between the Land's End and Scilly are rocks called in Cornish *Lethowsow;* by the English, *Seven-stones.*

"The Cornish call the places within the stones *Tregva,*—*i.e.,* a dwelling; —and it has been reported that windows and other stuff have been fished up, and that fishermen still see tops of houses under water. From the Land's End to Scilly, a tract of thirty miles, is an equal depth of water, and the bottom of the sea a plain, level surface. St Michael's Mount is called in Cornish, *Careg cowse in clowse—i.e.,* the hoary rock in the wood. Large trees with roots and bodies have been driven in by the sea of late years between St Michael's Mount and Penzance; and tradition says that at the time of the inundation which made the separation, one *Trevelyan* swam from thence on horseback; and in memory thereof the family, now in Somersetshire, bears gules a horse argent, from a less wavy argent, and azure, issuing out of a sea proper."—*Gough's Camden*, vol. i. p. 15.

"The flats, which stretched from one island to another, are plain evidences of a former union subsisting between many now distinct islands. The flats between Trescaw, Brêhar, and Sampson are quite dry at a springtide, and men easily pass dry-shod from one island to another over sandbanks (where, upon the shifting of the sands, walls and ruins are frequently discovered), upon which, at full sea, there are ten and twelve feet of water. From the southern side of St Martin there stretches out a large shoal towards Trescaw and St Mary's; and from St Mary's a flat called Sandy-bar, shoots away to meet it; and between these two shoals there are but four feet of water in the channel called Crow Sound,—all strong arguments that those islands were once one continued tract of land, though now, as to their low lands, overrun with the sea and sand. 'The Isles Cassiterides' (says Strabo, Geo., lib. 5) 'are ten in number, close to one another. One of them is desert and unpeopled; the rest are inhabited.' But see how the sea has multiplied these islands; there are now one hundred and forty. Into so many fragments are they divided; and yet there are but six inhabited."—*An Account of the Great Alteration which the Islands of Scylley have undergone, &c., by the Rev. Wm. Borlase, M.A., F.R.S., Phil. Trans.*, vol. xlviii. part 1.

"The Cornish land, from Plymouth, discovers itself to be devoured more and more to the westward, according to the aforesaid tradition of the tract of the Lionesse, being encroached upon above half the present distance from the Land's End to Scilly; whence it is probable that the low isthmus once joining Scilly and the Lionesse was first encroached upon in the same manner. The projecting land being exposed to the concurrence of the tides from the Irish, the Bristol, and British Channels, by whose violence and impetuosity, increased by the winds, the loose earth of the Gulf-rock might be worn away, leaving the resistible substance behind, standing as it is in the middle way betwixt Scilly and Cornwall."—*A Natural and Historical Account of the Islands of Scilly, by Robert Heath.*

The following notices are gathered from other local traditions :—

"From Rame-head to the two Looes very fertile valleys are stated to have extended at least a league southwards, over a tract now covered with sea; and around the coast in many places, we are assured, in twelve feet of water, trees are to be seen in the sea."

"The Black Rock in Falmouth Harbour is stated to have been a large island, which was surrounded by the sea only at high-water."

"Six miles south of St Michael's Mount waved, from Clement's Isle to Cudden Rock, a wood."

CUDDEN POINT AND THE SILVER TABLE

THIS point is situated in the parish of Perranuthnoe; the parish, it will be remembered, into which Trelawney escaped, aided by the fleetness of his horse, from the deluge which buried the lands between this and the Scilly Isles.

At the low-water of spring-tides, the children from all the neighbourhood flock to the sands around this point, in the hope of finding treasure, which they believe is buried in the sands beneath the sea, and which is, it is said, occasionally discovered. Amongst

N

other things, an especial search is made for a silver table, which was lost by a very wealthy lord, by some said to be the old Lord Pengerswick, who enriched himself by grinding down the poor. On one occasion, when the calmness of summer, the clearness of the skies, and the tranquillity of the waters invited the luxurious to the enjoyments of the sea, this magnate, with a party of gay and thoughtless friends, was floating in a beautiful boat lazily with the tide, and feasting from numerous luxuries spread on a silver table. Suddenly—no one lived to tell the cause—the boat sank in the calm, transparent waters ; and, long after the event, the fishermen would tell of sounds of revelry heard from beneath the waters, and some have said they have seen these wicked ones still seated around the silver table.

THE PADSTOW " HOBBY-HORSE." *

A T the time of the spring festival, which is observed at Helston as a revel in honour, probably, of Flora, and hence called the " Furry-day," and by the blowing of horns and gathering of the " May " in St Ives and other places, the people of Padstow were a few years since in the habit of riding the " hobby-horse " to water. This hobby-horse was, after it had been taken round the town, submerged in the sea. The old people said it was once believed that this ceremony preserved the cattle of the inhabitants from disease and death. The appearance of a white horse escaping from the flood which buried the Lioness, is told at several points, on both the north and south coast, and the riding of the hobby-horse probably belongs to this tradition. In support of this idea, we must not forget the mermaid story associated with the harbour of Padstow.

The water-horse is a truly Celtic tradition. We have it in the " Arabian Nights," and in the stories of all countries in the south of Europe. Mr Campbell, " West Highland Tales," says he finds the *horse* brought prominently forward in the Breton legends, and that animal figures largely in the traditions of Scotland and Ireland.

Has the miners' phrase—" a horse in the lode," applied to a mass of unproductive ground in the middle of a mineral lode ; or, " Black Jack rides a good horse," signifying that zinc ore gives good promise for copper—anything to do with these traditions?

* See Appendix P.

ST MICHAEL'S MOUNT—THE WHITE ROCK IN THE WOOD.

"An old legend of St Michael speaketh of a tounelet in this part (between Pensandes and Mousehole), now defaced, and lying under the water."
—*Leland's Itinerary.*

ALREADY it has been told how St Michael's Mount was built by the giants. So much for its Titanic origin. The tradition that the Mount was formerly called in old Cornish, *Careg-luz en kuz,** and that it rose from the midst of an extensive forest, is very prevalent. "A forest is supposed to have extended along the coast to St Michael's Mount, which was described as a 'hoare rock in a wood,' and stood five or six miles from the sea. The bay was said to have been a plain of five or six miles in extent, formed into parishes, each having its church, and laid out in meadows, corn-fields, and woods." † A similar tradition attaches itself to Mont St Michel, in Normandy.

By and by, when the Saxon rule was extended into Cornwall, this remarkable hill is seized upon, in common with many other such hills, as the residence of some anchorite. This holy recluse is visited by St Michael, who had an especial fondness for hill churches, and the hermit is directed to build a church on the summit, and dedicate it to St Michael.

> " In evile howre thou hentst in hond,
>   Thus holy hills to blame ;
> For sacred unto saints they stand,
>   And of them have their name.
> St Michael's Mount, who does not know,
>   That wards the western coast."
>
> —SPENSER.

Milton, in his delicately beautiful poem of "Lycidas," makes especial illusion to this monkish legend :—

> " Where'er thy bones are hurl'd,
> Whether beyond the stormy Hebrides,
> Where thou, perhaps, under the whelming tide,
> Visit'st the bottom of the monstrous world,
> Or, whether thou, to our moist vows denied,
> Sleep'st by the fable of Bellerus old,‡
> Where *the great vision of the guarded mount,*
> Look towards Namancos, and Bayona's hold ;

* Or *Careg Cowes in Clowse.*
† T. T. Blight.
‡ The name Bolerium has been especially given to the Land's End, but there is a cove near the Lizard now called Polurrian or Polerium.

Look homeward, angel, now, and melt with ruth,
And, O ye dolphins, waft the hapless youth."
—MILTON's *Lycidas*.

Warner, in his "Tour through Cornwall," with much assumption of learning, attempts to explain these lines. He tells us that the Land's End was called *Bellerium*, "so named from Bellerus, a Cornish giant. No such giant ever existed in Cornish fable, as far as can be ascertained. It is far more probable that Milton used the poet's license, and, from the name of the Land's End, Bellerium, created 'the fable of Bellerus old.'" What follows in Warner is worth extracting :—

"We learn from 'Caston's Golden Legende,' under the history of the Angel Michael, that, 'Th' apparacyon of this angell is manyfold. The fyrst is when he appeared in Mount of Gargan, &c.,' (edit. 1493, fol. cclxxxii. a). William of Worcester, who wrote his travels over England about 1490, says, in describing St Michael's Mount, there was an 'Apparicio Sancti Michaelis in monte Tumba antea vocato *Le Hore Rok in the Wodd*' (Itinerar., edit. Cantab., 1778, p. 102). *The Hoar Rock in the Wood* is this Mount or Rock of St Michael, anciently covered with thick wood, as we learn from Drayton and Carew. There is still a tradition, that a vision of St Michael seated on this crag, or St Michael's Chair, appeared to some hermits ; and that this circumstance occasioned the foundation of the monastery dedicated to St Michael. And hence this place was long renowned for its sanctity, and the object of frequent pilgrimages. Carew quotes some old rhymes much to our purpose, p. 154, *ut supra* :—

'Who knows not Mighel's Mount and Chaire,
The pilgrim's holy vaunt ?'

Nor should it be forgot that this monastery was a cell to another on a St Michael's Mount in Normandy, where was also a vision of St Michael. But to apply what has been said to Milton. This great vision is the famous apparition of St Michael, whom he, with much sublimity of imagination, supposes to be still throned on this lofty crag of St Michael's Mount in Cornwall, looking towards the Spanish coast. The guarded mount on which this great vision appeared is simply the *fortified* mount, implying the fortress above mentioned. And let us observe, that *Mount* is the peculiar appropriated appellation of this promontory. So in Daniel's Panegyricke on the King, st. 19, 'From Dover to the Mount.'"—P. 180.

"In the very corner is *Michael's Mount*, which gives name to the bay (the Mount's Bay) anciently called *Dinsol*, as in the book of Landaff, called by the inhabitants *Careg-Cowse*, or the Gray Rock—in Saxon, *Mychelyroz*, or Michael's Place." *

From Hals, Tonkin, and Gilbert, we learn yet further that " St Michael's Mount is so called, because our fathers, the Britons, believed that the appearance of the archangel St Michael in the year of our Lord 495 was in this place ; though in other countries they believe differently."

" Edward the Confessor, finding the place already celebrated for its holiness, founded an abbey of Benedictine monks, A.D. 1044, and also a chapel, which still stand, part of which is now converted into a dwelling-house.   Upon the tower of the chapel is the celebrated Kader Migell,—*i.e.*, Michael's Chair,—a seat artificially cut in the stone, very dangerous in the access, therefore holy for the adventure.

> " ' Who knows not Mighel's Mount and Chaire,
>   The pilgrim's holy vaunt ;
> Both land and island twice a day,
>   Both fort and port of haunt ? ' "

It is supposed by many persons to have been placed there for the pilgrims to complete their devotions at the Mount, by sitting in this chair, and showing themselves to the country around as pilgrims.   St Kenna, doubtless the same as St Keyna, once visited this Mount,—although the time of her visitation is not precisely known,—and she imparted the very same virtue to the chair as she bestowed on St Keyna's Well.   It is whichever, man or wife, sits in this chair first shall rule through life, and as it requires great resolution and steadiness of head to obtain the seat, one may be inclined to anticipate the supposed effect with greater certainty from its achievement, than from drinking water from St Keyna's Well.

It is not pleasant to destroy the romance of ages, but honesty compels me to pronounce this so-called chair to be nothing more than the remains of a stone lantern, built at the south-western angle of the tower.   The good monks, without doubt, placing a light therein, it could be seen by the fishermen far off at sea ; and probably they received some tribute of either fish or money for the support of this useful guide to the shore.

It is evident, from the following passage in Carew's Survey, that the " chair " formerly was not within the building at all, but on some rocks without the walls :—

* Gough's Camden's Britannia, vol. i. p. 4

" A little without the castle there is a bad seat in a craggy place called St Michael's Chaire, somewhat dangerous for accesse, and therefore holy for the adventure." *

GWAVAS LAKE.

ON the western side of the Mount's Bay, between the fishing-towns of Newlyn and Mousehole, is the well-known anchoring-place known by the above name. It is not a little curious that any part of the ocean should have been called a lake. Tradition, however, helps us to an explanation. Between the land on the western side of the bay, and St Michael's Mount on the eastern side, there, at one time, extended a forest of beech-trees. Within this forest, on the western side, was a large lake, and on its banks a hermitage. The saint of the lake was celebrated far and near for his holiness, and his small oratory was constantly resorted to by the diseased in body and the afflicted in mind. None ever came in the true spirit who failed to find relief. The prayers of the saint and the waters of the lake removed the severest pains from the limbs and the deepest sorrows from the mind. The young were strengthened and the old revived by their influences. The great flood, however, which separated the Islands of Scilly from England, submerged the forest, and destroyed the lands enclosing this lovely and almost holy lake, burying beneath the waters church and houses, and destroying alike the people and the priest. Those who survived this sad catastrophe built a church on the hill and dedicated it to the saint of the lake—or in Cornish, St Pol—modernised into St Paul.†

In support of this tradition, we may see, of a fine summer day, when the tide is low and the waters clear, the remains of a forest in the line passing from St Michael's Mount to Gwavas. At neap-tides the author has gathered beech-nuts from the sands below Chyandour, and cut the wood from the trees embedded in the sand. ‡

---

*. Carew, p. 154.

† Gwavas Lake. It is said that within historic times, tithes, or an equivalent for them, were collected from the land which surrounded this lake. I have been informed that the parish books of St Paul record the collection of tithes from lands which have disappeared. I applied for information on this point to the rector of the parish, but he has not yet favoured me with a reply.

‡ I have passed in a boat from St Michael's Mount to Penzance on a summer day, when the waters were very clear, and the tide low, and seen the black masses of trees in the white sands extending far out into the bay. On one occasion, while I was at school at Penzance, after a violent equinoctial gale, large trunks of trees were thrown up on the shore, just beyond Chyandour, and then with the other boys I went, at the lowest of

THE CITY OF LANGARROW OR LANGONA.*

WE cannot say how many years since, but once there stood on the northern shores of Cornwall, extending over all that country between the Gannell and Perranporth, a large city called Langarrow or Langona. The sand-hills which now extend over this part of the coast cover that great city, and the memory of the sad and sudden catastrophe still lingers among the peasantry. So settled is tradition, that no other time than 900 years since is ever mentioned as the period at which Langarrow was buried. This city in its prime is said to have been the largest in England, and to have had seven churches, which were alike remarkable for their beauty and their size. The inhabitants were wealthy, and according to received accounts, they drew their wealth from a large tract of level land, thickly wooded in some parts, and highly cultivated in others—from the sea, which was overflowing with fish of all kinds—and from mines, which yielded them abundance of tin and lead.

To this remote city, in those days, criminals were transported from other parts of Britain. They were made to work in the mines on the coast, in constructing a new harbour in the Gannell, and clearing it of sand, so that ships of large burden could in those days sail far inland. Numerous curious excavations in the rocks, on either side of this estuary, are still pointed out as being evidences of the works of the convicts. This portion of the population of Langarrow were not allowed to dwell within the city. The convicts and their families had to construct huts or dig caves on the wild moors of this unsheltered northern shore, and to this day evidences of their existence are found under the sand, in heaps of wood-ashes, amidst which are discovered considerable quantities of mussel and cockle shells, which we may suppose was

the tide, far out over the sands, and saw scores of trees embedded in the sands. We gathered nuts—they were beech-nuts—and leaves in abundance. It is not a little remarkable,—if it be true, as I am informed it is,—that the trees found in the Pentuan Stream Works, under some fifty or sixty feet of sand and silt, are beech-trees, and that they were destroyed when the fruit was upon them. I learn, that not far from Hull in Yorkshire there exists a submerged forest, where also the beech-trees evidently perished in the autumn. In Cardigan Bay a large tract of country is said to have been lost. May not all these traditions and evidences relate to one great cataclysm? See "A Week at the Land's End," by J. T. Blight, for an account of the submerged wood near Lariggan Rocks, between Penzance and Newlyn.

* "The vicarage church of Crantock is commonly called Languna or Langona,—that is to say, the hay temple or church,—and is suitable to its name, situate in a large hay meadow of rich land, containing about three acres, where, by ancient custom, the vicar's cattle all pasture over the dead bodies interred thereinto."—*Hals, as given by Gilbert.* See Appendix Q.

their principal food.   As far as I know, these are the first indications of anything resembling the Kjokkenmöddings, or refuse-heaps
of Denmark, which have been discovered in this country.

For a long period this city flourished in its prime, and its inhabitants were in the enjoyment of every luxury which industry
could obtain or wealth could purchase.   Sin, in many of its worst
forms, was however present amongst the people.   The convicts
sent to Langarrow were of the vilest.   They were long kept widely
separated ; but use breeds familiarity, and gradually the more
designing of the convicts persuaded their masters to employ them
within the city.   The result of this was, after a few years, an
amalgamation of the two classes of the population.   The
daughters of Langarrow were married to the criminals, and
thus crime became the familiar spirit of the place.   The progress
of this may have been slow—the result was, however, sure ; and
eventually, when vice was dominant, and the whole population
sunk in sensual pleasures, the anger of the Lord fell upon them.
A storm of unusual violence arose, and continued blowing, without intermitting its violence for one moment, for three days and
nights.   In that period the hills of blown sand, extending, with
few intervals, from Crantock to Perran were formed, burying the
city, its churches, and its inhabitants in a common grave.   To the
present time those sand-hills stand a monument of God's wrath ;
and in several places we certainly find considerable quantities of
bleached human bones, which are to many strong evidence of the
correctness of tradition.

Crantock was, according to tradition, once a trading town, and
it then had a religious house, with a dean and nine prebends.
The Gannell filling up ruined the town.   This must have happened when Langarrow was destroyed.

On Gwithian Sands the remains of what is supposed to have
been a church has been discovered, and according to Hals and
Gilbert, a similar tradition exists here of a buried town.   Gilbert
writes thus :—

"There has always existed a traditional account of the inundation of
sand in this parish, corroborated by the ecclesiastical valuations, which are
far too high for the actual extent of the land, and also said to be confirmed
by documents preserved in the Arundel family, carrying back the commencement of the evil nearly to the period of their acquiring the property.

" With respect to more recent inundations, Mr Hockin states to Mr
Lysons, that the Barton of Upton, one of the principal farms, was suddenly overwhelmed ; that his great-grandfather remembered the occupier
residing in the farmhouse, which was nearly buried in one night, the
family being obliged to make their escape through the chamber windows ;

and that in consequence of the wind producing a shifting of the sand, in the winter of 1808-9, the house, after having disappeared for more than a century, came again to view.

"The rector further stated that he himself remembered two fields being lost at Gwithian, and that they are now covered with sand to the depth of ten or twelve feet, and that the church-town would have been also lost, if the parish officers had not promptly resorted to the expedient of planting rushes. These stop the complete progress of sand, and greatly facilitate the growth of other vegetation on the surface, so as to create a thin turf, The hillocks of sand exhibit a model in miniature of the Alps."—*Gilbert*, vol. ii. p 149.

THE SANDS AT LELANT AND PHILLACK.

THERE is a tradition that Lelant and Phillack towns were all meadow land, and that the whole was covered with sand in a single night. Also that the low tract of land extended on both sides of Hayle far beyond the present bar, so that the sea has swallowed up some hundreds of acres. The people say that the sight of the ancient church and village of Lelant was somewhere seaward of the Black Rock;—the ancient burial-ground has been long washed away,—and that human teeth are still frequently found on the shore after a great *undertoe*, that takes the sand out to sea. Many circumstances seem to confirm the probability of the tradition. The sand was drifting inland at such a rate before the reed-like plant called by the present inhabitants *the spire* was planted, that the whole of the land about the village would have been rendered worthless ere this, but for the stability given to it. The land from which the sand has been cleared, on the sea side of the church, has evidently been ploughed, as the furrows are quite apparent between the ridges. They say that there was a market held in Lelant when St Ives was scarcely a village. Lelant being the mother church, would seem to prove this. One can easily understand how a large tract of land of the nature of that under Lelant sand-hills would be washed away in a comparatively short time, as the soil at the low-water level is a marly clay. This is constantly being washed down by high tides, and carried away by the undercurrent, as it contains no stone to form a pebbly beach, and therefore there is nothing left to protect the shore.

"THE ISLAND," ST IVES.

THE so-called island is now a peninsular mass of clay slate rocks, interpenetrated by very hard trappean masses. Between this and the town of St Ives is a low neck of land, which consists chiefly of sand and gravel, with some masses of clay slate broken into small angular fragments. On either side of this neck of land are good examples of raised beaches. Everything, therefore, favours the tradition which is preserved in the name.

One statement is, that " The Island " was *brought in from the sea ;* another, that it *rose out of the sea :—*

" This town, as Mr Camden saith, was formerly called Pendenis or Pendunes, the head fort, fortress, or fortified place, probably from the little island here, containing about six acres of ground, on which there stands the ruins of a little old fortification and a chapel."—*Hals's Cornwall.*

" On the island (or peninsula) work of St Ives standeth the ruins of an old chapel, wherein God was duly worshipped by our ancestors the Britons, before the Church of St Ives was erected or endowed."—*Tonkin's Cornwall.*

The beach on one side of the peninsula is called Porthmew, that on the other Porthgwidden ; and the name of the street between them is " Chyranchy," said to signify " the place of the breach," pointing, it might appear, to the action of the sea in wearing out the softer ground.

" Chyanchy " is another mode of pronouncing this name, " Chyan " signifying a house. Hence the name, it is thought by some, was given when two houses (chy-an-chy) stood alone on the spot.*

THE CHAPEL ROCK, PERRAN-PORTH.

THIS is one of the rocks—of which many exist—around the Cornish coast, upon which, at one time, there stood, in all probability, a small chapel or oratory. This rock is left dry at every tide, but stands far out in the sea at high-water. A curious fancy exists with respect to it. It is said that this rock can be approached on dry sand every day at eleven o'clock throughout the year. There is no truth in this statement, but strangers are gravely assured that this is the fact. From this rock to the sandy peninsula which runs out in the " porth," or port, is about five hundred yards—those, it is said, were, at one time, connected by cultivated land. From the circumstance that the evidences of a burial-place have been found on the little peninsula, it appears highly probable

---

* *Chyanwheal.* the house on the mine, is near St Ives. *Chyandour,* the house by the water, adjoins Penzance. *Chyangarrach,* the house on the road. The water-elder is called *skow-dower.*

that the island and it have been closely connected as church and graveyard. Tradition refers the destruction of the land to certain storms or convulsions which swept away the country, for a mile or two out at sea, marked by a line drawn from the rocks off St Agnes, known as "The Man and his Man," and "Carters' Rock," which is off Penhale Point.

FIRE WORSHIP.

" Safely hid
Beneath the purple pall of sacrifice
Did sleep our holy fire, nor saw the air,
Till to that pass we came, where whilom Brute
Planted his five hoar altars.   To our rites
Then swift we hasted, and in one short moment
The rocky piles were clothed with livid flame."
                    Caractacus—WM. MASON, M.A.

ROMANCES OF FIRE WORSHIP.

' An angel who at last in sight
Of both my parents all in flames ascended
From off the altar, where an offering burn'd,
As in a fiery column charioting
His god-like presence."
—*Samson Agonistes*—MILTON.

IT would not be profitable to pursue the inquiry into the value
of the numerous hypotheses which have been from time to
time raised in support of the assertion that a system of Fire Worship prevailed amongst the Britons of old Cornwall.

There can be no doubt but that the writings of Borlase, and
other earnest thinkers of his class, have done much to perpetuate
the belief in the existence of a Druidical priesthood in Cornwall,
who had their altars on the hills,—who made the huge piles of
granite rocks the instruments of their worship,—and who availed
themselves of the hollows formed in those rocks by nature, to
procure the unpolluted waters from heaven, with which to wash
away sins.

The antiquary has too frequently placed himself in the unfortunate position of Jonathan Oldbuck amidst the ancient fortifica-
tions at the Kaim of Kinprunes, when he was so rudely checked
in his theory by Edie Ochiltree, who would insist on it that he did
" mind the biggin' o' 't." But the modern historian and philosopher has gone as far wrong in the contrary direction. The
antiquaries formerly insisted that all the natural basins formed in
the granite rocks were of Druidic origin, and all the Logan stones
the result of Druid labours. The geologists and historians now
declare them, one and all, to be the result of disintegration, produced by ordinary atmospheric causes. Both are, I presume to
think, wrong. I am quite satisfied that I can point to rock-basins
upon which the hands of man have been busy, and to Logan stones
in which he has, for his own purposes, aided nature.

In the Sacrificing Rock on Carn Brae are a series of hollows so deeply cut, and so entirely unlike anything seen on any of the other rocks on that remarkable hill, although ordinary rock-basins are numerous, that I am disposed to believe in the tradition which gives it its name. On the Main or Men Rock in Constantine, I see, in like manner, evidences of the works of man, side by side with those of nature. The disintegration produced by the accumulation of water, at first in small quantities in a little hollow on the face of a rock, is a curious process. The first action is the separation of a few particles, or small crystals, of quartz or mica. These repose beneath the small deposit of water, until, by the beating of the rains and the action of the winds, they are made to serve as grinding materials, and carry on the work of weathering. The basins thus formed have a regular curvature, which does not belong to those deeper basins to which I have referred. The question, however, before us is, Have we any evidences, traditional or otherwise, which go to support the belief that the Phœnicians, or any other people, introduced the worship of fire into this country?

The influences of education, and the zeal with which religious teachers have penetrated into the remotest districts and taught the truth, have banished nearly every relic of this ancient idolatry. But still amidst the dead ashes a faint spark occasionally appears, to tell us that at one time our forefathers did use the rocks as altars, on which they kindled sacrificial fires; and that they had their periods of solemn feast, when every hill blazed with the emblem of life and dissolution. A few examples of these pale sparks will not be without value.

BAAL FIRES.

OF these Cornish Midsummer fires an account is given by a correspondent in Hone's "Year Book," which I quote entire, not because I can agree with the writer in all his views, but because he places the main question in a fair light:—

"An immemorial and peculiar custom prevails on the sea-coast of the western extremity of Cornwall, of kindling large bonfires on the Eve of June 24; and on the next day the country people, assembling in great crowds, amuse themselves with excursions on the water. I cannot help thinking it the remains of an ancient Druidical festival, celebrated on Midsummer-day, to implore the friendly influence of Heaven on their fields, compounded with that of the first of May, when the Druids kindled large fires on all their sacred places, and on the tops of all their cairns, in honour of Bel, or Belinus, the name by which they distinguished the sun, whose revolving course had again clothed the earth with beauty, and diffused joy and gladness through the creation. Their water parties on the 24th prove that they consider the summer season as now so fully established that they are not afraid to commit themselves to the mercy of the waves. If we reflect on the rooted animosity which subsisted between the Romans and the Druids, and that the latter, on being expelled from their former residences, found, together with the miserable remnants of the Britons, an asylum in the naturally fortified parts of the island, we shall not be surprised at their customs having been faintly handed down through such a long succession of ages. That Cornwall was one of their retreats is sufficiently proved by the numerous remains of their circular temples, cromlechs, cairns, &c. Even in the eleventh century, when Christianity was become the national religion, the people were so attached to their ancient superstitions, that we find a law of Canute the Great strictly prohibiting all his subjects from paying adoration to the sun, moon, sacred groves and woods, hallowed hills and fountains. If, then, this propensity to idolatry could not be rooted out of those parts of the kingdom exposed to the continual influx of foreigners, and the horrors of frequent war, how much more must it have flourished in Cornwall and those parts where the Druids long preserved their authority and influence? It may therefore be fairly inferred that, from their remote situation, and comparative insignificancy with the rest of England, they preserved those religious ceremonies unmolested ; and, corrupted as they must naturally be by long usage and tradition, yet are handed down to us to this to-day with evident marks of a Druidical origin." [*]

In Hone's " Every-Day Book " will be found several accounts of festivals which may be referred to Baal worship.

Mr Richard Edmonds, a native of Penzance, has given us a very faithful description of the proceedings at Penzance on Midsummer-eve. Although that gentleman states his belief in the true Celtic origin of this remarkable mode of celebrating the Midsummer festival, his description leads us to suppose that it is distinctly Roman :—

" It is the immemorial usage in Penzance and the neighbouring towns and villages to kindle bonfires and torches on Midsummer-eve ; and on Midsummer-day to hold a fair on Penzance quay, where the country folks assemble from the adjoining parishes in great numbers to make excursions on the water. St Peter's-eve is distinguished by a similar display of bonfires and torches, although the 'quay-fair' on St Peter's-day has been discontinued upwards of forty years.

" On these eves a line of tar-barrels, relieved occasionally by large bonfires, is seen in the centre of each of the principal streets in Penzance. On either side of this line young men and women pass up and down swinging round their heads heavy torches made of large pieces of folded canvas steeped in tar, and nailed to the ends of sticks between three and four feet long ; the flames of some of these almost equal those of the tar-barrels.

---

[*] In Ireland, May-day is called *la na Bealtina*, and the eve of May is *neen na Bealtina*, —the day and eve of Baal fires. Seeing the intimate relation of the inhabitants of Cornwall and those of Ireland, especially of the southern counties, may we not infer that the bonfires of May and those of Midsummer have a similar origin?

Rows of lighted candles also, when the air is calm, are fixed outside the windows or along the sides of the streets.   In St Just and other mining parishes the young miners, mimicking their fathers' employments, bore rows of holes in the rocks, load them with gunpowder, and explode them in rapid succession by trains of the same substance.   As the holes are not deep enough to split the rocks, the same little batteries serve for many years.   On these nights Mount's Bay has a most animating appearance, although not equal to what was annually witnessed at the beginning of the present century, when the whole coast, from the Land's End to the Lizard, wherever a town or village existed, was lighted up with these stationary or moving fires.   In the early part of the evening, children may be seen wearing wreaths of flowers,—a custom in all probability originating from the ancient use of these ornaments when they danced around the fires.   At the close of the fireworks in Penzance, a great number of persons of both sexes, chiefly from the neighbourhood of the quay, used always, until within the last few years, to join hand in hand, forming a long string, and run through the streets, playing 'thread the needle,' heedless of the fireworks showered upon them, and oftentimes leaping over the yet glowing embers.   I have on these occasions seen boys following one another, jumping through flames higher than themselves.   But whilst this is now done innocently in every sense of the word, we all know that the passing of children through fire was a very common act of idolatry ; and the heathen believed that all persons, and all living things, submitted to this ordeal, would be preserved from evil throughout the ensuing year.   A similar blessing was supposed to be imparted to their fields by running around them with flaming torches."—*Richard Edmonds— The Land's End District*, p. 66.

THE GARRICK ZANS, OR HOLY ROCK.

A FEW years—really but a few years—since, the stone altars on which the first inhabitants of these islands lit their holy fires had yet a place amongst us.   In the village of Roskestall stood one such altar ; in Treen was to be found another.   These huge masses of rock, rendered sacred by the memories surrounding them, have been wantonly removed, and employed in most cases in furnishing pillars at the " grand entrances " of the houses of the squire farmers of the Land's End district ; or they have been yet more rudely served, and are to be found at the entrance to a pigsty, or in the gate-posts to a potato-field.

The extinction of several of the old families is, to the present day, ascribed by the peasantry to the unholy act of removing or breaking up of the Garrick Zans in the village of Escols.   The rock in the village of Mayon was called indifferently *table-mayon* (mōn), or the Garrack Zans.   Within our memory is the gathering of the villagers around the Holy Rock.   It was their custom, when anything was stolen, or a misdemeanour committed, to light a fire on this altar, and when the fagots were in full blaze, all those who sought to prove their innocence took a burning stick from the rock and spat on the blazing end. If they could extinguish the fire by spitting on the stick, they were declared innocent; but if the mouth was so dry as not to generate sufficient moisture to be heard " frizzing " on it, that unfortunate individual was suspected, if not declared, to be guilty.* The Midsummer bonfire was first lighted on the rock in Escols, next on the Chapel Hill; then all the other beacon hills were soon ablaze. Many superstitious rites were formerly performed on the Garrack Zans, which are only found now as the amusements of young people on the eves of St Agnes and Midsummer.

FIRE ORDEAL FOR THE CURE OF DISEASE.

A MINER, who was also a small farmer, living in Zennor, once consulted me on the condition of his daughter, a little girl about five or six years of age. This child was evidently suffering from some scrofulous taint. She was of a delicate complexion, with, usually, a hectic flush on her cheeks; the skin being particularly fine, and so transparent that the course of the veins was marked by deep blue lines. This little girl had long suffered from indolent tumours, forming on the glands in various parts of the body; and, as her father said, " they had taken her to all the doctors in the country round, and the child got worse and worse."

I prescribed for this child; and for two or three weeks she was brought into Penzance on the market-day, that I might observe the influence of the remedial agent which I was employing. Right or wrong, however, the little girl was evidently benefited by the medicine I recommended.

Suddenly my patient was removed from my care, and many months passed away without my seeing either the child or the father. Eventually I met the parent in the market-place, and after some commonplace remarks, he informed me, on my inquiring for his daughter, that she was cured. I expressed satisfaction at hearing this, and inquired why he had not brought the child to me again. After some hesitation he said he had discovered what ailed the child—" *she was overlooked.*" Requiring some explanation of this, I got possession of his story, which was to the following purpose :—

* Boys at school, to prove the truth or falsehood of any charge, will take a stick from the fire and practise upon it in the same manner. May not the custom of joining hands and passing through the embers of a dying bonfire, for good luck, be a vestige of the same ritual?

At a short distance from their farm there resided an old woman who was feared by her neighbours, owing to her savage and uncontrollable temper, and who hated all around her in consequence of the system of ill-usage to which during a long life she had been subjected.

I have visited this miserable creature in her home. A stone-built hut in the wildest part of the bleak coast, forming but one room, was her dwelling. The door was rotten through age, and the two small windows, neither of them more than eighteen inches long by twelve inches wide, which had once been glazed, had been broken to pieces, and the holes were filled in with old rags. Consequently, when the door was closed, the hovel would have been dark, but for the light which descended through the hole in the roof, which we must call a chimney, and that which gained admission through the cracks in the door—these gave a tolerable amount of illumination.

A low truckle-bed in one corner, with very scanty, dirty, and ragged covering,—a small round table, roughly made and standing on four square legs,—a log of wood, and a three-legged stool, formed, with one exception, all the furniture in the place. This exception was the " dresser." Those who are not acquainted with western England will require to be told that no dwelling, however poor, is regarded as complete without the set of framed shelves and drawers which constitute the dresser.

This old woman's dresser was painted white and blue, and on its shelves were cups and saucers, a few plates, one or two dishes, and some mugs. Here was an orderly arrangement, and a tolerably clean display, strangely contrasting with the dirt and disorder of everything around. At the period of my visit this old woman was seated on the block of wood, with her naked arms folded before her, rocking herself to and fro. Margery Penwarne, for so she was called, though usually spoken of as " An'," or Aunt " Madge," must have been nearly eighty years old. Her hair was an iron gray, and it struggled out from under a cotton cap, which had once been white, in long thin locks. Her eyebrows were long enough to fall over her disagreeable gray eyes ; and this, with the accumulation of long hair around her toothless mouth, gave her a most repulsive appearance. There were still living two or three old people who had known Margery in her youth, and they spoke of her as having been a pretty girl. The general idea evidently being that she had sold her soul to the devil, and that it was the influence of her evil mind which gave her so wretched an aspect.

From Margery I had a long story of the wrongs she suffered, and I believe this sad example of humanity may be regarded as an instance of the reaction of uncontrolled passion. Ignorant in the extreme herself, and dwelling amongst a class of people who were at that time but little superior to her in any respect, Margery succeeded in exerting much power over them by her violence. In addition to this, she was more industrious than her neighbours, of which her small farm bore the evidences. Violence begat its like, and where Margery, by her energy, became the apparent conqueror, she called into play all kinds of low cunning against herself, and was always, in the end, the sufferer. Her crops were injured, her pigs died suddenly, her fowls were killed, and even her donkeys were lamed.

As age crept on, the power to provide the necessities of life failed her, and she had, at the time I speak of, been receiving pay from the parish for many years. With age Margery's infirmities of temper increased. She had long been used by the mothers of the parish as a means for frightening the children. Their tears were stopped more readily by a threat, " I 'll give 'e to An' Madge," than by any other means ; and good conduct was insured if An' Madge was to be sent for " to tak 'e away." From this state she passed into another stage. Margery, from being a terror to the young, became the fear of the old. No one would dare refuse her a drop of milk, a few potatoes, or any of those trifles which she almost demanded from her neighbours, every one trembling lest she should exert her evil eye, or vent her curses upon them.

This was the being who had "overlooked" the miner's daughter. He told me that the cause of this was that he caught Margery stealing some straw, and that he " kicked her out of the yard."

The gossips of the parish had for some time insisted upon the fact that the child had been ill-wished, and that she never would be better until " the spell was taken off her." The father, who was in many respects a sensible man, would not for a long period hear of this, but the reiteration of the assertion at length compelled him to give way, and he consulted some " knowing man " in the parish of St Just.

It was then formally announced that the girl could never recover unless three burning sticks were taken from the hearth of the " overlooker," and the child was made to walk three times over them when they were laid across on the ground, and then quench the fire with water.

The father had no doubt respecting the " overlooker," his

quarrel with Madge determined this in his mind ; but there were many difficulties in carrying out the prescribed means for effecting the cure. Without exposing themselves to the violence of the old woman it was impossible, and there was some fear that in forcibly entering her dwelling they might be brought "under the law," with which Margery had often threatened the people.

It was found, however, that nothing could be done for the child if they neglected this, and the father and two or three friends resolved to brave alike the old woman and the law.

One evening, the smoke, mixed with sparks, arising from the hole in the roof of Margery's cottage, informed them that the evil crone was preparing her supper, and as she evidently was burning dry furze, now was the time to procure the three blazing sticks. Accordingly three men and the little girl hurried to the hovel. The door was closed, but, not being secured on the inside, the father opened it. As they had planned, his two companions rushed in, and, without a word, seized the old woman, who fell from her block to the floor, to which, with unnecessary violence, they pinned her, she screaming with "the shriek of a goshawk." In the meantime the parent dragged three blazing pieces of furze from the hearth, hastened to the door, laid them one across the other, and then, without losing a moment, forced the trembling child across the fire three times, and compelled her to perform the other necessary portion of the ordeal by which the spell was to be broken.

Margery, weak, aged, and violent, was soon exhausted, and she probably fainted. I was, however, informed by the man, that as the fire was quenched in the sticks, the flames which appeared to kindle in her eyes gradually died away ; that all the colour forsook her lips, and that at last she murmured, " My heart ! my heart ! bring me the girl, and I'll purge her of the spell ; " upon which they left her as though dead upon the rough earth floor on which she had fallen.

Many other examples might have been given of the existence of a belief in the " virtue of fire," as I have heard it expressed.

BURNING ANIMALS ALIVE.

THERE can be no doubt but that a belief prevailed, until a very recent period, amongst the small farmers in the districts remote from towns, in Cornwall, that a living sacrifice appeased the wrath of God. This sacrifice must be by fire ; and I have heard it argued that the Bible gave them warranty for this belief.

The accompanying notes, from Hone's " Every-Day Book," and from Drew and Hitchen's " Cornwall," prove the prevalence— at least at the commencement of this century—of this idea. I have lately been informed that within the last few years a calf has been thus sacrificed by a farmer, in a district where churches, chapels, and schools abound.

The burning of blood, drawn from a deceased animal, has been a very common mode of appeasing the spirits of disease.

" There are too many obvious traces of the fact to doubt its truth, that the making of bonfires, and the leaping through them, are vestiges of the ancient worship of the heathen god Bal; and therefore it is, with propriety, that the editor of "Time's Telescope" adduces a recent occurrence from Drew and Hitchin's " History of Cornwall," as a probable remnant of pagan superstition in that country. He presumes that the vulgar notion which gave rise to it was derived from the Druidical sacrifice of beasts : ' An ignorant old farmer in Cornwall, having met with some severe losses in his cattle about the year 1800, was much afflicted with his misfortunes. To stop the growing evil, he applied to the farriers in his neighbourhood, but unfortunately he applied in vain. The malady still continuing, and all remedies failing, he thought it necessary to have recourse to some extraordinary measure. Accordingly, on consulting with some of his neighbours, equally ignorant with himself, and evidently not less barbarous, they recalled to their recollections a tale, which tradition had handed down from remote antiquity, that the calamity would not cease until he had actually *burned alive the finest calf which he had upon his farm ;* but that, when this sacrifice was made, the murrain would afflict his cattle no more. The old farmer, influenced by this counsel, resolved immediately on reducing it to practice ; that, by making the detestable experiment, he might secure an advantage which the whisperers of tradition and the advice of his neighbours had conspired to assure him would follow. He accordingly called several of his friends together on an appointed day, and having lighted a large fire, brought forth his best calf, and without ceremony or remorse, pushed it into the flames. The innocent victim, on feeling the intolerable heat, endeavoured to escape ; but this was in vain. The barbarians that surrounded the fire were armed with pitchforks, or *pikes,* as in Cornwall they are generally called ; and, as the burning victim endeavoured to escape from death, with these instruments of cruelty the wretches pushed back the tortured animal into the flames. In this state, amidst the wounds of pitchforks, the shouts of unfeeling ignorance and cruelty, and the corrosion of flames, the dying victim poured out its expiring groan, and was consumed to ashes. It is scarcely possible to reflect on this instance of superstitious barbarity without tracing a kind of resemblance between it and the ancient sacrifices of the Druids. This *calf* was *sacrificed to fortune,* or *good luck,* to avert impending calamity, and to insure future prosperity, and was selected by the farmer as the finest among his herd.' Every intelligent native of Cornwall will perceive that this extract from the history of his county is here made for the purpose of shaming the brutally ignorant, if it be possible, into humanity." *

The remarks in Drew and Hitchin are as follows :—

"There is a tradition in Cornwall, which has been handed down from remote antiquity, that farmers may prevent any calamity by burning alive the finest calf they possess. This was so fully believed, that even as late as the year 1800, an ignorant old farmer, having met with some severe losses in his cattle, determined on being advised by some neighbours, not less barbarous than himself, to try this remedy. He accordingly, on an appointed day, called his friends together, lighted a large fire, brought forth his best calf, and without ceremony or remorse, pushed it into the flames."

[While correcting these sheets, I am informed of two recent instances of this superstition. One of them was the sacrifice of a calf by a farmer near Portreath, for the purpose of removing a disease which had long followed his horses and his cows. The other was the burning of a living lamb, to save, as the farmer said, "his flock from spells which had been cast on 'em."]

* Burning a Calf Alive.—Hone's "Every-Day Book," June 24, p. 431.

DEMONS AND SPECTRES.

"A ghost, shrouded and folded up
In its own formless horror."

The Cenci—SHELLEY

"I woke; it was the midnight hour,
The clock was echoing in the tower;
But though my slumber was gone by,
This dream it would not pass away—
It seems to live upon my eye!"

Christabel—COLERIDGE

ROMANCES OF DEMONS, SPECTRE

ETC.

THE HOOTING CAIRN.

"On either hand, to left to right,
Heath, pasture, stream, and lake,
Glanced dazzling by, too swift for sight;
The thundering bridges quake.
'Dost fear, my love? The moon shines bright.
Hurrah! The dead ride swift to-night;
And art thou of the dead afraid?'
'Oh no! but name them not—the dead.'"
—BÜRGER's *Leonora, Herschel's Translation.*

CAIRN Kenidzhek, pronounced Kenidjack, signifying Hooting Cairn, is on the north road from St Just to Penzance, and is strikingly distinguished from other hills by its rugged character. Hoary stones, bleached by the sunshine of ages, are reared in fantastic confusion. The spirits of the Celts, possibly the spirits of a yet older people, dwell amidst those rocks. Within the shadow of this hill are mounds and barrows, and mystic circles, and holed stones, and rude altars, still telling of the past. The dead hold undisputed possession of all around; no ploughshare has dared to invade this sacred spot, and every effort made by modern man to mark his sway is indicated by its ruin. Nothing but what the Briton planted remains, and, if tales tell true, it is probable long years must pass before the Englishman can banish the Celtic powers who here hold sovereign sway.

"A weird tract is that of Kenidzhek and the Gump, and of ill repute. The old, half-starved horses on the common, with their hides grown rusty brown, like dried and withered grass, by exposure, are ridden by the archfiend at night. He is said to hunt lost souls over this heath; and an old stile hard by bears an evil name, for there the souls are sure to be caught, none being able to get over it. The people tell of midnight fights by demons, and of a shadowy form holding a lantern to the combatants." —*Blight.*

One of the tales which I have heard may be given as a strange mixture of the Celtic and the monastic legend.

Two miners who had been working in one of the now abandoned mines in Morvah, had, their labours being over, been, as was common, " half-pinting " in the public-house in Morvah Churchtown. It was after dark, but not late ; they were very quiet men, and not drunk. They had walked on, talking of the prospects of the mine, and speculating on the promise of certain " pitches," and were now on the Common, at the base of the Hooting Cairn. No miner ever passed within the shadow of Cairn Kenidzhek who dared to indulge in any frivolous talk : at least, thirty years since, the influence akin to fear was very potent upon all.

Well, our two friends became silent, and trudged with a firm, a resolved footstep onward.

There was but little wind, yet a low moaning sound came from the cairn, which now and then arose into a hoot. The night was dark, yet a strange gleaming light rendered the rocks on the cairn visible, and both the miners fancied they saw gigantic forms passing in and about the intricate rocks. Presently they heard a horse galloping at no great distance behind them. They turned and saw, mounted on a horse which they knew very well, since the bony brute had often worked the " whim " on their mine, a dark man robed in a black gown, and a hood over his head, partly covering his face.

" Hallo ! hallo ! " shouted they, fearing the rider would-ride over them.

" Hallo to you," answered a gruff voice.

" Where be'st goen then ? " asked the bravest of the miners.

" Up to the cairn to see the wrestling," answered the rider ; " come along ! come along ! "

Horse and rider rushed by the two miners, and, they could never tell why, they found themselves compelled to follow.

They did not appear to exert themselves, but without much effort they kept up with the galloping horse. Now and then the dark rider motioned them onward with his hand, but he spoke not. At length the miners arrived at a mass of rocks near the base of the hill, which stopped their way ; and, since it was dark, they knew not how to get past them. Presently they saw the rider ascending the hill, regardless of the masses of rock ; passing unconcernedly over all, and, as it seemed to them, the man, the horse, and the rocks were engaged in a " three man's song," * the chorus to which was a piercing hoot. A great number of uncouth figures were gathering together, coming, as it seemed, out of the rocks themselves. They were men of great size and strength, with savage faces, rendered more terrible by the masses of uncombed hair which hung about them, and the colours with which they had painted their cheeks. The plain in front of the rocks which had checked the miners' progress was evidently to be the wrestling ground. Here gathered those monstrous-looking men, all anxiety, making a strange noise. It was not long ere they saw the rider, who was now on foot, descending the hill with two giants of men, more terrible than any they had yet seen.

A circle was formed ; the rider, who had thrown off his black gown, and discovered to the miners that he was no other than Old Nick, placed the two men, and seated himself in a very odd manner upon the ground.

The miners declared the wrestlers were no other than two devils, although the horns and tail were wanting. There was a shout, which, as if it indicated that the light was insufficient, was answered by the squatting demon by flashing from his eyes two beams of fire, which shed an unearthly glow over everything. To it the wrestlers went, and better men were never seen to the west of Penzance. At length one of them, straining hard for the mastery, lifted his antagonist fairly high in the air, and flung him to the ground, a fair back fall. The rocks trembled, and the ground seemed to thunder with the force of the fall. Old Nick still sat quietly looking on, and notwithstanding the defeated wrestler lay as one dead, no one went near him. All crowded around the victor, and shouted like so many wild beasts. The love of fair play was strong in the hearts of the miners ; they scorned the idea of deserting a fallen foe ; so they scrambled over the rocks, and made for the prostrate giant, for so, for size, he might well be called. He was in a dreadful strait. Whether his bones were smashed or not by the fall, they could not tell, but he appeared " passing away." The elder miner had long been a professor of religion. It is true he had fallen back ; but still he knew the right road. He thought, therefore, that even a devil might repent, and he whispered in the ear of the dying man the Christian's hope.

If a thunderbolt had fallen amongst them, it could not have

" They have also *Cornish* three men's songs, cunningly contrived for the ditty, and pleasant for the note."—*Carew*, p. 72.

produced such an effect as this. The rocks shook with an earth-quake; everything became pitchy dark; there was a noise of rushing hither and thither, and all were gone, dying man and all, they knew not whither. The two miners, terrified beyond measure, clung to each other on their knees; and, while in this position, they saw, as if in the air, the two blazing eyes of the demon passing away into the west, and at last disappear in a dreadfully black cloud. These two men were, although they knew the ground perfectly well, inextricably lost; so, after vainly endeavouring to find the right road off the Common, they lay down in each other's arms under a mass of granite rock, praying that they might be protected till the light of day removed the spell which was upon them.

JAGO'S DEMON.

THE vicar of Wendron, who bore the name of Jago, appears to have had strange intercourse with the invisible world; or, rather, the primitive people of this district believe him to have possessed supernatural powers. Any one visiting the parish of Wendron will be struck with many distinguishing features in its inhabitants. It would appear as if a strange people had settled down amidst the races already inhabiting the spot, and that they had studiously avoided any intimate connection with their neighbours. The dialect of the Wendron people is unlike any other in Cornwall, and there are many customs existing amongst them which are not found in any other part of the county. Until of late years, the inhabitants of Wendron were quite uneducated;— hence the readiness with which they associate ancient superstitions with comparatively modern individuals.

The Reverend Mr Jago was no doubt a man who impressed this people with the powers of his knowledge. Hence we are told that no spirit walking the earth could resist the spells laid upon him by Jago. By his prayers—or powers—many a night wanderer has been put back into his grave, and so confined that the poor ghost could never again get loose. To the evil-disposed Mr Jago was a terror. All Wendron believed that every act was visible to the parson at the moment it was done—day or night it mattered not. He has been known to pick a thief at once out of a crowd, and criminal men or women could not endure the glance of his eye. Many a person has at once confessed to guilty deeds of which they have been suspected the moment they have been brought before Mr Jago.

We are told that he had spirits continually waiting upon him, though invisible until he desired them to appear. The parson rode far and wide over the moorland of his parish. He never took a groom with him; for, the moment he alighted from his horse, he had only to strike the earth with his whip, and up came a demon-groom to take charge of the steed.

PETER THE DEVIL.

THE church at Altarnun is said to have been built from the remains of an ancient nunnery which had been founded in the early days of Christianity by the saint to whom it was dedicated.

There was a peculiar sanctity about all that surrounded this little church and its holy well, and few were unfaithful enough to scoff at any of the holy traditions of the sacred place.

About the time of Charles II., an under-clerk or deacon of this church was called Peter, and he is said to have been a man of exceedingly bad character. He scoffed at holy things, and—unless he was belied—he made use of his position for merely temporal benefit, and was not remarkable for his honesty. He was, moreover, the terror of the neighbourhood. Common report insisting on it that Peter had been known to disentomb the dead, whether for the purpose of stealing rings and other trinkets which may have been buried, as some said, or for the purpose of renewing his youth, as others suggested, by mysterious contact with the dead, was not clearly made out. He was invariably called Peter Jowle, or Joule—that is, Peter the Devil. At the age of a hundred he was a gray-headed, toothless man; but then, by some diabolical incantation, he is said to have caused new black hairs to spring forth amongst those which were white with age, and then also new teeth grew in his jaws. Peter is said to have died when he was more than a hundred and fifty years old.

DANDO AND HIS DOGS.

IN the neighbourhood of the lovely village of St Germans formerly lived a priest connected with the old priory church of this parish, whose life does not appear to have been quite consistent with his vows.

He lived the life of the traditional "jolly friar." He ate and drank of the best the land could give him, or money buy; and it is said that his indulgences extended far beyond the ordinary limits of good living. The priest Dando was, notwithstanding all his vices, a man liked by the people. He was good-natured, and therefore blind to many of their sins. Indeed, he threw a cloak over his own iniquities, which was inscribed " charity," and he freely forgave all those who came to his confessional.

As a man increases in years he becomes more deeply dyed with the polluted waters through which he may have waded. It rarely happens that an old sinner is ever a repentant one, until the decay of nature has reduced him to a state of second childhood. As long as health allows him to enjoy the sensualities of life, he continues to gratify his passions, regardless of the cost. He becomes more selfish, and his own gratification is the rule of his existence. So it has ever been, and so was it with Dando.

The sinful priest was a capital huntsman, and scoured the country far and near in pursuit of game, which was in those days abundant and varied, over this well-wooded district. Dando, in the eagerness of the chase, paid no regard to any kind of property. Many a corn-field has been trampled down, and many a cottage garden destroyed by the horses and dogs which this impetuous hunter would lead unthinkingly over them. Curses deep, though not loud, would follow the old man, as even those who suffered by his excesses were still in fear of his priestly power.

Any man may sell his soul to the devil without going through the stereotyped process of signing a deed with his blood. Give up your soul to Satan's darling sins, and he will help you for a season, until he has his chains carefully wound around you, when the links are suddenly closed, and he seizes his victim, who has no power to resist.

Dando worshipped the sensual gods which he had created, and his external worship of the God of truth became every year more and more a hypocritical lie. The devil looked carefully after his prize. Of course, to catch a dignitary of the church was a thing to cause rejoicings amongst the lost; and Dando was carefully lured to the undoing of his soul. Health and wealth were secured to him, and by and by the measure of his sins was full, and he was left the victim to self-indulgences—a doomed man. With increasing years, and the immunities he enjoyed, Dando became more reckless. Wine and wassail, a board groaning with dishes which stimulated the sated appetite, and the company of both sexes of dissolute habits, exhausted his nights. His days were devoted to the pursuits of the field ; and to maintain the required excitement, ardent drinks were supplied him by his wicked companions. It mattered not to Dando,—provided the day was an auspicious one, if the scent would lie on the ground,—even on the Sabbath, horses and hounds were ordered out, and the priest would be seen in full cry.

One Sabbath morning, Dando and his riotous rout were hunting over the Earth estate ; game was plenty, and sport first-rate. Exausted with a long and eager run, Dando called for drink.   He had already exhausted the flasks of the attendant hunters.

" Drink, I say ; give me drink," he cried.

" Whence can we get it ? " asked one of the gang.

" Go to hell for it, if you can't get it on Earth," said the priest, with a bitter laugh at his own joke on the Earth estate. ·

At the moment, a dashing hunter, who had mingled with the throng unobserved, came forward, and presented a richly-mounted flask to Dando, saying,—

" Here is some choice liquor distilled in the establishment you speak of.   It will warm and revive you, I 'll warrant.   Drink deep, friend, drink."

Dando drank deep ; the flask appeared to cling to his lips. The strange hunter looked on with a rejoicing yet malignant expression, a wicked smile playing over an otherwise tranquil face.

By and by Dando fetched a deep sigh, and removed the flask, exclaiming, " By hell ! that was a drink indeed.   Do the gods drink such nectar ? "

" Devils do," said the hunter.

" An they do, I wish I were one," said Dando, who now rocked to and fro in a state of thorough intoxication ; " methinks the drink is very like "—— The impious expression died upon his lips.

Looking round with a half-idiotic stare, Dando saw that his new friend had appropriated several head of game.   Notwithstanding his stupid intoxication, his selfishness asserted its power, and he seized the game, exclaiming, in a guttural, half-smothered voice, " None of these are thine."

" What I catch I keep," said the hunter.

" By all the devils they 're mine," stammered Dando.

The hunter quietly bowed.

Dando's wrath burst at once into a burning flame, uncontrolled by reason.   He rolled himself off his horse, and rushed, staggering as he went, at the steed of his unknown friend, uttering most frightful oaths and curses.

The strange hunter's horse was a splendid creature, black as night, and its eyes gleamed like the brightest stars with unnatural lustre.   The horse was turned adroitly aside, and Dando fell to the earth with much force.   The fall appeared to add to his fury, and he roared with rage. Aided by his attendants, he was speedily on his legs, and again at the side of the hunter, who shook with laughter, shaking the game in derision, and quietly uttering, " They 're mine."

" I 'll go to hell after them, but I 'll get them from thee," shouted Dando.

" So thou shalt," said the hunter; and seizing Dando by the collar, he lifted him from the ground, and placed him, as though he were a child, before him on the horse.

With a dash, the horse passed down the hill, its hoofs striking fire at every tread, and the dogs, barking furiously, followed impetuously. These strange riders reached the banks of the Lynher, and with a terrific leap, the horse and its riders, followed by the hounds, went out far in its waters, disappearing at length in a blaze of fire, which caused the stream to boil for a moment, and then the waters flowed on as tranquilly as ever over the doomed priest. All this happened in the sight of the assembled peasantry. Dando never more was seen, and his fearful death was received as a warning by many, who gave gifts to the church. One amongst them carved a chair for the bishop, and on it he represented Dando and his dogs, that the memory of his wickedness might be always renewed. There, in St German's Church, stands to this day the chair, and all who doubt the truth of this tradition may view the story carved in enduring oak. If they please, they can sit in the chair until their faith is so far quickened that they become true believers. On Sunday mornings early, the dogs of the priest have been often heard as if in eager pursuit of game. Cheney's hounds and the Wish hounds of Dartmoor are but other versions of the same legend.*

Mr T. Q. Couch, in his " Folk Lore of a Cornish Village," tells the story in a somewhat different form :—

THE DEVIL AND HIS DANDY-DOGS.

" A POOR herdsman was journeying homeward across the moors one windy night, when he heard at a distance among the Tors the baying of hounds, which he soon recognised as the dismal chorus of the dandy-dogs. It was three or four miles to his house; and very much alarmed, he hurried onward as fast as the treacherous nature of the soil and the uncertainty of the path would allow; but, alas! the melancholy yelping of the hounds, and the dismal holloa of the hunter came nearer and nearer. After a considerable run, they had so gained upon him, that on looking back,—oh horror! he could distinctly see hunter and dogs. The former was terrible to look at, and had the usual complement of *saucer-eyes*, horns, and tail, accorded by common consent to the legendary devil. He was black, of course, and carried in his hand a long hunting-pole. The dogs, a numerous pack, blackened the small patch of moor that was visible; each snorting fire, and uttering a yelp of indescribably frightful tone. No cottage, rock, or tree was near to give the herdsman shelter, and nothing apparently remained to him but to abandon himself to their fury, when a happy thought suddenly flashed upon him and suggested a resource. Just as they were about to rush upon him, he fell on his knees in prayer. There was strange power in the holy words he uttered; for immediately, as if resistance had been offered, the hell-hounds stood at bay, howling more dismally than ever, and the hunter shouted, ' Bo Shrove,' which (says my informant) means in the old language, '*The boy prays,*' at which they all drew off on some other pursuit and disappeared."

THE SPECTRAL COACH.*

"You have heard of such a spirit, and well you know
　The superstitious, idle-headed eld
　Received and did deliver to our age
　This tale of Herne the Hunter for a truth."
　　　　　　　—MERRY WIVES OF WINDSOR.

THE old vicarage-house at Talland, as seen from the Looe road, its low roof and gray walls peeping prettily from between the dense boughs of ash and elm that environed it, was as picturesque an object as you could desire to see. The seclusion of its situation was enhanced by the character of the house itself. It was an odd-looking, old-fashioned building, erected apparently in an age when asceticism and self-denial were more in vogue than at present, with a stern disregard of the comfort of the inhabitant, and in utter contempt of received principles of taste. As if not secure enough in its retirement, a high wall, enclosing a courtelage in front, effectually protected its inmates from the prying passenger, and only revealed the upper part of the house, with its small Gothic windows, its slated roof, and heavy chimneys partly hidden by the evergreen shrubs which grew in the enclosure. Such was it until its removal a few years since; and such was it as it lay sweetly in the shadows of an autumnal evening one hundred and thirty years ago, when a stranger in the garb of a country labourer knocked hesitatingly at the wicket-gate which conducted to the court. After a little delay a servant-girl appeared, and finding that the countryman bore a message to the vicar, admitted him within the walls, and conducted him along a paved passage to the little, low, damp parlour where sat the good man. The Rev. Mr Dodge was in many respects a remarkable man.

* Contributed by T. Q. Couch, Esq.

You would have judged as much of him as he sat before the fire in his high-back chair, in an attitude of thought, arranging, it may have been, the heads of his next Sabbath's discourse. His heavy eyebrows throwing into shade his spacious eyes, and indeed the whole contour of his face, marked him as a man of great firmness of character and of much moral and personal courage. His suit of sober black and full-bottomed periwig also added to his dignity, and gave him an appearance of greater age. He was then verging on sixty. The time and the place gave him abundant exercise for the qualities we have mentioned, for many of his parishioners obtained their livelihood by the contraband trade, and were mostly men of unscrupulous and daring character, little likely to bear with patience reflections on the dishonesty of their calling. Nevertheless, the vicar was fearless in reprehending it, and his frank exhortations were, at least, listened to on account of the simple honesty of the man, and his well-known kindness of heart. The eccentricity of his life, too, had a wonderful effect in procuring him the respect, not to say the awe, of a people superstitious in a more than ordinary degree. Ghosts in those days had more freedom accorded them, or had more business with the visible world, than at present; and the parson was frequently required by his parishioners to draw from the uneasy spirit the dread secret which troubled it, or by the aid of the solemn prayers of the Church to set it at rest for ever. Mr Dodge had a fame as an exorcist, which was not confined to the bounds of his parish, nor limited to the age in which he lived.

"Well, my good man, what brings you hither?" said the clergyman to the messenger.

"A letter, may it please your reverence, from Mr Mills of Lanreath," said the countryman, handing him a letter.

Mr Dodge opened it and read as follows :—

"My dear brother Dodge,—I have ventured to trouble you, at the earnest request of my parishioners, with a matter, of which some particulars have doubtless reached you, and which has caused, and is causing, much terror in my neighbourhood. For its fuller explication, I will be so tedious as to recount to you the whole of this strange story as it has reached my ears, for as yet I have not satisfied my eyes of its truth. It has been told me by men of honest and good report (witnesses of a portion of what they relate), with such strong assurances that it behoves us to look more closely into the matter. There is in the neighbourhood of this village a barren bit of moor which had no owner, or rather more than one, for the lords of the adjoining manors debated its ownership between themselves, and both determined to take it from the poor, who have for many years past regarded it as a common. And truly, it is little to the credit of these gentlemen, that they should strive for a thing so worthless as scarce to bear the cost of law, and yet of no mean value to poor labouring people. The two litigants, however, contested it with as much violence as if it had been a field of great price, and especially one, an old man (whose thoughts should have been less set on earthly possessions, which he was soon to leave), had so set his heart on the success of his suit, that the loss of it, a few years back, is said to have much hastened his death. Nor, indeed, after death, if current reports are worthy of credit, does he quit his claim to it ; for at night-time his apparition is seen on the moor, to the great terror of the neighbouring villagers. A public path leads by at no great distance from the spot, and on divers occasions has the labourer, returning from his work, been frightened nigh unto lunacy by sight and sounds of a very dreadful character. The appearance is said to be that of a man habited in black, driving a carriage drawn by headless horses. This is, I avow, very marvellous to believe, but it has had so much credible testimony, and has gained so many believers in my parish, that some steps seem necessary to allay the excitement it causes. I have been applied to for this purpose, and my present business is to ask your assistance in this matter, either to reassure the minds of the country people, if it be only a simple terror ; or, if there be truth in it, to set the troubled spirit of the man at rest. My messenger, who is an industrious, trustworthy man, will give you more information if it be needed, for, from report, he is acquainted with most of the circumstances, and will bring back your advice and promise of assistance.

"Not doubting of your help herein, I do, with my very hearty commendation, commit you to God's protection and blessing, and am,

"Your very loving brother,

"ABRAHAM MILLS."

This remarkable note was read and re-read, while the countryman sat watching its effects on the parson's countenance, and was surprised that it changed not from its usual sedate and settled character. Turning at length to the man, Mr Dodge inquired, "Are you, then, acquainted with my good friend Mills ? "

" I should know him, sir," replied the messenger, " having been sexton to the parish for fourteen years, and being, with my family, much beholden to the kindness of the rector."

" You are also not without some knowledge of the circumstances related in this letter. Have you been an eye-witness to any of those strange sights ? "

" For myself, sir, I have been on the road at all hours of the night and day, and never did I see anything which I could call worse than myself. One night my wife and I were awoke by the rattle of wheels, which was also heard by some of our neighbours, and we are all assured that it could have been no other than the black coach. We have every day such stories told in the villages by so many creditable persons, that it would not be proper in a plain, ignorant man like me to doubt it."

" And how far," asked the clergyman, " is the moor from Lanreath ? "

" About two miles, and please your reverence. The whole parish is so frightened, that few will venture far after nightfall, for it has of late come much nearer the village. A man who is esteemed a sensible and pious man by many, though an Anabaptist in principle, went a few weeks back to the moor ('tis called Blackadon) at midnight, in order to lay the spirit, being requested thereto by his neighbours, and he was so alarmed at what he saw, that he hath been somewhat mazed ever since."

" A fitting punishment for his presumption, if it hath not quite demented him," said the parson. " These persons are like those addressed by St Chrysostom, fitly called the golden-mouthed, who said, ' Miserable wretches that ye be ! ye cannot expel a flea, much less a devil !' It will be well if it serves no other purpose but to bring back these stray sheep to the fold of the Church. So this story has gained much belief in the parish ? "

" Most believe it, sir, as rightly they should, what hath so many witnesses," said the sexton, " though there be some, chiefly young men, who set up for being wiser than their fathers, and refuse to credit it, though it be sworn to on the book."

" If those things are disbelieved, friend," said the parson, " and without inquiry, which your disbeliever is ever the first to shrink from, of what worth is human testimony ? That ghosts have returned to the earth, either for the discovery of murder, or to make restitution for other injustice committed in the flesh, or compelled thereto by the incantations of sorcery, or to communicate tidings from another world, has been testified to in all ages, and many are the accounts which have been left us both in sacred and profane authors. Did not Brutus, when in Asia, as is related by Plutarch, see "——

Just at this moment the parson's handmaid announced that a person waited on him in the kitchen,—or the good clergyman would probably have detailed all those cases in history, general and biblical, with which his reading had acquainted him, not much, we fear, to the edification and comfort of the sexton, who had to return to Lanreath, a long and dreary road, after nightfall. So, instead, he directed the girl to take him with her, and give him such refreshment as he needed, and in the meanwhile he prepared a note in answer to Mr Mills, informing him that on the morrow he was to visit some sick persons in his parish, but that on the following evening he should be ready to proceed with him to the moor.

On the night appointed the two clergymen left the Lanreath rectory on horseback, and reached the moor at eleven o'clock. Bleak and dismal did it look by day, but then there was the distant landscape dotted over with pretty homesteads to relieve its desolation. Now, nothing was seen but the black patch of sterile moor on which they stood, nothing heard but the wind as it swept in gusts across the bare hill, and howled dismally through a stunted grove of trees that grew in a glen below them, except the occasional baying of dogs from the farmhouses in the distance. That they felt at ease, is more than could be expected of them; but as it would have shown a lack of faith in the protection of Heaven, which it would have been unseemly in men of their holy calling to exhibit, they managed to conceal from each other their uneasiness. Leading their horses, they trod to and fro through the damp fern and heath with firmness in their steps, and upheld each other by remarks on the power of that Great Being whose ministers they were, and the might of whose name they were there to make manifest. Still slowly and dismally passed the time as they conversed, and anon stopped to look through the darkness for the approach of their ghostly visitor. In vain. Though the night was as dark and murky as ghost could wish, the coach and its driver came not.

After a considerable stay, the two clergymen consulted together, and determined that it was useless to watch any longer for that night, but that they would meet on some other, when perhaps it might please his ghostship to appear. Accordingly, with a few words of leave-taking, they separated, Mr Mills for the rectory, and Mr Dodge, by a short ride across the moor, which shortened his journey by half a mile, for the vicarage at Talland.

The vicar rode on at an ambling pace, which his good mare sustained up hill and down dale without urging. At the bottom of a deep valley, however, about a mile from Blackadon, the animal became very uneasy, pricked up her ears, snorted, and moved from side to side of the road, as if something stood in the path before her. The parson tightened the reins, and applied whip and spur to her sides, but the animal, usually docile, became very unruly, made several attempts to turn, and, when prevented, threw herself upon her haunches. Whip and spur were applied again and again, to no other purpose than to add to the horse's terror. To the rider nothing was apparent which could account for the sudden restiveness of his beast. He dismounted, and attempted in turns to lead or drag her, but both were impracticable, and attended with no small risk of snapping the reins. She was remounted with great difficulty, and another attempt was made to urge her forward, with the like want of success. At length the eccentric clergyman, judging it to be some special signal from Heaven, which it would be dangerous to neglect, threw the reins on the neck of his steed, which, wheeling suddenly round, started backward in a direction towards the moor, at a pace which rendered the parson's seat neither a pleasant nor a safe one. In an astonishingly short space of time they were once more a Blackadon.

By this time the bare outline of the moor was broken by a large black group of objects, which the darkness of the night prevented the parson from defining. On approaching this unaccountable appearance, the mare was seized with fresh fury, and it was with considerable difficulty that she could be brought to face this new cause of fright. In the pauses of the horse's prancing, the vicar discovered to his horror the much-dreaded spectacle of the black coach and the headless steeds, and, terrible to relate, his friend Mr Mills lying prostrate on the ground before the sable driver. Little time was left him to call up his courage for this fearful emergency; for just as the vicar began to give utterance to the earnest prayers which struggled to his lips, the spectre shouted, "Dodge is come! I must begone!" and forthwith leaped into his chariot, and disappeared across the moor.

The fury of the mare now subsided, and Mr Dodge was enabled to approach his friend, who was lying motionless and speechless, with his face buried in the heather.

Meanwhile the rector's horse, which had taken fright at the apparition, and had thrown his rider to the ground on or near the spot where we have left him lying, made homeward at a furious speed, and stopped not until he had reached his stable door. The sound of his hoofs as he galloped madly through the village awoke the cottagers, many of whom had been some hours in their beds. Many eager faces, staring with affright, gathered round the rectory, and added, by their various conjectures, to the terror and apprehensions of the family.

The villagers, gathering courage as their numbers increased, agreed to go in search of the missing clergyman, and started off in a compact body, a few on horseback, but the greater number on foot, in the direction of Blackadon. There they discovered their rector, supported in the arms of Parson Dodge, and recovered so far as to be able to speak. Still there was a wildness in his eye, and an incoherency in his speech, that showed that his reason was, at least, temporarily unsettled by the fright. In this condition he was taken to his home, followed by his reverend companion.

Here ended this strange adventure; for Mr Mills soon completely regained his reason, Parson Dodge got safely back to Talland, and from that time to this nothing has been heard or seen of the black ghost or his chariot.*

SIR FRANCIS DRAKE AND HIS DEMON.

SIR FRANCIS DRAKE—who appears to have been especially befriended by his demon—is said to drive at night a black hearse drawn by headless horses, and urged on by running devils and yelping, headless dogs, through Jump, on the road from Tavistock to Plymouth.

Sir Francis, according to tradition, was enabled to destroy the Spanish armada by the aid of the devil. The old admiral went to Devil's Point, a well-known promontory jutting into Plymouth Sound. He there cut pieces of wood into the water, and by the power of magic and the assistance of his demon these became at once well-armed gunboats.

The Queen, Elizabeth, gave Sir Franois Drake Buckland Abbey; and on every hand we hear of Drake and his familiars.

An extensive building attached to the abbey—which was no doubt used as barns and stables after the place had been deprived of its religious character—was said to have been built by the devil in three nights. After the first night, the butler, astonished at the work done, resolved to watch and see how it was performed. Consequently, on the second night, he mounted into a large tree, and hid himself between the forks of its five branches. At midnight the devil came, driving several teams of oxen; and as some of them were lazy, he plucked this tree from the ground and used

---

* The Parson Dodge, whose adventure is related, was vicar of Talland from 1713 till his death. So that the name as well as the story is true to tradition. Bond ("History of East and West Love") says of him: "About a century since the Rev. Richard Dodge was vicar of this parish of Talland, and was, by traditionary account, a very singular man. He had the reputation of being deeply skilled in the black art, and would raise ghosts, or send them into the Dead Sea, at the nod of his head. The common people, not only in his own parish, but throughout the neighbourhood, stood in the greatest awe of him, and to meet him on the highway at midnight produced the utmost horror; he was then driving about the evil spirits; many of them were seen, in all sorts of shapes, flying and running before him, and he pursuing them with his whip in a most daring manner. Not unfrequently he would be seen in the churchyard at dead of night to the terror of passers-by. He was a worthy man, and much respected, but had his eccentricities."

it as a goad. The poor butler lost his senses, and never recovered them.

Drake constructed the Channel, carrying the waters from Dartmoor to Plymouth. Tradition says he went with his demon to Dartmoor, walked into Plymouth, and the waters followed him.* Even now,—as old Betty Donithorne, formerly the housekeeper at Buckland Abbey, told me,—if the warrior hears the drum which hangs in the hall of the abbey, and which accompanied him round the world, he rises and has a revel.

Some few years since a small box was found in a closet which had been long closed, containing, it is supposed, family papers. This was to be sent to the residence of the inheritor of this property. The carriage was at the abbey door, and a man easily lifted the box into it. The owner having taken his seat, the coachman attempted to start his horses, but in vain. They would not—they could not move. More horses were brought, and then the heavy farm-horses, and eventually all the oxen. They were powerless to start the carriage. At length a mysterious voice was heard, declaring that the box could never be moved from Buckland Abbey. It was taken from the carriage easily by one man, and a pair of horses galloped off with the carriage.

THE PARSON AND CLERK.

NEAR Dawlish stand, out in the sea, two rocks, of red sandstone conglomerate, to which the above name is given.

Seeing that this forms a part of Old Cornwall, I do not go beyond my limits in telling the true story of these singular rocks.

The Bishop of Exeter was sick unto death at Dawlish. An ambitious priest, from the east, frequently rode with his clerk to make anxious inquiries after the condition of the dying bishop. It is whispered that this priest had great hopes of occupying the bishop's throne in Exeter Cathedral.

The clerk was usually the priest's guide; but somehow or other, on a particularly stormy night, he lost the road, and they were wandering over Haldon. Excessively angry was the priest, and very provoking was the clerk. He led his master this way and that way, but they were yet upon the elevated country of Haldon.

* " Here Sir Francis Drake first extended the point of that liquid line wherewith (as an emulator of the sunnes glorie) he encompassed the world."—*The Survey of Cornwall, Carew.*

At length the priest, in a great rage, exclaimed, " I would rather have the devil for a guide than you." Presently the clatter of horse's hoofs were heard, and a peasant, on a moor pony, rode up. The priest told of his condition, and the peasant volunteered to guide them. On rode peasant, priest, and clerk, and presently they were at Dawlish. The night was tempestuous, the ride had quickened the appetite of the priest, and he was wet through, —therefore, when his friend asked him to supper, as they approached an old ruined house, through the windows of which bright lights were shining, there was no hesitation in accepting the invitation.

There were a host of friends gathered together—a strange, wild-looking lot of men. But as the tables were laden with substantial dishes, and black-jacks were standing thick around, the parson, and the clerk too, soon made friends with all.

They ate and drank, and became most irreligiously uproarious. The parson sang hunting songs, and songs in praise of a certain old gentleman, with whom a priest should not have maintained any acquaintance. These were very highly appreciated, and every man joined loudly in the choruses. Night wore away, and at last news was brought that the bishop was dead. This appeared to rouse up the parson, who was only too eager to get the first intelligence, and go to work to secure the hope of his ambition. So master and man mounted their horses, and bade adieu to their hilarious friends.

They were yet at the door of the mansion—somehow or other the horses did not appear disposed to move. They were whipped and spurred, but to no purpose.

" The devil's in the horses," said the priest.

" I b'lieve he is," said the clerk.

" Devil or no devil, they shall go," said the parson, cutting his horse madly with his heavy whip.

There was a roar of unearthly laughter.

The priest looked round—his drinking friends were all turned into demons, wild with glee, and the peasant guide was an arch little devil, looking on with a marvellously curious twinkle in his eyes. The noise of waters was around them ; and now the priest discovered that the mansion had disappeared, and that waves beat heavy upon his horse's flanks, and rushed over the smaller horse of his man.

Repentance was too late.

In the morning following this stormy night, two horses were

found straying on the sands at Dawlish ; and clinging with the
grasp of death to two rocks, were found the parson and the clerk.
There stand the rocks to which the devil had given the forms of
horses—an enduring monument to all generations.

THE HAUNTED WIDOWER.

A LABOURING man, very shortly after his wife's death,
sent to a servant girl, living at the time in a small ship-
ping port, requesting her to come to the inn to him. The girl
went, and over a " ha' pint " she agreed to accept him as her
husband.

All went on pleasantly enough for a time. One evening the
man met the girl. He was silent for some time and sorrowful,
but at length he told her his wife had come back.

" What do'st mean ? " asked the girl ; " have 'e seen hur ? "

" Naw, I han't seed her."

" Why, how do'st knaw it is her then ? "

The poor man explained to her, that at night, when in bed, she
would come to the side of it, and " flop " his face ; and there was
no mistaking her " flop."

" So you knawed her flop, did 'e ? " asked the girl.

" Ay, it couldn't be mistook."

" If she do hunt thee," said the girl, " she 'll hunt me ; and if
she do flop 'e, she 'll flop me,—so it must be off atween us."

The unfortunate flop of the dead wife prevented the man from
securing a living one.

THE SPECTRE BRIDEGROOM.

LONG, long ago a farmer named Lenine lived in Boscean.
He had but one son, Frank Lenine, who was indulged into
waywardness by both his parents. In addition to the farm servants, there was one, a young girl, Nancy Trenoweth, who especially assisted Mrs Lenine in all the various duties of a small
farmhouse.

Nancy Trenoweth was very pretty, and although perfectly uneducated, in the sense in which we now employ the term education,
she possessed many native graces, and she had acquired much
knowledge, really useful to one whose aspirations would probably
never rise higher than to be mistress of a farm of a few acres. Educated by parents who had certainly never seen the world beyond
Penzance, her ideas of the world were limited to a few miles around

the Land's End. But although her book of nature was a small one, it had deeply impressed her mind with its influences. The wild waste, the small but fertile valley, the rugged hills, with their crowns of cairns, the moors rich in the golden furze and the purple heath, the sea-beaten cliffs, and the silver sands, were the pages she had studied, under the guidance of a mother who conceived, in the sublimity of her ignorance, that everything in nature was the home of some spirit form. The soul of the girl was imbued with the deeply religious dye of her mother's mind, whose religion was only a sense of an unknown world immediately beyond our own. The elder Nancy Trenoweth exerted over the villagers around her considerable power. They did not exactly fear her. She was too free from evil for that ; but they were conscious of a mental superiority, and yielded without complaining to her sway.

The result of this was, that the younger Nancy, although compelled to service, always exhibited some pride, from a feeling that her mother was a superior woman to any around her.

She never felt herself inferior to her master and mistress, yet she complained not of being in subjection to them. There were so many interesting features in the character of this young servant girl that she became in many respects like a daughter to her mistress. There was no broad line of division in those days, in even the manorial hall, between the lord and his domestics, and still less defined was the position of the employer and the employed in a small farmhouse. Consequent on this condition of things, Frank Lenine and Nancy were thrown as much together as if they had been brother and sister. Frank was rarely checked in anything by his over-fond parents, who were especially proud of their son, since he was regarded as the handsomest young man in the parish. Frank conceived a very warm attachment for Nancy, and she was not a little proud of her lover. Although it was evident to all the parish that Frank and Nancy were seriously devoted to each other, the young man's parents were blind to it, and were taken by surprise when one day Frank asked his father and mother to consent to his marrying Nancy.

The Lenines had allowed their son to have his own way from his youth up ; and now, in a matter which brought into play the strongest of human feelings, they were angry because he refused to bend to their wills.

The old man felt it would be a degradation for a Lenine to marry a Trenoweth, and, in the most unreasoning manner, he resolved it should never be.

The first act was to send Nancy home to Alsia Mill, where

her parents resided ; the next was an imperious command to his son never again to see the girl.

The commands of the old are generally powerless upon the young where the affairs of the heart are concerned. So were they upon Frank. He, who was rarely seen of an evening beyond the garden of his father's cottage, was now as constantly absent from his home. The house, which was wont to be a pleasant one, was strangely altered. A gloom had fallen over all things ; the father and son rarely met as friends—the mother and her boy had now a feeling of reserve. Often there were angry altercations between the father and son, and the mother felt she could not become the defender of her boy in his open acts of disobedience, his bold defiance of his parents' commands.

Rarely an evening passed that did not find Nancy and Frank together in some retired nook. The Holy Well was a favourite meeting-place, and here the most solemn vows were made. Locks of hair were exchanged ; a wedding-ring, taken from the finger of a corpse, was broken, when they vowed that they would be united either dead or alive ; and they even climbed at night the granite-pile at Treryn, and swore by the Logan Rock the same strong vow.

Time passed onward thus unhappily, and, as the result of the endeavours to quench out the passion by force, it grew stronger under the repressing power, and, like imprisoned steam, eventually burst through all restraint.

Nancy's parents discovered at length that moonlight meetings between two untrained, impulsive youths, had a natural result, and they were now doubly earnest in their endeavours to compel Frank to marry their daughter.

The elder Lenine could not be brought to consent to this, and he firmly resolved to remove his son entirely from what he considered the hateful influences of the Trenoweths. He resolved to go to Plymouth, to take his son with him, and, if possible, to send him away to sea, hoping thus to wean him from his folly, as he considered this love-madness. Frank, poor fellow, with the best intentions, was not capable of any sustained effort, and consequently he at length succumbed to his father ; and, to escape his persecution, he entered a ship bound for India, and bade adieu to his native land.

Frank could not write, and this happened in days when letters could be forwarded only with extreme difficulty, consequently Nancy never heard from her lover.

A baby had been born into a troublesome world, and the infant became a real solace to the young mother. As the child grew, it became an especial favourite with its grandmother; the elder Nancy rejoiced over the little prattler, and forgot her cause of sorrow. Young Nancy lived for her child, and on the memory of its father. Subdued in spirit she was, but her affliction had given force to her character, and she had been heard to declare that wherever Frank might be she was ever present with him; whatever might be the temptations of the hour, that her influence was all-powerful over him for good. She felt that no distance could separate their souls, that no time could be long enough to destroy the bond between them.

A period of distress fell upon the Trenoweths, and it was necessary that Nancy should leave her home once more, and go again into service. Her mother took charge of the babe, and she found a situation in the village of Kimyall, in the parish of Paul. Nancy, like her mother, contrived by force of character to maintain an ascendancy amongst her companions. She had formed an acquaintance, which certainly never grew into friendship, with some of the daughters of the small farmers around. These girls were all full of the superstitions of the time and place.

The winter was coming on, and nearly three years had passed away since Frank Lenine left his country. As yet there was no sign. Nor father, nor mother, nor maiden had heard of him, and they all sorrowed over his absence. The Lenines desired to have Nancy's child, but the Trenoweths would not part with it. They went so far even as to endeavour to persuade Nancy to live again with them, but Nancy was not at all disposed to submit to their wishes.

It was All-hallows Eve, and two of Nancy's companions persuaded her—no very difficult task—to go with them and sow hemp-seed.

At midnight the three maidens stole out unperceived into Kimyall town-place to perform their incantation. Nancy was the first to sow, the others being less bold than she.

Boldly she advanced, saying, as she scattered the seed,—

> " Hemp-seed I sow thee,
> Hemp-seed grow thee;
> And he who will my true love be,
> Come after me
> And shaw thee."

This was repeated three times, when, looking back over her left shoulder, she saw Lenine; but he looked so angry that she shrieked with fear, and broke the spell. One of the other girls, however, resolved now to make trial of the spell, and the result of her labours was the vision of a white coffin. Fear now fell on all, and they went home sorrowful, to spend each one a sleepless night.

November came with its storms, and during one terrific night a large vessel was thrown upon the rocks in Bernowhall Cliff, and, beaten by the impetuous waves, she was soon in pieces. Amongst the bodies of the crew washed ashore, nearly all of whom had perished, was Frank Lenine. He was not dead when found, but the only words he lived to speak were begging the people to send for Nancy Trenoweth, that he might make her his wife before he died.

Rapidly sinking, Frank was borne by his friends on a litter to Boscean, but he died as he reached the town-place. His parents, overwhelmed in their own sorrows, thought nothing of Nancy, and without her knowing that Lenine had returned, the poor fellow was laid in his last bed, in Burian Churchyard.

On the night of the funeral, Nancy went, as was her custom, to lock the door of the house, and as was her custom too, she looked out into the night. At this instant a horseman rode up in hot haste, called her by name, and hailed her in a voice that made her blood boil.

The voice was the voice of Lenine. She could never forget that ; and the horse she now saw was her sweetheart's favourite colt, on which he had often ridden at night to Alsia.

The rider was imperfectly seen ; but he looked very sorrowful, and deadly pale, still Nancy knew him to be Frank Lenine.

He told her that he had just arrived home, and that the first moment he was at liberty he had taken horse to fetch his loved one, and to make her his bride.

Nancy's excitement was so great, that she was easily persuaded to spring on the horse behind him, that they might reach his home before the morning.

When she took Lenine's hand a cold shiver passed through her, and as she grasped his waist to secure herself in her seat, her arm became as stiff as ice. She lost all power of speech, and suffered deep fear, yet she knew not why. The moon had arisen, and now burst out in a full flood of light, through the heavy clouds which had obscured it. The horse pursued its journey with great rapidity, and whenever in weariness it slackened its speed, the peculiar voice of the rider aroused its drooping energies. Beyond this no word was spoken since Nancy had mounted behind her lover. They now came to Trove Bottom, where there was no bridge at that time ; they dashed into the river. The moon shone full in their faces. Nancy looked into the stream, and saw that the rider was in a shroud and other grave-clothes. She now knew that she was being carried away by a spirit, yet she had no power to save herself; indeed, the inclination to do so did not exist.

On went the horse at a furious pace, until they came to the blacksmith's shop near Burian Church-town, when she knew by the light from the forge fire thrown across the road that the smith was still at his labours. She now recovered speech. " Save me ! save me ! save me ! " she cried with all her might. The smith sprang from the door of the smithy, with a red-hot iron in his hand, and as the horse rushed by, caught the woman's dress and pulled her to the ground. The spirit, however, also seized Nancy's dress in one hand, and his grasp was like that of a vice. The horse passed like the wind, and Nancy and the smith were pulled down as far as the old Almshouses, near the churchyard. Here the horse for a moment stopped. The smith seized that moment, and with his hot iron burned off the dress from the rider's hand, thus saving Nancy, more dead than alive ; while the rider passed over the wall of the churchyard, and vanished on the grave in which Lenine had been laid but a few hours before.

The smith took Nancy into his shop, and he soon aroused some of his neighbours, who took the poor girl back to Alsia. Her parents laid her on her bed. She spoke no word, but to ask for her child, to request her mother to give up her child to Lenine's parents, and her desire to be buried in his grave. Before the morning light fell on the world, Nancy had breathed her last breath.

A horse was seen that night to pass through the Church-town like a ball from a musket, and in the morning Lenine's colt was found dead in Bernowhall Cliff, covered with foam, its eyes forced from its head, and its swollen tongue hanging out of its mouth. On Lenine's grave was found the piece of Nancy's dress which was left in the spirit's hand when the smith burnt her from his grasp.

It is said that one or two of the sailors who survived the wreck related after the funeral, how, on the 30th of October, at night, Lenine was like one mad ; they could scarcely keep him in the ship. He seemed more asleep than awake, and, after great excitement, he fell as if dead upon the deck, and lay so for hours. When he came to himself, he told them that he had been taken to the village of Kimyall, and that if he ever married the woman who had cast the spell, he would make her suffer the longest day she had to live for drawing his soul out of his body.

Poor Nancy was buried in Lenine's grave, and her companion in sowing hemp-seed, who saw the white coffin, slept beside her within the year.

This story bears a striking resemblance to the " Lenore " of Bürger, which remarkable ballad can scarcely have found its way, even yet, to Boscean.

DUFFY AND THE DEVIL.*

MANY of the superstitions of our ancestors are preserved in quaint, irregular rhymes, the recitation of which was the amusement of the people in the long nights of winter. These were sung, or rather said, in a monotone, by the professional Drolls, who doubtless added such things as they fancied would increase the interest of the story to the listeners. Especially were they fond of introducing known characters on the scene, and of mixing up events which had occurred within the memory of the old people, with the more ancient legend. The following story, or rather parts of it, formed the subject of one of the Cornish Christmas plays. When I was a boy, I well remember being much delighted with the coarse acting of a set of Christmas players, who exhibited in the " great hall " of a farmhouse at which I was visiting, and who gave us the principal incidents of Duffy and the Devil Terrytop ; one of the company doing the part of Chorus, and filling up by rude descriptions—often in rhyme— the parts which the players could not represent.

It was in cider-making time. Squire Lovel of Trove, or more correctly, Trewoof, rode up to Burian Church-town to procure help. Boys and maidens were in request, some to gather the

* The incidents of this story are strikingly similar to those in " *Rumpel-stiizchen.*" The maiden in that tale has to spin straw into gold thread, and she, like Duffy, has to discover the name of the spirit who has befriended her.

Mr Robert Chambers, in his " Popular Rhymes of Scotland," has a fairy tale in which the fairy threatens the mother that she will have her "lad bairn" unless "ye can tell me my right name." The anxious mother takes a walk in the wood, and she hears the fairy singing—

> " Little kens our gude dame at hame
> That 'Whuppity Stoorie' is my name."

Of course, when the fairy comes to claim the "lad bairn," she is addressed as "Whuppity Stoorie," and she at once disappears.

In "Who Built Reynir Church?" in the " Icelandic Legends" of Jon Arnason, the story turns on the discovery of the name of the builder.—*Icelandic Legends*, p. 49.

apples from the trees, others to carry them to the cider-mill. Passing along the village as hastily as the dignity of a squire would allow him, his attention was drawn to a great noise—scolding in a shrill treble voice, and crying—proceeding from Janey Chygwin's door. The squire rode up to the cottage, and he saw the old woman beating her step-daughter Duffy about the head with the skirt of her swing-tail gown, in which she had been carrying out the ashes. She made such a dust, that the squire was nearly choked and almost blinded with the wood ashes.

"What cheer, Janey?" cries the squire; "what's the to-do with you and Duffy?"

"Oh, the lazy hussy!" shouts Janey, "is all her time courseying and courranting with the boys! she will never stay in to boil the porridge, knit the stockings, or spin the yarn."

"Don't believe her, your honour," exclaims Duffy; "my knitting and spinning is the best in the parish."

The war of tongues continued in this strain for some time, the old squire looking calmly on, and resolving in his mind to take Duffy home with him to Trove, her appearance evidently pleasing him greatly. Squire Lovel left the old and young woman to do the best they could, and went round the village to complete his hiring. When he returned, peace had been declared between them; but when Lovel expressed his desire to take Duffy home to his house to help the housekeeper to do the spinning, "A pretty spinner she is!" shouted old Janey at the top of her voice. "Try me, your honour," said Duffy, curtsying very low; "my yarns are the best in the parish."

"We'll soon try that," said the squire; "Janey will be glad to get quits of thee, I see, and thou'lt be nothing loath to leave her; so jump up behind me, Duffy."

No sooner said than done. The maid Duffy, without ceremony, mounted behind the squire on the horse, and they jogged silently down to Trove.

Squire Lovel's old housekeeper was almost blind—one eye had been put out by an angry old wizard, and through sympathy she was rapidly losing the power of seeing with the other.

This old dame was consequently very glad of some one to help her in spinning and knitting.

The introduction over, the housekeeper takes Duffy up into the garret where the wool was kept, and where the spinning was done in the summer, and requests her to commence her work.

The truth must be told; Duffy was an idle slut, she could

neither knit nor spin. Well, here she was left alone, and, of course, expected to produce a good specimen of her work.

The garret was piled from the floor to the key-beams with fleeces of wool. Duffy looked despairingly at them, and then sat herself down on the "turn"—the spinning-wheel—and cried out,

"Curse the spinning and knitting! The devil may spin and knit for the squire for what I care."

Scarcely had Duffy spoken these words than she heard a rustling noise behind some woolpacks, and forth walked a queer-looking little man, with a remarkable pair of eyes, which seemed to send out flashes of light. There was something uncommonly knowing in the twist of his mouth, and his curved nose had an air of curious intelligence. He was dressed in black, and moved towards Duffy with a jaunty air, knocking something against the floor at every step he took.

"Duffy dear," said this little gentleman, "I'll do all the spinning and knitting for thee."

"Thank 'e," says Duffy, quite astonished.

"Duffy dear, a lady shall you be."

"Thank 'e, your honour," smiled Duffy.

"But, Duffy dear, remember," coaxingly said the queer little man,—"remember, that for all this, at the end of three years, you must go with me, unless you can find out my name."

Duffy was not the least bit frightened, nor did she hesitate long, but presently struck a bargain with her kind but unknown friend, who told her she had only to wish, and her every wish should be fulfilled; and as for the spinning and knitting, she would find all she required under the black ram's fleece.

He then departed. How, Duffy could not tell, but in a moment the queer little gentleman was gone.

Duffy sung in idleness, and slept until it was time for her to make her appearance. So she wished for some yarns, and looking under the black fleece she found them.

Those were shown by the housekeeper to the squire, and both declared "they had never seen such beautiful yarns."

The next day Duffy was to knit this yarn into stockings. Duffy idled, as only professed idlers can idle; but in due time, as if she had been excessively industrious, she produced a pair of stockings for the old squire.

If the yarn was beautiful, the stockings were beyond all praise. They were as fine as silk, and as strong as leather.

Squire Lovel soon gave them a trial; and when he came home at night after hunting, he declared he would never wear any

Q

other than Duffy's stockings. He had wandered all day through brake and briar, furze and brambles; there was not a scratch on his legs, and he was as dry as a bone. There was no end to his praise of Duffy's stockings.

Duffy had a rare time of it now—she could do what she pleased, and rove where she willed.

She was dancing on the mill-bed half the day, with all the gossiping women who brought their grist to be ground.

In those "good old times" the ladies of the parish would take their corn to mill, and serge the flour themselves. When a few of them met together, they would either tell stories or dance whilst the corn was grinding. Sometimes the dance would be on the mill-bed, sometimes out on the green. On some occasions the miller's fiddle would be in request, at others the "crowd" * was made to do the duty of a tambourine.

So Duffy was always finding excuses to go to mill, and many "a round" would she dance with the best people in the parish.

Old Bet, the miller's wife, was a witch, and she found out who did Duffy's work for her. Duffy and old Bet were always the best of friends, and she never told any one about Duffy's knitting friend, nor did she ever say a word about the stockings being unfinished. *There was always a stitch down.*

On Sundays the people went to Burian Church, from all parts, to look at the squire's stockings; and the old squire would stop at the Cross, proud enough to show them. He could hunt

> " Through brambles and furze in all sorts of weather ;
> His old shanks were as sound as if bound up in leather."

Duffy was now sought after by all the young men of the country ; and at last the squire, fearing to lose a pretty girl, and one who was so useful to him, married her himself, and she became, according to the fashion of the time and place, Lady Lovel ; but she was commonly known by her neighbours as the Duffy Lady.

Lady Lovel kept the devil hard at work. Stockings, all sorts of fine underclothing, bedding, and much ornamental work, the like of which was never seen, was produced at command, and passed off as her own.

Duffy passed a merry time of it, but somehow or other she was never happy when she was compelled to play the lady. She passed much more of her time with the old crone at the mill, than in the drawing-room at Trove. The squire sported and

* Crowd,—a sieve covered with sheep-skin.

drank, and cared little about Duffy, so long as she provided him with knitted garments.

The three years were nearly at an end. Duffy had tried every plan to find out the devil's name, but had failed in all.

She began to fear that she should have to go off with her queer friend, and Duffy became melancholy. Old Bet endeavoured to rouse her, persuading her that she could from her long experience and many dealings with the imps of darkness, at the last moment put her in the way of escaping her doom.

Duffy went day after day to her garret, and there each day was the devil gibing and jeering till she was almost mad.

There was but another day. Bet was seriously consulted now, and, as good as her word, she promised to use her power.

Duffy Lady was to bring down to the mill that very evening a jack of the strongest beer she had in the cellar. She was not to go to bed until the squire returned from hunting, no matter how late, and she was to make no remark in reply to anything the squire might tell her.

The jack of beer was duly carried to the mill, and Duffy returned home very melancholy to wait up for the squire.

No sooner had Lady Lovel left the mill than old Bet came out with the "crowd" over her shoulders, and the blackjack in her hand. She shut the door, and turned the water off the mill-wheel,—threw her red cloak about her, and away.

She was seen by her neighbours going towards Boleit. A man saw the old woman trudging past the Pipers, and through the Dawnse Main into the downs, but there he lost sight of her, and no one could tell where old Bet was gone to at that time of night.

Duffy waited long and anxiously. By and by the dogs came home alone. They were covered with foam, their tongues were hanging out of their mouths, and all the servants said they must have met the devil's hounds without heads.

Duffy was seriously alarmed. Midnight came but no squire. At last he arrived, but like a crazy, crack-brained man, he kept singing,—

> "Here's to the devil,
> With his wooden pick and shovel."

He was neither drunk nor frightened, but wild with some strange excitement. After a long time Squire Lovel sat down, and began, "My dear Duffy, you haven't smiled this long time ; but now I'll tell 'e something that would make ye laugh if ye're dying. If you'd seen what I've seen to-night, ha, ha, ha !

' Here's to the devil,
With his wooden pick and shovel.' "

True to her orders, Duffy said not a word, but allowed the squire to ramble on as he pleased. At length he told her the following story of his adventures, with interruptions which have not been retained, and with numerous coarse expressions which are best forgotten :—

THE SQUIRE'S STORY OF THE MEETING OF THE WITCHES IN THE FUGOE HOLE.

" Duffy dear, I left home at break of day this morning. I hunted all the moors from Trove to Trevider, and never started a hare all the livelong day. I determined to hunt all night, but that I'd have a brace to bring home. So, at nightfall I went down Lemorna Bottoms, then up Brene Downses, and as we passed the Dawnse Main up started a hare, as fine a hare as ever was seen. She passed the Pipers, down through the Reens, in the mouth of the dogs half the time, yet they couldn't catch her at all. As fine a chase as ever was seen, until she took into the Fugoe Hole.* In went the dogs after her, and I followed, the owls and bats flying round my head. On we went, through water and mud, a mile or more, I'm quite certain. I didn't know the place was so long before. At last we came to a broad pool of water, when the dogs lost the scent, and ran back past me howling and jowling, terrified almost to death ! A little farther on I turned round a corner, and saw a glimmering fire on the other side the water, and there were St Leven witches in scores. Some were riding on ragwort, some on brooms, some were floating on their three-legged stools, and some, who had been milking the little good cows in Wales, had come back astride of the largest leeks they could find. Amongst the rest there was our Bet of the Mill, with her ' crowd ' in her hand, and my own blackjack slung across her shoulders.

" In a short time the witches gathered round the fire, and blowed it up, after a strange fashion, till it burned up into a

* There is a tradition, firmly believed on the lower side of Burian, that the Fugoe Hole extends from the cliffs underground so far that the end of it is under the parlour of the Tremewen's house in Trove, which is the only remaining portion of the old mansion of the Lovels.

Here the witches were in the habit of meeting the devil, and holding their Sabbath. Often his dark Highness has been heard piping, while the witches danced to his music.

A pool of water some distance from the entrance prevents any adventurer from exploring the "Hole" to its termination.

Hares often take refuge in the Fugoe Hole, from which they have never been known to return.

brilliant blue flame. Then I saw amongst the rest a queer little man in black, with a long forked tail, which he held high in the air, and twirled around. Bet struck her 'crowd' as soon as he appeared, and beat up the tune,—

> ' Here's to the devil,
> With his wooden pick and shovel,
> Digging tin by the bushel,
> With his tail cock'd up ! '

Then the queer little devil and all danced like the wind, and went faster and faster, making such a clatter, ' as if they had on each foot a pewter platter.'

" Every time the man in black came round by old Bet, he took a good pull from my own blackjack, till at last, as if he had been drinking my best beer, he seemed to have lost his head, when he jumped up and down, turned round and round, and roaring with laughter, sung,—

> ' Duffy, my lady, you'll never know—what ?—
> That my name is Terrytop, Terrytop—top ! ' "

When the squire sung those lines, he stopped suddenly, thinking that Duffy was going to die. She turned pale and red, and pale again. However, Duffy said nothing, and the squire proceeded:—

" After the dance, all the witches made a ring around the fire, and again blew it up, until the blue flames reached the top of the 'Zawn.' * Then the devil danced through and through the fire, and springing ever and anon amongst the witches, kicked them soundly. At last—I was shaking with laughter at the fun—I shouted, ' Go it, Old Nick ! ' and, lo, the lights went out, and I had to fly with all my speed, for every one of the witches were after me. I scampered home somehow, and here I am. Why don't you laugh, Duffy ? " Duffy did laugh, and laugh right heartily now, and when tired of their fun, the squire and the lady went to bed.

The three years were up within an hour. Duffy had willed for an abundant supply of knitted things, and filled every chest in the house. She was in the best chamber trying to cram some more stockings into a big chest, when the queer little man in black appeared before her.

" Well, Duffy, my dear," said he, " I have been to my word, and served you truly for three years as we agreed, so now I hope you will go with me, and make no objection." He bowed very

* Zawn,—a cavernous gorge.

obsequiously, almost to the ground, and regarded Duffy Lady with a very offensive leer.

"I fear," smiled Duffy, "that your country is rather warm, and might spoil my fair complexion."

"It is not so hot as some people say, Duffy," was his reply; "but come along, I've kept my word, and of course a lady of your standing will keep your word also. Can you tell me my name?"

Duffy curtsied, and smilingly said, "You have behaved like a true gentlemen; yet I wouldn't like to go so far." The devil frowned, and approached as if he would lay forcible hands upon her. "Maybe your name is Lucifer?"

He stamped his foot and grinned horridly. "Lucifer! Lucifer! He's no other than a servant to me in my own country." Suddenly calming again, he said, quietly, "Lucifer! I would scarcely be seen speaking to him at court. But come along. When I spin for ladies I expect honourable treatment at their hands. You've two guesses more. But they're of little use; my name is not generally known on earth."

"Perhaps," smiled Duffy again, "my lord's name is Beelzebub?"

How he grinned, and his sides shook with convulsive joy. "Beelzebub!" says he; "why, he's little better than the other, a common devil he. I believe he's some sort of a cousin—a Cornish cousin, you know."

"I hope your honour," curtsied Duffy, "will not take offence. Impute my mistake to ignorance."

Our Demon was rampant with joy; he danced around Duffy with delight, and was, seeing that she hesitated, about to seize her somewhat roughly.

"Stop! stop!" shouts Duffy; "perhaps you will be honest enough to admit that your name is Terrytop."

The gentleman in black looked at Duffy, and she steadily looked him in the face. "Terrytop! deny it if you dare," says she.

"A gentleman never denies his name," replied Terrytop, drawing himself up with much dignity. "I did not expect to be beaten by a young minx like you, Duffy; but the pleasure of your company is merely postponed." With this Terrytop departed in fire and smoke, and all the devil's knitting suddenly turned to ashes.

Squire Lovel was out hunting, away far on the moors; the day was cold and the winds piercing. Suddenly the stockings dropped from his legs and the homespun from his back, so that he came home with nothing on but his shirt and his shoes, almost dead with cold. All this was attributed by the squire to the influence of old Bet, who, he thought, had punished him for pursuing her with his dogs when she had assumed the form of a hare.

The story, as told by the Drolls, now rambles on. Duffy cannot furnish stockings. The squire is very wroth. There are many quarrels—mutual recriminations. Duffy's old sweetheart is called in to beat the squire, and eventually peace is procured, by a stratagem of old Bet's, which would rather shock the sense of propriety in these our days.

THE LOVERS OF PORTHANGWARTHA.*

THE names of the youth and maiden who fixed the term of the Lover's Cove upon this retired spot have passed from the memory of man. A simple story, however, remains, the mere fragment, without doubt, of a longer and more ancient tale.

The course of love with this humble pair did not run smooth. On one side or the other the parents were decidedly opposed to the intimacy which existed, and by their persecutions, they so far succeeded, that the young man was compelled to emigrate to some far distant land.

In this cove the lovers met for the last time in life, and vowed under the light of the full moon, that living or dead they would meet at the end of three years.

The young woman remained with her friends—the young man went to the Indies. Time passed on, and the three years, which had been years of melancholy to both, were expiring.

One moonlight night, when the sea was tranquil as a mirror, an old crone sat on the edge of the cliff " making her charms." She saw a figure—she was sure it was a spirit, very like the village maiden—descend into the cove, and seat herself upon a rock, around two-thirds of which the light waves were rippling. On this rock sat the maiden, looking anxiously out over the sea, until, from the rising of the tide, she was completely surrounded. The old woman called ; but in vain—the maiden was unconscious of any voice. There she sat, and the tide was rising rapidly around her. The old woman, now seeing the danger in which she was, resolved to go down into the cove, and, if possible, awaken the maiden to a sense of her danger. To do this, it was necessary to go round a projecting pile of rocks. While doing this, she lost sight of the object of her interest, and much was her surprise, when she again saw the maiden, to perceive a young sailor by her side, with his

* This is said to mean the Lover's Cove.

arm around her waist. Conceiving that help had arrived, the old woman sat herself down on the slope of the descending path, and resolved patiently to await the arrival of the pair on shore, and then to rate the girl soundly.

She sat watching this loving and lovely pair, lighted as they were on the black rock by a full flood of moonshine. There they sat, and the tide rose and washed around them. Never were boy and girl so mad, and at last the terrified old woman shrieked with excitement. Suddenly they appeared to float off upon the waters. She thought she heard their voices; but there was no sound of terror. Instead of it a tranquil murmuring music, like the voice of doves, singing,—

> " I am thine,
> Thou art mine,
>   Beyond control ;
> In the wave
> Be the grave
>   Of heart and soul."

Down, down into the sea passed the lovers. Awestruck, the old woman looked on, until, as she said, " At last they turned round, looked me full in the face, smiling like angels, and, kissing each other, sank to rise no more."

They tell us that the body of the young woman was found a day or two after in a neighbouring cove, and that intelligence eventually reached England that the young man had been killed on this very night.

THE GHOST OF ROSEWARNE.

"EZEKIEL GROSSE, gent., attorney-at-law," bought the lands of Rosewarne from one of the De Rosewarnes, who had become involved in difficulties, by endeavouring, without sufficient means, to support the dignity of his family. There is reason for believing that Ezekiel was the legal adviser of this unfortunate Rosewarne, and that he was not over-honest in his transactions with his client. However this may be, Ezekiel Grosse had scarcely made Rosewarne his dwelling-place, before he was alarmed by noises, at first of an unearthly character, and subsequently, one very dark night, by the appearance of the ghost himself in the form of a worn and aged man. The first appearance was in the park, but he subsequently repeated his visits in the house, but always after dark. Ezekiel Grosse was not a man to be terrified at trifles, and for some time he paid but slight attention to his nocturnal visitor. Howbeit, the repetition of visits, and certain mysterious indications on the part of the spectre, became annoying to Ezekiel. One night, when seated in his office examining some deeds, and being rather irritable, having lost an important suit, his visitor approached him, making some strange indications which the lawyer could not understand. Ezekiel suddenly exclaimed, " In the name of God, what wantest thou ? "

" To show thee, Ezekiel Grosse, where the gold for which thou longest lies buried."

No one ever lived upon whom the greed of gold was stronger than on Ezekiel, yet he hesitated now that his spectral friend had spoken so plainly, and trembled in every limb as the ghost slowly delivered himself in sepulchral tones of this telling speech.

The lawyer looked fixedly on the spectre, but he dared not utter a word. He longed to obtain possession of the secret, yet he feared to ask him where he was to find this treasure. The spectre looked as fixedly at the poor trembling lawyer, as if enjoying the sight of his terror. At length, lifting his finger, he beckoned Ezekiel to follow him, turning at the same time to leave the room. Ezekiel was glued to his seat ; he could not exert strength enough to move, although he desired to do so.

" Come ! " said the ghost, in a hollow voice. The lawyer was powerless to come.

" Gold ! " exclaimed the old man, in a whining tone, though in a louder key.

" Where ? " gasped Ezekiel.

" Follow me, and I will show thee," said the ghost. Ezekiel endeavoured to rise, but it was in vain.

" I command thee, come ! " almost shrieked the ghost. Ezekiel felt that he was compelled to follow his friend ; and by some supernatural power rather than his own, he followed the spectre out of the room, and through the hall, into the park.

They passed onward through the night—the ghost gliding before the lawyer, and guiding him by a peculiar phosphorescent light, which appeared to glow from every part of the form, until they arrived at a little dell, and had reached a small cairn formed of granite boulders. By this the spectre rested ; and when Ezekiel had approached it, and was standing on the other side of the cairn, still trembling, the aged man, looking fixedly in his face, said, in low tones—

" Ezekiel Grosse, thou longest for gold, as I did. I won the glittering prize, but I could not enjoy it. Heaps of treasure are buried beneath those stones ; it is thine, if thou diggest for it.

Win the gold, Ezekiel. Glitter with the wicked ones of the world; and when thou art the most joyous, I will look in upon thy happiness." The ghost then disappeared, and as soon as Grosse could recover himself from the extreme trepidation,— the result of mixed feelings,—he looked about him, and finding himself alone, he exclaimed, " Ghost or devil, I will soon prove whether or not thou liest ! " Ezekiel is said to have heard a laugh, echoing between the hills, as he said those words.

The lawyer noted well the spot; returned to his house ; pondered on all the circumstances of his case ; and eventually resolved to seize the earliest opportunity, when he might do so unobserved, of removing the stones, and examining the ground beneath them.

A few nights after this, Ezekiel went to the little cairn, and by the aid of a crowbar, he soon overturned the stones, and laid the ground bare. He then commenced digging, and had not proceeded far when his spade struck against some other metal. He carefully cleared away the earth, and he then felt—for he could not see, having no light with him—that he had uncovered a metallic urn of some kind. He found it quite impossible to lift it, and he was therefore compelled to cover it up again, and to replace the stones sufficiently to hide it from the observation of any chance wanderer.

The next night Ezekiel found that this urn, which was of bronze, contained gold coins of a very ancient date. He loaded himself with his treasure, and returned home. From time to time, at night, as Ezekiel found he could do so without exciting the suspicions of his servants, he visited the urn, and thus by degrees removed all the treasure to Rosewarne house. There was nothing in the series of circumstances which had surrounded Ezekiel which he could less understand than the fact that the ghost of the old man had left off troubling him from the moment when he had disclosed to him the hiding-place of this treasure.

The neighbouring gentry could not but observe the rapid improvements which Ezekiel Grosse made in his mansion, his grounds, in his personal appearance, and indeed in everything by which he was surrounded. In a short time he abandoned the law, and led in every respect the life of a country gentleman. He ostentatiously paraded his power to procure all earthly enjoyments, and, in spite of his notoriously bad character, he succeeded in drawing many of the landed proprietors around him.

Things went well with Ezekiel. The man who could in those days visit London in his own carriage and four was not without a large circle of flatterers.　The lawyer who had struggled hard, in the outset of life, to secure wealth, and who did not always employ the most honest means for doing so, now found himself the centre of a circle to whom he could preach honesty, and receive from them expressions of the admiration in which the world holds the possessor of gold.　His old tricks were forgotten, and he was put in places of honour.　This state of things continued for some time ; indeed, Grosse's entertainments became more and more splendid, and his revels more and more seductive to those he admitted to share them with him.　The Lord of Rosewarne was the Lord of the West.　To him every one bowed the knee : he walked the Earth as the proud possessor of a large share of the planet.

It was Christmas eve, and a large gathering there was at Rosewarne.　In the hall the ladies and gentlemen were in the full enjoyment of the dance, and in the kitchen all the tenantry and the servants were emulating their superiors.　Everything went joyously ; and when mirth was in full swing, and Ezekiel felt to the full the influence of wealth, it appeared as if in one moment the chill of death had fallen over every one.　The dancers paused, and looked one at another, each one struck with the other's paleness ; and there, in the middle of the hall, every one saw a strange old man looking angrily, but in silence, at Ezekiel Grosse, who was fixed in terror, blank as a statue.

No one had seen this old man enter the hall, yet there he was in the midst of them.　It was but for a minute, and he was gone.　Ezekiel, as if a frozen torrent of water had thawed in an instant, roared with impetuous laughter.

" What do you think of that for a Christmas play ?　There was an old Father Christmas for you !　Ha ! ha ! ha ! ha !　How frightened you all look !　Butler, order the men to hand round the spiced wines !　On with the dancing, my friends !　It was only a trick, ay, and a clever one, which I have put upon you On with your dancing, my friends ! "

Notwithstanding his boisterous attempts to restore the spirit of the evening, Ezekiel could not succeed.　There was an influence stronger than any which he could command ; and one by one, framing sundry excuses, his guests took their departure, every one of them satisfied that all was not right at Rosewarne.

From that Christmas eve Grosse was a changed man.　He tried to be his former self ; but it was in vain.　Again and again he called his gay companions around him ; but at every feast there appeared one more than was desired.　An aged man—

weird beyond measure—took his place at the table in the middle of the feast ; and although he spoke not, he exerted a miraculous power over all.   No one dared to move ; no one ventured to speak.   Occasionally Ezekiel assumed an appearance of courage, which he felt not ; rallied his guests, and made sundry excuses for the presence of his aged friend, whom he represented as having a mental infirmity, as being deaf and dumb.   On all such occasions the old man rose from the table, and looking at the host, laughed a demoniac laugh of joy, and departed as quietly as he came.

The natural consequence of this was that Ezekiel Grosse's friends fell away from him, and he became a lonely man, amidst his vast possessions—his only companion being his faithful clerk, John Call.

The persecuting presence of the spectre became more and more constant ; and wherever the poor lawyer went, there was the aged man at his side.   From being one of the finest men in the county, he became a miserably attenuated and bowed old man.   Misery was stamped on every feature—terror was indicated in every movement.   At length he appears to have besought his ghostly attendant to free him of his presence.   It was long before the ghost would listen to any terms ; but when Ezekiel at length agreed to surrender the whole of his wealth to any one whom the spectre might indicate, he obtained a promise that upon this being carried out, in a perfectly legal manner, in favour of John Call, that he should no longer be haunted.

This was, after numerous struggles on the part of Ezekiel to retain his property, or at least some portion of it, legally settled, and John Call became possessor of Rosewarne and the adjoining lands.   Grosse was then informed that this evil spirit was one of the ancestors of the Rosewarne, from whom by his fraudulent dealings he obtained the place, and that he was allowed to visit the earth again for the purpose of inflicting the most condign punishment on the avaricious lawyer.   His avarice had been gratified, his pride had been pampered to the highest ; and then he was made a pitiful spectacle, at whom all men pointed, and no one pitied.   He lived on in misery, but it was for a short time.   He was found dead : and the country people ever said that his death was a violent one ; they spoke of marks on his body, and some even asserted that the spectre of De Rosewarne was seen rejoicing amidst a crowd of devils, as they bore the spirit of Ezekiel over Carn Brea.

Hals thus quaintly tells this story :—

"Rosewarne, in this parish, gave to its owner the name of De Rosewarne, one of which tribe sold those lands, temp. James I., to Ezekiel Grosse, gent., attorney-at-law, who made it his dwelling, and in this place got a great estate by the inferior practice of the law ; but much more, as tradition saith, by means of a spirit or apparition that haunted him in this place, till he spake to it (for it is notable that sort of things called apparitions are such proud gentry, that they never speak first) ; whereupon it discovered to him where much treasure lay hid in this mansion, which, according to the (honest) ghost's direction, he found, to his great enriching. After which, this phantasm or spectrum became so troublesome and direful to him, day and night, that it forced him to forsake this place (as rich, it seems, as this devil could make him), and to quit his claim thereto, by giving or selling it to his clerk, John Call ; whose son, John Call, gent., sold it again to Robert Hooker, gent., attorney-at-law, now in possession thereof. The arms of Call were, in a field three trumpets—in allusion to the name in English ; but in Cornish-British, 'call,' 'cal,' signifies any hard, flinty, or obdurate matter or thing, and 'hirgorue' is a trumpet."*

THE SUICIDE'S SPEARMAN.

A FAMILY of the name of Spearman has lived in Cornwall for many ages, their native centre having been somewhere between Ludgvan and St Ives.

Years long ago, an unfortunate man, weary of life, destroyed himself ; and the rude laws of a remote age, carrying out, as they thought, human punishments even after death, decreed that the body should be buried at the four cross-roads, and quicklime poured on the corpse.

Superstition stepped in, and somewhat changed the order of burial. To prevent the dead man from "walking," and becoming a terror to all his neighbours, the coffin was to be turned upside down, and a spear was to be driven through it and the body, so as to pin it to the ground.

It was with some difficulty that a man could be found to perform this task. At length, however, a blacksmith undertook it. He made the spear ; and after the coffin was properly placed, he drove his spear-headed iron bar through it. From that day he was called "the spearman," and his descendants have never lost the name.

In making a new road not many years since, the coffin and spear were found, and removed. From that time several old men and women have declared that the self-murderer "walks the earth."

* See Gilbert's "Parochial History of Cornwall," 1838, vol. i p. 162.

THE SUICIDE'S GHOST.

ON the bleak road between Helston and Wendron Church-town, at its highest and wildest spot, three roads meet about a quarter of a mile from the latter place. Here, at " Three Cross," as the place is called, years ago, when the Downs being unenclosed, it was more desolate than it is even now, a poor suicide, named " Tucker," was buried. Few liked to pass up Row's Lane, leading there, after nightfall ; for Tucker's shade had more than once been seen. One man, however, valiant in his cups, on his return from Helston market, cracked his whip, and shouted lustily, " Arise, Tucker !" as he passed the place. It is said Tucker did arise, and fixed himself on the saddle behind the man as he rode on horseback, and accompanied him—how far it is not said. This was often repeated, until the spirit, becoming angry, refused any more to quit his disturber, and continued to trouble him, till " Parson Jago " was called in to use his skill, which was found effectual, in " laying " Tucker's spirit to rest.

THE "HA-AF" A FACE.

JAMES BERRYMAN said, " Fa-ather took a house doun to Lelant, whear we lived for a bra' bit. Very often after I ben in bed, our ould cat wud tear up, coover its ars like a ma-aged thing, jump uppon the bed, and dig her ould hed under the clothes, as if she wud git doun to bottom, and jest after, a man's face, with a light round un, wud cum in ; 'twas ha-af a face like, and it wud stop at the bottom of the bed. I 've sen it many times ; and fa-ather, though he didn't say nothin', was glad enough to leave the place. I was tould that the house belonged to an ould man, and that two rich gentlemen, brothers, who lived close by, wanted the place, and put on law, and got the place from the poor ould man. When they war goin' to turn un out, the poor fellow stopped and looked round crying, and then fell down in a fit, was put to bed, and died in the house ; and 'twas he, they said, that used to come back."

THE WARNING.

THE following instance is given me, as from the party to whom it happened, " a respectable person, of undoubted veracity." " When a young man, fearing and caring for no one, I was in the habit of visiting Sancreed from Penzance, and of returning in the evening. One night I took up my hat to return, and went out at the door. It was a most beautiful night, when, without the most remote assignable reason, I was seized in a manner I never experienced either before or since. I was absolutely 'terror-stricken,' so that I was compelled to turn back to the house, a thing I had never done before, and say, 'I must remain here for the night.' I could never account for it; and without caring to be called superstitious, have regarded it as a special interposition of Providence. It was reported that shortly before, a lad, who had driven home a farmer's daughter to her father's house in the neighbourhood, had suddenly been missed, and no clue to his whereabouts had ever been found. About four or six weeks after my adventure, a gang of sheep-stealers who had carried on their depredations for a long time previous, were discovered in the neighbourhood; their abode, indeed, adjoined the road from Sancreed to Penzance, and I cannot help believing it probable, that had I returned that night I should have encountered the gang, and perhaps lost my life. Years afterwards, one of the gang confessed that the boy had come suddenly upon them during one of their nefarious expeditions. He was seized, and injudiciously said, 'Well, you may get off once or twice, but you're sure to be hanged in the end.' 'Thee shan't help to do it,' said one, and the poor boy was murdered, and his body thrown into a neighbouring shaft."

LAYING A GHOST.

"TO the ignorance of men in our age in this particular and mysterious part of philosophy and religion,—namely, the communication between spirits and men,—not one scholar out of ten thousand, though otherwise of excellent learning, knows anything of it, or the way how to manage it. This ignorance breeds fear and abhorrence of that which otherwise might be of incomparable benefit to mankind."

Such is the concluding paragraph of "An Account of an Apparition, attested by the Rev. Wm. Ruddell, Minister at Launceston, in Cornwall," 1665.

A schoolboy was haunted by Dorothy Dingley; we know not why, but the boy pined. He was thought to be in love; but when, at the wishes of his friends, the parson questioned him, he told him of his ghostly visitor, and he took the parson to the field in which he was in the habit of meeting the apparition; and the reverend gentleman himself saw the spectral Dorothy, and afterwards he showed her to the boy's father and mother. Then comes the story of the laying. " The next morning being Thursday, I went out very early by myself, and walked for about an hour's space in meditation and prayer in the field next adjoining to the Quartiles. Soon after five, I stepped over the stile into the disturbed field, and had not gone above thirty or forty paces before the ghost appeared at the further stile. I spoke to it with a loud voice, in some such sentences as the way of these dealings directed me; whereupon it approached, but slowly, and when I came near it it moved not. I spoke again, and it answered again in a voice which was neither very audible nor intelligible. I was not the least terrified, therefore I persisted until it spake again and gave me satisfaction. But the work could not be finished at this time; wherefore the same evening, an hour after sunset, it met me again, near the same place, and after a few words on each side *it quietly vanished*, and neither doth appear since, nor ever will more to any man's disturbance." *

A FLYING SPIRIT.

ABOUT the year 1761 a pinnacle was thrown down, by lightning, from the tower of the church at Ludgvan. The effect was then universally imputed to the vengeance of a perturbed spirit, exorcised from Treassow, and passing eastward, towards the usual place of banishment—THE RED SEA.

The following story is given as a remarkable example of the manner in which very recent events become connected with exceedingly old superstitious ideas. The tales of Tregeagle have shown us how the name of a man who lived about two centuries since is made to do duty as a demon belonging to the pagan times. In this story we have the name of a woman who lived about the commencement of the present century, associated with a legend belonging to the earliest ages.

THE EXECUTION AND WEDDING.

A WOMAN, who had lived at Ludgvan, was executed at Bodmin for the murder of her husband. There was but little doubt that she had been urged on to the diabolical deed by a horsedealer, known as Yorkshire Jack, with whom, for a long period, she was generally supposed to have been criminally acquainted.

* "Historical Survey of Cornwall," C. S. Gilbert.

Now, it will be remembered that this really happened within the present century. One morning, during my residence in Penzance, an old woman from Ludgvan called on me with some trifling message. While she was waiting for my answer, I made some ordinary remark about the weather.

" It's all owing to Sarah Polgrain," said she.

" Sarah Polgrain !" said I ; "and who is Sarah Polgrain ? "

Then the voluble old lady told me the whole story of the poisoning, with which we need not, at present, concern ourselves. By and by the tale grew especially interesting, and there I resume it.

Sarah had begged that Yorkshire Jack might accompany her to the scaffold when she was led forth to execution. This was granted ; and on the dreadful morning, there stood this unholy pair, the fatal beam on which the woman's body was in a few minutes to swing, before them.

They kissed each other, and whispered words passed between them.

The executioner intimated that the moment of execution had arrived, and that they must part. Sarah Polgrain, looking earnestly into the man's eyes, said,

" You will ? "

Yorkshire Jack replied, " I will !" and they separated. The man retired amongst the crowd, the woman was soon a dead corpse, pendulating in the wind.

Years passed on. Yorkshire Jack was never the same man as before, his whole bearing was altered. His bold, his dashing air deserted him. He walked, or rather wandered, slowly about the streets of the town, or the lanes of the country. He constantly moved his head from side to side, looking first over one, and then over the other shoulder, as though dreading that some one was following him.

The stout man became thin, his ruddy cheeks more pale, and his eyes sunken.

At length he disappeared, and it was discovered—for Yorkshire Jack had made a confidant of some Ludgvan man—that he had pledged himself, " living or dead, to become the husband of Sarah Polgrain, after the lapse of years."

To escape, if possible, from himself, Jack had gone to sea in the merchant service.

Well, the period had arrived when this unholy promise was to be fulfilled. Yorkshire Jack was returning from the Mediterranean in a fruit-ship. He was met by the devil and Sarah Polgrain far out at sea, off the Land's-End. Jack would not accompany them willingly; so they followed the ship for days, during all which time she was involved in a storm. Eventually Jack was washed from the deck, by such a wave as the oldest sailor had never seen ; and presently, amidst loud thunders and flashing lightnings, riding as it were in a black cloud, three figures were seen passing onward. These were the devil, Sarah Polgrain, and Yorkshire Jack; and this was the cause of the storm.

"It is all true, as you may learn if you will inquire," said the old woman ; "for many of her kin live in Church-town."

THE LUGGER OF CROFT PASCO POOL.

IN the midst of the dreary waste of Gornhilly, which occupies a large portion of the Lizard promontory, is a large piece of water known as "Croft Pasco Pool," where it is said at night the form of a ghostly vessel may be seen floating with lug-sails spread. A more dreary, weird spot could hardly be selected for a witches' meeting ; and the Lizard folks were always—a fact—careful to be back before dark, preferring to suffer inconvenience, to risking a sight of the ghostly lugger. Unbelieving people attributed the origin of the tradition to a white horse seen in a dim twilight standing in the shallow water ; but this was indignantly rejected by the mass of the residents.